RUMBLES LEFT AND RIGHT

A Book About Troublesome People and Ideas

Rumbles
Left and Right

A BOOK ABOUT

TROUBLESOME PEOPLE AND IDEAS

Wm. F. Buckley, Jr.

Introduction by Russell Kirk

G. P. PUTNAM'S SONS New York

© *1963 by Wm. F. Buckley, Jr.*

Library of Congress Catalog
Card Number: 63-9654

 72

MANUFACTURED IN THE UNITED STATES OF AMERICA

VAN REES PRESS • NEW YORK

To my mother, Aloïse Steiner Buckley,
from her troublesome,
but always devoted, son

Some of the material in this book has appeared
before in: *Harper's, Coronet, National Review,
The American Legion Magazine, The Saturday
Review, Newsday, Ave Maria, Monocle, Esquire,
Playboy, Motor Boating,* and *The Skipper.* My thanks
to them for permission to reprint. My thanks also to
Mr. Tom Wallace, of Putnam's, for his encouragement,
to Mrs. Gertrude E. Vogt for her superintending
intelligence, and to Mr. Russell Kirk for the nice
champagne.   W.F.B.

Stamford, Conn.
January, 1963

CONTENTS

9

INTRODUCTION
by Russell Kirk

A BORN debater, Mr. William F. Buckley, Jr. has made himself into a formidable knight-errant of twentieth-century politics and letters. This book, *Rumbles Left and Right*, though on the surface a collection of his occasional pieces, really amounts to more than a series of jousts with the men-at-arms of liberalism and radicalism. Through these essays runs a strong consistency: a concerted assault on the fallacies of a decadent age.

The controversies with which Mr. Buckley deals may be forgotten a generation from now, if not sooner; some are dusty already, perhaps. Yet, as Mr. T. S. Eliot observes, there are no lost causes, because there are no gained causes. And the follies which Mr. Buckley scourges rise ghastly from their graves in every generation. The reader of this book, then, is to take these essays not as ephemera, but as political and social criticism worthy of survival in their own right. It is not inconceivable that, thirty years from now, Americans seeking to understand the curious moods of the 50's and 60's may find in *Rumbles Left and Right* a sturdy thread to lead them through the Minoan labyrinth of political and literary controversy in the times of Eisenhower and Kennedy. As Pope immortalized in *The Dunciad* a crew of poetasters who otherwise would have been snuffed out like tallow drips, so Buckley may preserve in the amber of his humorous invective a collection of insects that otherwise would have been consigned to the trash burner of remorseless fate. Yet I doubt whether many of his adversaries will be sufficiently grateful for this solicitude of the curator.

Some of these portraits, to be sure, are framed with deep affection, notably those of Whittaker Chambers and Barry Goldwater. The former probably is Mr. Buckley's best piece of writing; and it penetrates beneath the shallow passion of recent years to the springs of character and the disillusion of our century. Here Mr. Buckley does the rising generation an enduring service by his analysis—marked with a strong pathos—of a man courageous and wise enough to escape from the clutch of a consuming ideology, though so burnt by that self-emancipation that he could not live. In fiction, Mr. Lionel Trilling's character Maxim, in *The Middle of the Journey*, curiously anticipates the real Chambers. Mr. Buckley's examination of that melancholy and symbolic author of *Witness* may do much to help the searchers of Anno Domini 1990 or 2000 understand this age of ideology.

Not long ago, Mr. Norman Thomas and I were fellow travelers on the way to an airport. In our company was an intelligent girl college student who never had heard of Whittaker Chambers or Alger Hiss; so Mr. Thomas and I had to describe for her the intricate web of circumstance, significant of so much in the tribulations of this age, which involved the Communist intriguer and his reluctant accuser. If such controversies already are obscure to the rising generation, they will be incomprehensible a generation from now without the illumination of Mr. Buckley's moving words.

Similarly, William Buckley thrusts through the bramble thickets of passing partisanship to take the measure of such journalists—gentlemen of widely differing talents—as Richard Rovere, Herbert Matthews, Kenneth Tynan, and Murray Kempton. These he does not love, except possibly Mr. Kempton; but he discerns in them, as in Edward Bennett Williams and in Robert Hutchins, manifestations of the modern temper. For one so accustomed to exchange cut and thrust with these gentlemen, Mr. Buckley writes almost charitably. Though theirs are the voices of Babel, Buckley does not charge them with having built the Tower: rather, he exhibits them to his increasing audience as specimens of bewilderment.

Apropos of such specimens, one hopes that in future Mr. Buckley may tilt a lance at some of the greater and grimmer champions of neoterism—at Lord Bertrand Russell and Sir Charles Snow, for instance, whom he drubs only casually in these pages. Though Mr. Buckley is anything but a freak, his talent for showmanship has led him to repeated tests of strength in Nightmare Alley; and, somewhat ironically, probably he is best known to the general American public through his television debates with such oddities as Gore Vidal and Norman Mailer. But Mr. Buckley's dissection of freakishness, as in the essay on Mailer, has a worth greater than the subject of its mordant wit—quite as Whittaker Chambers' review of *Atlas Shrugged*, published in *National Review*, broke a butterfly—or, rather, broke a lunar moth—on the wheel. The criticism of Buckley and Chambers will remain worth reading when the next wave of literary flotsam litters our beaches with little dying marine monsters and jellyfish. The chief value of polemical silliness is the wisdom of the reaction it sometimes provokes. No one nowadays knows Price's sermon on the Old Jewry, which irritated Edmund Burke into writing his *Reflections on the Revolution in France.* So it must be said in apology for the Mailers and Rands of this century that without them we should lose the civilized fun of the Buckleys.

Much though he is detested by some gentlemen of the Academy, Mr. William Buckley is eminently a civilized man. Not much liking the education to which he was exposed at Yale—and liking still less the higher learning at other universities and colleges—Buckley set out to scandalize these United States. He found that Christianity was indeed a scandal in his time—as, indeed, it always has been and ought to be—and that modern orthodoxy was enforced by the "Liberal Establishment." Upon his unrepentant head the outraged devotees of the Establishment heaped coals of fire and poured oil of vitriol. Yet Mr. Buckley was undismayed. In 1955 he founded the weekly review which now has become the most widely discussed and widely circulated journal of opinion in this country. Now he is a power in the land, chiefly through his talent for "scarifying." But in the rough and tumble of scores of literary combats and hundreds of sardonic speeches, he has not lost the urbanity of real culture; nor has he forgotten what Burke described as the roots of our civilization, the spirit of religion and the spirit of a gentleman.

It seems to me, indeed, that Mr. Buckley has grown stronger and wiser during his hard years in the lists. Even though he assailed the ritualistic liberalism that had made its way into Yale, at first he bore himself certain marks of that nineteenth-century liberalism which Santayana labeled a mere transitory stage between the old polity and the coming collectivism. In his witty wrath at the corruption of tolerance, he assailed academic freedom (*God and Man at Yale*)— which, properly understood, is more than a shibboleth, to my mind. In his justified contempt for the "little dogs and all, Blanche, Tray, and Sweetlips" who nipped at the ankles of Joseph McCarthy *after* that leader of demos had begun to slip from influence, Mr. Buckley became the most eloquent defender of a politician who, after all—as Whittaker Chambers said—"can't lead anybody because he can't think." And in flaying the puerilities of the Left, when he began to publish *National Review,* occasionally he mistook for useful auxiliaries people who were quite as silly and doctrinaire—in another direction—as the latter-day liberals he disdained.

But the reader will not find in *Rumbles Left and Right* these weaknesses. Taught consistency through adversity, Mr. Buckley objects as strongly as ever to the mentality of "no enemies to the Left"; yet his mordant objections are founded upon a good understanding of the first principles of order and justice and freedom. Far from being exacerbated by the immoderate denunciations of his enemies in the Academy and out of it, Buckley actually has grown more urbane, though not thick-skinned. The snarling enmity which he has encountered on such television shows as those of Mike Wallace, Jack Paar, and David Susskind has taught him the character of his opposition, without souring his temper. A vivacious female admirer who saw Mr. Buckley in his first clash with Mike Wallace remarked that though Buckley had much the better of the fight, he seemed like a man without a skin, cut and bruised by vicious epithet, and yet enduring every ferocity for the sake of a cause, and dealing back deadly thrusts that paralyzed even the hardened television ruffians who had expected to drag him down.

Parenthetically, one may inquire why William Buckley suffers or even invites the unscrupulous and ignorant operations of television's M.C.'s, and condescends to debate with pseudo-literary denizens of Nightmare Alley unable to apprehend what he is talking about. The answer, I suppose, is that Mr. Buckley—like the old Templars—has sworn an oath never to refuse battle to less than three adversaries at once; and that he likes a hot fight, even with ignorant armies clashing by night; and that someone has to take up arms against even the surliest brute who abides by no rules of chivalry. In the mass age, Caliban has to be taken seriously and cudgeled from time to time, disagreeable though it is to contend with masterless men and sturdy beggars. Like it or not, Mr. Buckley is compelled to play Brasidas, although a smiling and subtle Brasidas, to the Cleon of the Left. Unless people like William Buckley wage this fight before the mass audience, Chaos and Old Night come mowing round Rockefeller Plaza and Lafayette Square.

So what ties together the essays in this collection is Mr. Buckley's consistent determination to wage the good fight in defense of ordered freedom; in defense of the traditions of civility; in defense of life with purpose. The "troublesome people and ideas" that he assails, sword in hand and tongue in cheek, are—most of them—either willing or unconscious servants of Chaos and Old Night. Though most of his chapters touch upon politics, Buckley is no ideologue. As a conservative, he knows that politics is not the most interesting thing in life, let alone the end of life. The purpose of life is to know God and enjoy Him forever—not to march potvaliantly toward the mirage of the Terrestrial Paradise. Like other thinking conservatives, Mr. Buckley turns to politics only defensively—to prevent the energumen or the well-intentioned zealot from giving us the Terrestrial Hell. As the reader will gather from "The Threat to the Amateur Sailor," Buckley would prefer yachting to polemicizing.* Yet none of us will be free to sail yachts, or even row dinghies, unless we set our face against the enemies of order—and of leisure.

Thus fanatic slogans, à la John Brown, about immediate integration have something to do with the passivity of most moderns before feckless or insolent waiters; thus the problem of Catholics and ideology is joined, in some fashion, with the Formosan resistance to Communism. Our present disorder is both external and internal. Most of our discontents are caused not so much by malice as by an eagerness to evade the pain of thinking. Mr. Buckley has gone to some pains to object; and he objects thoughtfully, unlike the quasi-professional decrier of "conformity" who himself conforms to cant and slogan.

Life is an arena where we are tested for our fortitude and our faith. If this fight ever should cease, we literally would be bored to death. If William Buckley has struck some fierce strokes in this arena, his are no backhanded blows. He objects to mediocrity for the sake of normality; he detests the

* Though now and again I have my differences of opinion with Mr. Buckley, we sail in the same vessel: indeed, I once piloted his *Panic*—in a most landlubberly fashion—across Long Island Sound. For my part, I am a swamp navigator, rejoicing in the exploration of the haunts of coot and hern by leaky boat in my Mecosta County. Mr. Buckley can have the gull's way and the whale's way. But either we all bail together, or we all sink separately.

monster because he cherishes the true man. Like Tailfer riding out from the Norman host, tossing his sword and laughing, Buckley has challenged to single combat one after another the champions of the opposing array. Yet if he charges into the press at Hastings, I do not think he will go down under the weight of his adversaries.

Inside Politics

THE GENTEEL NIGHTMARE
OF RICHARD ROVERE

RICHARD ROVERE has written an elegant spoof on the theme of an American Establishment, from which he has recently got a lot of footage. Almost certainly he will get more still, since his hypothesis—that there *is* what one might call an American Establishment—is inherently fascinating, whether presented with mock solemnity (as Rovere did it in *Esquire*), or with considerable seriousness (as Rovere did it in *The American Scholar*).

It is the leg-pull version that Rovere has slid into his latest book,* which otherwise contains a number of essays and studies, written for the most part for *The New Yorker;* and, at the moment, he finds it most convenient, or effective, or sophisticated, to say of the hypothesis that it is "pure nonsense"—those were his words on the Mike Wallace television program a few weeks ago. On the same occasion he rejoiced at being able to relate that he had succeeded in completely taking in a literal-minded young Congressman, a member of the John Birch Society, who seized on Rovere's *Esquire* essay as the Inside Word on the Apparatus that runs America, and rushed to introduce the essay into the *Congressional Record,* confident that, at last, someone had turned the key in the door that all these years has kept hidden from sight the mysteries of American political power.

That was a silly thing the Congressman did, to get taken in by a piece which—while maintaining that an Establish-

---

* Richard H. Rovere, *The American Establishment and Other Reports, Opinions, and Speculations,* Harcourt, Brace & World, 1962.

ment pretty well governs America, every bit as seriously as Swift once maintained that the only solution to the dietary problem in Ireland lay in eating babies—is full of rollicking giveaways, many of them instantly recognizable as imitations of the formulae of the sociologist of gamesmanship, Mr. Stephen Potter. *"Hilary Masters, a leading member of the Dutchess County school of sociologists, defined [the Establishment] in a recent lecture as the 'legitimate Mafia.'"* Footnote: *"Before the Edgewater Institute, Barrytown, N. Y., July 4, 1961. Vide Proceedings, 1961, pp. 37-51. Also see Masters' first-rate monograph Establishment Watering Places, Shekomeko Press, 1957."* Again, *"American students [of the Establishment] number few trained historians."* Footnote: *"Arthur Schlesinger, Jr., has done fairly decent work in the past* (vide The General and the President, *with Richard H. Rovere) but his judgments are suspect because of his own connections with the Establishment."*

The yuks aside, Rovere is clearly up to something (though he will deny it) more serious than catching up gullible Congressmen for the delectation of the *Esquire* set. If the piece was intended as sheer fantasy, it is the first venture in that precarious form that Mr. Rovere has ever taken, so far as I, one of his dutiful readers, am aware. The fact of the matter is that Mr. Rovere's disavowals notwithstanding, there *is* a thing which, properly understood, might well be called an American Establishment; and the success of Mr. Rovere's essay wholly depends on a sort of nervous apprehension of the correctness of the essential insight. Moreover, appealing now from Richard drunk (*Esquire*) to Richard sober (*American Scholar*), the author gives every indication of knowing that the idea of an Establishment is *not* sheer nonsense.

So our Establishment is different from the British Establishment, a designation which Macaulay and Carlyle, stretching the original and merely religious meaning of the term, attached to the dominant men and institutions of England— the established order. So what? The English Establishment

is more frozen than our own, primarily because theirs is a
society based on class. Their Establishment has rites and
honorifics and primogenitive continuities, and rests on deeply
embedded institutional commitments against which the Socialists, the angry young men, the disestablishmentarians,
have railed and howled and wept altogether in vain.

The "Establishment" Mr. Rovere is talking, or not talking,
about is precariously perched; and every now and then it
gets a terrific shellacking from its opponents. In the English
Establishment, membership is to a considerable extent ex
officio (even non-U dukes belong); in ours, far less so (though
it is inconceivable, at least to this observer, that the head of
the Ford Foundation could be an outsider). The chances are
better that you might earn a berth in the American Establishment if you have gone to Groton and Yale; but no one has an
automatic right to membership in it, not even the President
of the United States (as Rovere, even in his flippant mood,
admits). And membership in it is to an extent far greater than
in England dependent on a man's opinions (and the way they
are expressed); England, by contrast, has no trouble at all in
countenancing Socialist earls.

It tends to be true in England that the Establishment prevails. It is less true in the United States: for the Establishment
here is not so much of the governing class, as of the class that
governs the governors. The English Establishment mediates
the popular political will through perdurable English institutions. The American Establishment seeks to set the bounds of
permissible opinion. And on this, it speaks ex cathedra. It
would not hesitate to decertify Mr. Rovere. But he gives no
indication of waywardness.

Mr. Rovere's technique in the essay is to make a generality about the Establishment and quickly undermine it by a
ludicrous particularization.

• *"The Establishment has always favored foreign aid."*
Quite true. *"It is, in fact, a matter on which Establishment
discipline may be invoked."* The reader is supposed to sigh

with relief—obviously there are no disciplinary commissions lying around, visible or invisible, set up to weigh complaints of dogmatic infidelity, and issue bulls of excommunication. Does it not follow from this buffoonery that what went before is also nonsense? That the Establishment does not in fact always favor foreign aid? Does it not follow, even, that the very idea of an Establishment is a hoax?

• *"Within the next couple of years ... Congress will spend a good part of its time fighting the Establishment program for a great revision of American trade practices and for eventual American association with the European Common Market."* Quite so. But then quickly: *"This whole scheme was cooked up at a three-day meeting of the Executive Committee [of the Establishment] at the Sheraton Park in Washington immediately after President Kennedy's inauguration on January 20, 1961."*

• Again: *"If it were not for the occasional formation of public committees such as the Citizens Committee for International Development scholars would have a difficult time learning who the key figures are."* Hmm. Then the payoff: *"A working principle agreed upon by Establishment scholars is this. If in the course of a year a man's name turns up fourteen times in paid advertisements in, or collective letters to, the* New York Times, *the official Establishment daily, it is about fourteen to one that he is a member of the Executive Committee. (I refer, of course, to advertisements and letters pleading Establishment causes.)"*

But then on other statements about the Establishment, Rovere does not bother to frolic; he is simply asseverative:

"The accepted range [of Establishment opinion] is from about as far left as, say, Walter Reuther to about as far right as, say, Dwight Eisenhower. A man cannot be for less welfarism than Eisenhower, and to be farther left than Reuther is considered bad taste." (A significant disjunction: Erich Fromm is merely bad taste; Ludwig von Mises is intolerable.)

"Racial equality is another matter on which the Establishment forbids dissent."

"In matters of public policy, it may be said that those principles and policies that have the editorial support of The New York Times *are at the core of Establishment doctrine."*

And so on. It is at best difficult to undermine a truism. Rovere's sense of style prevents him from taking them all on. The result is that most of his readers walk away from his piece not like the Congressman, grimly tracking down every *jeu de mots* for Social Truth, but aware that Rovere has, in spite of himself, limned the outlines of a great force in American affairs, which is slowly acquiring self-consciousness.

Why should the concept of an American Establishment, first introduced into American journalism, according to Rovere, by *National Review,* be so fascinating to so many people? The answer is complicated. It has to do, first, with the difference in attitude, in England and here, toward a national Establishment. In England, most influential people like to feel they are in the Establishment. Here, especially among intellectuals, the desire is to be thought of as too independent a spirit to be a part of any movement which is powerful and institutionalized, let alone one of which it might be said that it is also an apparatus.

Thus, when Rovere writes that his buddy Arthur Schlesinger, Jr. "has connections with the Establishment" it becomes dismally complicated to sort out everything Rovere is trying to communicate. At least this much he seems to be trying to say: 1) There is no Establishment, so anything I say about Arthur's connection with it is playful, and not to be taken seriously. However, 2) what I say must have at least a superficial plausibility, if I am to bring off this spoof; and it is of course true that Arthur is very well connected with very powerful people; for instance, at the national level, the President of the United States; at the professional level,

Harvard University; at the level of highbrow journalism, myself. And I, er, know the President pretty well, who, of course, is an overseer of Harvard, where he has known Arthur for years, and of course Arthur wrote a lot of his speeches for him and a book, *Kennedy or Nixon: Does It Make Any Difference?*, which may have swung as many votes as the margin Kennedy won by, who knows? And then, Arthur and I wrote a book together—yes, it is plausible to suggest that Arthur has connections with something that might be called the Establishment. But remember!—there is no such thing.

Another difference: in England, the Establishment is conceded to concern itself with what is clearly the national consensus. In America, by contrast, there is a deep division between the views of the putative Establishment and those whose interests it seeks to forward. For in this country there are two consensuses, that of the people (broadly speaking) and that of the intellectuals (narrowly speaking). These differences the Establishment is not eager to stress. Having prescribed what is permissible opinion, it is reassuring to hold that those who drink deep in impermissible opinions are a) a minority; and b) an ignorant minority, at that.

The tension between the two consensuses persists, as Mr. Rovere acknowledges in indicating which are the great bases of the Establishment's strength. For thirty years now, the Establishment has pretty well succeeded in dominating the Executive and the Judiciary—but not the Congress (which is still capable of passing a McCarran Internal Security Bill, trimming drastically a foreign aid bill, and filibustering to death a civil rights bill). As Mr. Rovere is careful to say, the Establishment has accumulated the power not to put one of its own "agents" (to go along with the terminology of the apparatus) in any sensitive spot it wishes, but to see to it that a real outsider does not get in. Thus Willkie, then Dewey, then Eisenhower, two insiders and one fellow traveler of the Establishment, took the nomination away from the outsider Taft—major operations for an anxious Establishment. Nixon came along and posed a clear threat; the Establishment huffed and puffed (did you ever see Walter Lippmann so highly mobilized?) and narrowly squeaked by. In short, the whole thing is easier to conceive if one bears in mind that the Establishment in question is not altogether establishmentarianized. That is why those who started using the term—Frank Meyer, Willmoore Kendall, James Burnham, William Henry Chamberlin—usually speak of the "Liberal Establishment."

Professor Willmoore Kendall, a well-known enemy of the Establishment, several years ago reviewed Professor Samuel Stouffer's book, *Communism, Conformity, and Civil Liberties.* "The title of the book," Kendall began, "should have been *Sam Stouffer Discovers America"*—for here were Professor Stouffer's anguished statistical revelations that the overwhelming majority of the American people do not believe that civil liberties should be enjoyed by Communists, or that atheists should teach in the public schools! *Obviously* that is what the body of Americans believes, Kendall observed; and it is an indication of the otherworldliness of Establishment scholarship that statistical verification of a fact as plain as Jimmy Durante's nose should come as such a shock.

What is all the more galling is that the people have their own scholars; precious few of them, to be sure. But is this because the people's point of view is, *sub specie aeternitatis* (an anti-Establishment concept), indefensible? Not altogether. There are other reasons, Kendall and others have been suggesting, and these other reasons have been coming forward armed with imposing credentials. *Anti-Establishment scholars are not given true equality,* a true opportunity to set up their stands, unencumbered by the censors of the Establishment, in the academic market place. The Establishment loves dissent as a theoretical proposition. In practice, it is not easy to get a hearing, in high circles of the Establishment, for heretical doctrine. In our time, the Willmoore Kendalls, not the Robert Oppenheimers, are the Galileos.

Come now, let us acknowledge that it is as difficult for a camel to pass through a needle's eye as for a true dissenter to receive a favorable review of an anti-Establishment book in *The New York Times Book Review* section. I say "as difficult," in order to acknowledge that such a thing does occasionally happen. But not often.

Here, then, is what Rovere is really getting at. He knows there is a body of political and social thought which prevails in the centers of American intellectual and polemical power. What he resists so fiercely, for reasons he has not thought through, is the insinuation a) that what one might call the Liberal Establishment holds to a definable orthodoxy (his going on to adumbrate that orthodoxy was sheer brinkmanship); and b) that the keepers of that orthodoxy resort to conventional means to maintain it, even to means which, officially, its theorists disdain. Especially, he shudders at the use of the word "conspiracy." He has a hard enough time acknowledging that the Communists are, from time to time, successful conspirators. It is more than he can bear that it is sometimes suggested that the Liberal Establishment engages in conspiratorial practices.

Elsewhere in this book, Rovere rails explicitly against the "conspiracy view of history." Mr. Rovere is fond of laying down fine distinctions, but in this regard he is an absolutist—conspiracies, to judge from his writings, don't exist; or if they do, they never accomplish anything. So absolute is his commitment to nonconspiracy that he wrote an entire volume about Senator McCarthy without mentioning a) the conspiracy whose target was the Institute of Pacific Relations; or b) the curious affair (involving a number of his friends) whose focal point was the anti-McCarthy "independent investigator," Paul Hughes.

What, after all, does it mean, to conspire? Usually something less, as Father John Courtney Murray has reminded

Sidney Hook, than to meet your partner under the bridge with complementary parts of a bomb. "To plot, devise, contrive," "to combine in action or aims: to concur, cooperate as by intention," says the dictionary. That kind of thing goes on all the time. In the White House, for instance. Within the Department of Government at Harvard, for instance. The question whether there is an Establishment some of whose members conspire together raises merely the question whether there is, or has been, coordination of purpose between people who administer in the White House, teach at Harvard, write in *The New Yorker,* and preach at St. John the Divine. Of course there is coordination, however informal, and it is as naïve to believe there is not as it is naïve to support that *only* conspiratorial action is responsible for historical events.

The word conspiracy, at another level, has a highly pejorative meaning, spelled out in the definition (Oxford's): "To combine ... to do something criminal, illegal, or reprehensible." It is not necessarily reprehensible for Bishop Pike and Bishop Sherrill to agree to denounce the Radical Right during the next fortnight—why shouldn't they? (What would God think if they *didn't*?) It *is* reprehensible for Joseph L. Rauh, Jr. (ADA) and Al Friendly (Washington *Post*) and Clayton Fritchey (*Democratic Digest*) to have conspired with Paul Hughes, a secret informer, in an attempt to penetrate a congressional committee. Surely it is reprehensible if professors within a department of economics or government conspire against the promotion of a scholar because his views are different from their own (assuming the professors announce themselves as advocates of academic freedom).

Granted, then, that a sane man might seek to designate whatever figurative edifice shelters the household gods of American Liberalism, its high priests, its incense makers, and its catechetical press—is "Establishment" a good word for it? I think the term is useful, if one is careful to remember that it is a figure of speech, even as it has been understood to be in

England for over a hundred years. It is preposterous to take seriously (as the Congressman evidently did) Mr. Rovere's statement that "Spruille Braden . . . was read out of the Establishment on April 14, 1960." It is by no means preposterous to recognize that while Braden was once a member of the Establishment, now he no longer is, though the alienation was attended by no formal rites of excommunication, and took place over a considerable period of time. You need not be taken in by the solemn whisper that the Establishment has a president, an executive committee, a constitution, by-laws, and formal membership requirements, to believe that there do exist people of varying prestige and power within American Liberaldom; that we speak here of the intellectual plutocrats of the nation, who have at their disposal vast cultural and financial resources; and that it is possible at any given moment to plot with fair accuracy the vectors of the Establishment's position on everything from birth control to Moise Tshombe. That is what the excitement is about.

Mr. Rovere writes, as always, with precision and wit. In this volume he turns his attention to any number of things, about some of which he feels strongly, about some of which he does not seem to feel at all. In this particular book, he is clearly vexed only by Douglas MacArthur, and by certain things (about the Establishment) Peter Viereck has written; and by the personal shortcomings of Harold Ickes—no, come to think of it, he isn't really vexed by them at all. Mr. Rovere is fun to read, easy to read, interesting to read. But he needs to watch out. *The New Yorker* encourages good literary needlework; but Rovere has always fancied himself *l'homme engagé*. There are those who wish he would discover other evils than Joe McCarthy. Address your complaints to the Assignment Editor, the American Establishment, care of your local post office.

BARRY GOLDWATER AND THE
THUNDER ON THE RIGHT

IF THE American people *really* wanted a New Frontier, they could always turn for leadership to Barry Morris Goldwater, junior Senator from Arizona, and one of the few genuine radicals in American public life. A radical conservative—a man who, if he were President, would change the face of the nation: in that sense he's a "radical." He would reorient America back in the direction of a) minimum government, and b) maximum personal responsibility: in that sense he's a "conservative."

Agriculture? *"The government of the United States has no business taking money from one group of people to give it to another."* The government, in other words, should get out of agriculture.

Labor unions? *"I've never understood why if monopolies are bad when they are exercised by businessmen, why they aren't also bad when they are exercised by labor union leaders."* An end, in a word, to industry-wide bargaining and the union shop.

The Negro problem? *"I believe justice and morality require that persons of different races attend the same schools. But I'm not going to impose my ideas of morality and justice on other people. The Constitution of the United States gave me no warrant to tell South Carolinians how to run their schools."*—So put a stop to federal efforts to impose integration—if necessary, by a constitutional amendment.

And so it goes. Every one of Senator Goldwater's domestic proposals derives from two central beliefs. The first is that

31

the Constitution of the United States enumerates the powers of Congress and explicitly denies Congress the right to do the kind of thing that has been going under the name of the New Deal, the Fair Deal, and the New Frontier. Second, human freedom is best served by keeping the government small.

That kind of drastic conservatism is not easy to find these days. Even so, Senator Goldwater firmly believes that the United States is a profoundly conservative country, if only the people had a chance to get a taste of the real thing, and realized more fully where they are headed under statism. But if it should turn out that he is wrong, that Americans reject Goldwater's brand of individualism, it is unlikely it would make the least difference to him: he'd go on believing what he now believes, a set of principles rooted—he has publicly maintained—in the very nature of man. Beliefs of that intensity are not changed by Gallup polls. Sometimes they even make friends. "I *like* Goldwater, as a man and as a politician," William S. White of *Harper's* wrote recently. "I wholly disagree with most of his views. But I own to a bias for a man so full of principle."

It's astonishing that a man holding to such rigidly conservative views should be so strikingly successful in politics almost thirty years after Franklin Roosevelt came, saw, and conquered. Goldwater's emergence has a lot to do, of course, with organic political and social developments in America. Many people are disillusioned with the kind of world we live in, and seek other solutions than those that have been advanced by the Liberals during the years of our decline. But Goldwater's rise is to a considerable extent the result of Goldwater. Very few people escape from exposure to him completely unscathed. You can find diehard left-wingers who will tell you Goldwater has no personal attraction whatever, just as you could find diehard right-wingers who would say the same thing about Franklin Roosevelt: both are fooling themselves. Goldwater, like Roosevelt, has a first-class political personality. And again like Roosevelt, Goldwater is accepted as a partisan of a political position. So that in backing him, his followers can fuse personal and ideological passions.

That is what accounts for Goldwater's success, notwithstanding a political position that can hardly be considered to be in vogue. It is generally suggested that Senator Goldwater is so conservative he's just out of this world. Senator Humphrey twitted him at a cocktail party recently. "You're one of the handsomest men in America," Humphrey said. "You ought to be in the movies. In fact, I've made just that proposal to 18th Century Fox." Goldwater's enemies, to be sure, are legion; but they are not—yet—mortally engaged against him, nor even, for the most part, waspish in their references to him. (That isn't true of Walter Reuther and his circle, to be sure. Goldwater got fired up one day and called Reuther more dangerous than the Communists, whereupon Reuther replied that Goldwater should be taken away in a white suit, and the colorful vendetta goes on.) And that isn't because Goldwater is not powerful, and therefore can be indulged as one would, say, a vegetarian. Goldwater is among the three most important Republicans in the GOP. When at the Republican Convention in 1960 he and Rockefeller and Nixon stood before the cameras, arm in arm, the idea was that *all* the forces in the Republican Party were present and accounted for: Left, Center, and Right. The camera had never been off Goldwater during the hectic few days before the Convention, beginning the day Nixon traveled to see Rockefeller in New York, there to consummate what Goldwater publicly denounced as a "Munich Conference," and ending with the exhortation by Goldwater to his fellow conservatives to fight hard for a Nixon victory.

Here was a remarkably versatile man, who on Sunday could denounce Nixon as an appeaser on the scale of Neville Chamberlain, and on Wednesday, in the interest of party unity, embrace him *and* the man to whom Nixon had allegedly betrayed the Republican Party. There was a flurry of resentment, a sense of disappointment here and there among his followers. "I got quite a lot of nasty mail," Goldwater commented, "some of it calling me yellow, and other worse things—no, nothing worse. There isn't anything worse." But Goldwater gained, rather than lost, prestige. He had proved he is what most truly successful American politicians have to be: an Insider. He had made his criticisms of Nixon, of Rockefeller, of "Progressive Republicanism," in language absolutely remarkable for its candor: but now it was time to strike camp and move on. And Goldwater is, and always will be, a member of the Republican team. Here is a key to his durability—an organizational fidelity that Joe McCarthy renounced when, after the vote of censure, he apologized to the American people for having urged them to vote for Eisenhower. It was the end of McCarthy.

He is a man so attractive, so plausible, so energetic, as to cause the kingmakers to deplore his single and obtrusive disqualification, his "ultraconservatism"—a designation, by the way, that Goldwater deeply resents, because of its emotive overhead. ("Why don't they call Humphrey, Stevenson, Williams and that gang 'ultraliberals'?") The feeling in these quarters is that Goldwater represents a remarkable conjunction of politically negotiable assets—"if only he would drop the antisocial security crap," as one old pro put it. Barry Goldwater is: amiable, good-looking, fluent, earnest, a veteran, an active jet pilot, one part Jewish, a practicing Christian, head of a handsome family, a successful businessman, a best-selling author, a syndicated columnist, and a tough campaigner who won a smashing victory in 1958 when he was re-elected Senator in a solidly Democratic state, against the bitter opposition of organized labor. "He could go very, very far," the old pro mused, his face as sad as though he were looking at an uncontrolled oil gusher, spouting its yellow gold wantonly onto the ground.

Others point out that Goldwater *has* come very far, and

quite possibly wouldn't have except for the ardent support of American conservatives. One can argue whether his stout conservatism has helped or hurt him thus far. The big question is whether the Senator might, but for his adamant conservatism, successfully contend for the presidential nomination in 1964.

How did he get that way? He is the son of an Episcopalian mother and a Jewish father, who brought him up in Arizona, where his grandparents had settled and founded a little trading store which soon grew into a prosperous chain. When he was a freshman at college his father died, and Barry decided to quit school and tend the store while his brothers continued their education. The three of them worked hard, and the business flourished. The employees of Goldwater's, incidentally, have never been able to understand the bitter opposition to Senator Barry from organized labor. They earn more than their competitors, and yet they work a 37-hour week, and enjoy fringe benefits ranging from an employees' swimming pool to a retirement fund.

"Flying in a jet airplane from California to Arizona as I often do," Goldwater remarks, "I often marvel at the ordeal my grandfather and his brother went through in making that trek over plain and desert—those really were new frontiers, not made in Madison Avenue. They went without sufficient food or water, and with Indians harassing them all the way. But they did it, and their whole generation did it, and that's the kind of spirit that created America. That was a spiritual energy that came out of the loins of the people. It didn't come out of Washington. And it never will. Washington's principal responsibility is to get out of the way of the creative impulses of the people." It's one thing to intone generalities about human freedom and the American Constitution—every politician does that as a matter of course ("Ask not what the government can do for you," declaimed President Kennedy, a couple of days before suggesting about thirty-

seven new things the government could do for me . . .). But
Goldwater means it. If he had his way, the farmer's checks
would stop coming in, the labor union leader would face a
law telling him he couldn't strike an entire industry, the
businessman wouldn't get his cozy little tariff, the apartment
dweller wouldn't have his rent frozen, the unemployed
wouldn't get a federal check, nor the teacher federal money,
nor the Little Rock Negroes their paratroops. It's all very
well to venerate the Constitution and individual freedom
where the other fellow is concerned, but Barry Goldwater
is for it all the way.

What would Goldwater do if he were President today?
The ideal candidate for public office, he wrote in his best-
selling book, *The Conscience of a Conservative,* would speak
to the people as follows: "I have little interest in streamlining
government or in making it more efficient, for I mean to
reduce its size. I do not undertake to promote welfare, for I
propose to extend freedom. My aim is not to pass laws, but
to repeal them. It is not to inaugurate new programs, but to
cancel old ones that do violence to the Constitution, or that
have failed in their purpose, or that impose on the people
an unwarranted financial burden. I will not attempt to discover whether legislation is 'needed' before I have first determined whether it is constitutionally permissible. And if I
should later be attacked for neglecting my constituents' 'interests,' I shall reply that I was informed their main interest
is liberty and that in that cause I am doing the very best I
can."

That is a staggering statement, the likes of which have not
been heard from any President since Grover Cleveland.

What, specifically, would Barry Goldwater have the government do? Here are his most "ultra" domestic proposals.
He would: 1) Get the government out of agriculture and
welfare—altogether. 2) Apply antimonopoly legislation
against the big labor unions. 3) Abolish the progressive income tax. In foreign affairs, he would: 1) Eliminate foreign

aid except to nations actively prepared to assist in the anti-Communist enterprise. 2) Eliminate economic and cultural exchange programs, which he views as counterfeit considering the actual relationship between the Soviet Union and the United States. 3) Continue nuclear testing. And 4) "be prepared to undertake military programs against vulnerable Communist regimes" in the cause of pressing for victory over the Soviet Union. For instance, a Monroe Doctrine for Africa, imposed by the NATO powers. A striking force of anti-Communist Asiatics that would help the pro-Western government in Laos, the rebels in Indonesia.

Such a program is completely at odds with the programs adopted in 1960, by both the Democratic and the Republican parties. Both these programs called for soft living at home, and send the bill to Washington; and abroad, more of the same—endless negotiations with the Soviet Union, based on the assumption that we can soften Communism by a massive parliamentary offensive, plus foreign aid for everybody. Does it follow that Goldwater's program can never guide the country? Goldwater is anything but hopeless. He once reminded a student that the difference between his program and the official program of the Republican Party is not nearly so great as the difference between the official Democratic program of 1932 (in which Roosevelt promised to cut down federal spending!) and the program of the New Deal (in which spending was elevated to a Sacred National Duty). Yet the New Deal, when it came up for ratification in 1936, was solidly endorsed. Roosevelt spent, and the people flipped.

But Goldwater, if ever he were to run for President, would not dissemble, as Roosevelt did. He seems to be temperamentally incapable of doing so. The columnist Holmes Alexander wrote about him recently, "He must be the frankest political speaker who has ever gone the rounds, because his practice is not to dissemble at all, for any reason whatever. A year or so ago he made one of his typical speeches at the

National Press Club and left his critics gaping with astonish-
ment. He admitted his own mistakes. He laughed at himself,
and kidded his party. He refused to vilify Walter Reuther,
although disapproving of the labor leader's 'power complex.'
Goldwater even told how he'd publicly sought the endorsement of a Communist-tainted union, because he knew the
membership to be composed of loyal Americans. Was there
ever such a politician as this?"

Not in recent years, certainly. And yet Goldwater is nothing more than a political curio if his political program is
trivial, insubstantial, merely eccentric.

And this is the point at which the blows are exchanged
between Liberals and conservatives. Goldwater's admirers
believe that a hard dose of Goldwater could revive this country as very little else could. It is Goldwater's program, of all
those extant, that most faithfully reflects the political philosophy of the men who forged this country, and hammered
out its Constitution. On this point there simply isn't any
doubt. Our Constitution was drafted by men who thought
the federal government should have enough power to maintain order, but no more. Thomas Jefferson thought that government best which governed least; and once he commented
that any program of federal aid to education should be introduced as an amendment to the Constitution, since control
over education was not among the specified powers granted
to the federal government by the Constitution.

The question is whether the insights of men like Hamilton
and Jefferson and Madison and Marshall hold good for today.
Goldwater thinks they do, that they have not been, essentially, invalidated: that government, unless it is kept in hand,
grows tyrannical; that the diffusion of governmental power,
among the respective states, is the key to the maintenance of
individual liberty.

For instance, Goldwater disapproves of segregated schooling. But he can find no warrant in the Constitution for giving
to the federal government any say whatever on matters of

education. Hence he believes it is for the individual state to decide for itself what will be its educational practices.

Social security is best effected, he believes, by maximizing the national wealth. In America, as in all free market economies, the only (lawful) way for one man to acquire wealth is by contributing to the wealth of other men. That is why in America it has never been the case that the rich got richer while the poor got poorer. Throughout our history, the well-being of the lower class has (in defiance of the laws of Marx) increased. If, to look after the very few who for whatever reason cannot survive in a free market economy, we must have social security programs, then let the individual states handle them, with reference to local resources, and local needs. If an individual state chooses not to have a social security law, leaving charity for the local communities to exercise, why that is for the majority of the citizens of that state to decide, just as it is the privilege of New York State to levy an income tax, and the privilege of Connecticut *not* to levy such a tax. "And who will say," Goldwater asks, "that the government of New York is 'better,' or 'more humane,' or 'more progressive,' than Connecticut's?"

"The genius of the federal system," Goldwater has said, "is that it allows the individual state to experiment. If the state makes an unwise move, the contrast with surrounding states is enough to bring quick reform. But when the decision is made by the federal government, binding on all fifty states, the mistake is totalized: and you lose the means by which to make your comparisons."

In foreign policy, the Goldwater program is fashioned out of hard steel, and is not distinctively Republican. In fact it happens to be almost identical with the policy of Senator Thomas Dodd, a Democrat who votes on the other side of Goldwater on most domestic issues. Even so, it consistently reflects Goldwater's concern for freedom—not only here, but abroad. Goldwater's enthusiasm for liberating the slaves of Communism relates historically to the nineteenth-century abolitionist fervor to liberate the slaves. Goldwater's premises are: 1) Soviet Communism intends to colonize the entire world, if necessary by force of arms. 2) The United States will never surrender. 3) The best means of opposing Communism is also the best means of effecting peace: we must fight, fight hard, at every front, with courage to oppose Soviet advances by the threat of the use of force.

Again, that is, at first glance, not very different from the Truman-Eisenhower-Kennedy program. But the similarities are, again, mostly rhetorical. Goldwater would have followed MacArthur's recommendations to bomb north of the Yalu; he would right now be testing nuclear bombs, to perfect our arms flexibility; he would not have traveled to the summit, neither to Geneva in 1953, nor to Camp David in 1959, nor to Paris in 1960; nor be sending aid to Sukarno, Tito, and Gomulka; nor have permitted the UN army to protect Gizenga's pro-Communist regime in the Congo. *"Goldwater will end up in a pine box,"* Moscow's *Pravda* thundered in a lead editorial last year, commenting on Goldwater's book, *The Conscience of a Conservative.* "If Communism took over the world," Goldwater commented, "that's just where I'd want to be."

What will come of this phenomenon? The chances are very much against Goldwater's nomination for the presidency—unless President Kennedy, by pursuing a hard-left policy at home, and apeasement abroad, should bring the nation to catastrophe. If there is runaway inflation, if Communism marches into Latin America on a frightening scale, if our alliances begin to crumble, the people may turn to a man who offers a genuine alternative. The tough and persuasive voice of Barry Goldwater would sound loud and clear.

But if Kennedy's course is moderate, as probably it will be, Goldwater will surely be passed up by the Republican convention, in favor of a moderate, or even a left-moderate: a Nixon, a Rockefeller. Still, he will continue to exercise an important influence, as already he has done. Every measure that comes up before Congress, every proposal advanced in a party caucus, every executive order issued from the White House, he will assess according to traditional constitutional principles, and the realities of our war against the Soviet Union. And his enormous appeal, throughout the country, will give weight to that assessment. He is a hero not merely to the members and followers of the National Association of Manufacturers, but to all the Right-minded youth of the nation, for whom he seems to embody the Politician Unchained from the dreary, federalized, temporizing, circumlocutory, bureaucratized politics of the Welfare State, the way station on the road to 1984. And on the other hand, it isn't just youthful enthusiasts who like Goldwater—it is just about every American conservative. "In the stomping, roaring ovation that followed [Goldwater's] speech," *Time* magazine recently commented, "it was clear that conservatives of all ages had found their most persuasive voice since Robert Alphonso Taft."

Senator Goldwater will, then, in the months to come, act as a potent inhibiting influence on government; and on the side, as a political educator. When that political re-education is complete—perhaps during Goldwater's lifetime—a man such as he, with a program such as his, could lead the country. On that day the faculty of Harvard University, associated in the public mind as the GHQ of American Liberalism, would undoubtedly dive for their bomb shelters, and classify themselves a Depressed Area. But it would be up to the Commonwealth of Massachusetts—not the federal government—to look after them.

ON THE VISIT OF KHRUSHCHEV TO THE UNITED STATES IN 1959 *

THE damage Khrushchev can do to the United States on this trip is not comparable to the damage we have done to ourselves. Khrushchev is here. And his being here profanes the nation. But the harm we have done, we have done to ourselves; and for that we cannot hold Khrushchev responsible. There is nothing he is in a position to do, as he passes through our land, that can aggravate the national dishonor. We can only dishonor ourselves. Mr. Eisenhower invited him to come. But that was a transient damage that might have been laid to the vagaries of personal diplomacy. The lasting damage is related to the national acquiescence in Mr. Eisenhower's aberration. That acquiescence required the lapse of our critical and moral faculties. And for so long as they are in suspension, regeneration is not possible.

I deplore the fact that Khrushchev travels about this country—having been met at the frontier by our own prince, who arrived with his first string of dancing girls, and a majestic caravan of jewels and honey and spices; I mind that he will wend his lordly way from city to city, where the Lilliputians will fuss over his needs, weave garlands through the ring in his nose, shiver when he belches out his threats, and labor in panic to sate his imperial appetites. I mind that Khrushchev is here; but I mind more that Eisenhower invited him. I mind that Eisenhower invited him, but I mind much more the defense of that invitation by the *thought* leaders of the nation. Khrushchev cannot by his presence here permanently

* An address, delivered at Carnegie Hall.

42

damage us, I repeat; and neither can Mr. Eisenhower by inviting him. But we are gravely damaged if it is true that in welcoming Khrushchev, Eisenhower speaks for America; for in that case the people have lost their reason; and we cannot hope to live down the experience until we have recovered our reason, and regained our moral equilibrium.

I mind, in a word, the so-called "reasons" that have been advanced—and accepted—as to why Mr. Eisenhower issued the invitation. I mind first that "reasons" are being put forward, but mostly that they are being accepted. Khrushchev's visit has been successfully transmuted into a "diplomatic necessity"; and many even speak of it as a stroke of diplomatic genius. If the invitation had been rendered by President Eisenhower in his capacity as principal agent of American foreign policy, the deed would have been explosive enough. But the true dimensions of our national crisis became visible on the appearance of the concentric ripples of assent that followed upon the issuance of the invitation. *A splendid idea*, said the chairman of the Foreign Relations Committee of the Senate. And all the world concurs.

And in a matter of days, we were being solemnly advised by the majority of the editorial writers of the nation that a) the invitation was bound to meet with the approval of all those who favor peace in the world and good will toward men; and that b) in any event, those who opposed the invitation have no alternative save to abide by the spirit that moved the President—as a matter of loyalty. "If you have to throw something at him," said Mr. Nixon upon touching ground after his visit to Moscow, "throw flowers." And then Mr. Gallup confirmed the popularity of the President's decision—which, it turns out, exceeds even the popularity of the President himself.

I do not recall that six months earlier Mr. Gallup had canvassed the American people on the question whether Mr. Khrushchev should be invited to this country, but I doubt that anyone would dispute my guess that as emphatic a majority would then have voted *against* the visit.

What happened? The sheer cogency of the invitation evidently struck the people as forcibly as the superiority of round as against square wheels is said one day to have struck our primitive ancestors. *Obviously* the visit is in order, the people seem to have grasped, giving way before the intuitions and analyses of their leaders. How mischievous is the habit of adducing reasons behind everything that is done! I can, happily and unassailably, delight in lobster and despise crabmeat all my life—so long as I refrain from giving *reasons* why the one food suits and the other sickens. But when I seek rationally to motivate my preferences, I lose my authority. If only the publicists had refrained from shoring up the President's caprice with a Gothic rational structure! But no. We are a rational people. We do nothing without cause. There must be cause behind the invitation; and so the reasons for it are conjured up.

I have not heard a "reason" why Khrushchev should come to this country that is not in fact a reason why he should *not* come to this country. *He will see for himself the health and wealth of the land?* Very well; and having confirmed the fact, what are we to expect? That he will weaken in his adherence to his maniacal course? Because the average American has the use of one and two-thirds toilets? One might as well expect the Bishop of Rome to break the apostolic succession upon being confronted by the splendid new YMCA in Canton, Ohio. Does Khrushchev really *doubt* that there are 67 million automobiles in this country? What is he to do now that he is here? Count them? And if it is true that he doubts the statistics on American production and the American way of life, statistics that have been corroborated by his own technicians—then what reason is there to believe that he will trust the evidence of his own eyes as more reliable?

And what will he do if there is a discrepancy? Fire Alger Hiss?

If Khrushchev were a man to be moved by empirical brushes with reality, how could he continue to believe in Communism? He cannot turn a corner in the Soviet Union without colliding against stark evidence of the fraudulence of Marxist theory. Where is the workers' paradise? In the two-room apartments that house five families? In the frozen reaches where he commits to slavery the millions who fail to appreciate the fact that under the Marxist prescription they have been elevated to a state of total freedom? In the head-quarters of the secret police where files are kept on every citizen of the Soviet Union on the *presumption* that every citizen is an enemy of the proletarian state?

Any man who is capable of being affected by the evidence of things as they are need not leave Russia to discover that the major premises of Karl Marx are mistaken. Dante culti-vated a love of heaven by demonstrating the horrors of hell. It did not occur to him that the devil might be converted by taking him around the glories of the court of the Medici. What reason have we to believe that a man who knows Russia and *still* has not rejected Marx will be moved by the sight of Levittown?

But even if Khrushchev fails to readjust his views after witnessing the economic miracles wrought by capitalism— in which connection it is relevant to recall the amazement of American industrial leaders on discovering during Mikoyan's visit that he knew more about American industrial accom-plishments than they did—even if Khrushchev finds out that Mikoyan was right all along, will he learn that other great lesson which the President advanced as a principal "reason" why Khrushchev should come? Is he going to encounter that firmness of American resolution which will cause him, when he returns to Russia, to furrow his brow in anxiety on resum-ing the war against us?

I suggest that this brings us to the major reason why

Khrushchev should *not* have been invited. If indeed the nation is united behind Mr. Eisenhower in this invitation, then the nation is united behind an act of diplomatic sentimentality which can only confirm Khrushchev in the contempt he feels for the dissipated morale of a nation far gone, as the theorists of Marxism have all along contended, in decrepitude. That he should be invited to visit here as though he were susceptible to a rational engagement! That he should achieve orthodox diplomatic recognition not three years after shocking history itself by the brutalities of Budapest; months after endorsing the shooting down of an unarmed American plane; only weeks since he last shrieked his intention, in *Foreign Affairs,* of demolishing the West should it show any resistance to the march of socialism; only days since publishing in an American magazine his undiluted resolve to enslave the citizens of Free Berlin—that such an introduction should end up constituting his credentials for a visit to America will teach him something about the West some of us wish he might never have known.

What is it stands in the way of Communism's march? The little homilies of American capitalism? A gigantic air force which depends less on gasoline than on the pronouncements of the Committee for a Sane Nuclear Policy to know whether it can ever be airborne? Have we not something more to face Khrushchev with? Is this indeed the nature of the enemy? Khrushchev is entitled to wonder exultantly, after twelve days of giddy American cameraderie—will he not cherish as never before the pronouncements of Marx about the weakness of the capitalist opposition? Will he not return convinced that behind the modulated hubbub at the White House, in the State Department, at the city halls, at the economic clubs, at the industrial banquets, he heard—*with his own ears*—the death rattle of the West? Is there a *reason* why we should voluntarily expose to the enemy the great lesion of the West—our deficient understanding—which saps the will without which we can never save the world for freedom? Will Khrushchev respect us more as, by our deeds, we proclaim and proclaim again and again our hallucination, in the grinding teeth of the evidence, that we and the Soviet Union can work together for a better world?

It is the imposture of irrationality in the guise of rationality that frightens. The visit is timely, we are told. Why? State one reason. Why was it not timely, if it is timely now, a year ago? If Eisenhower is correct now in welcoming Khrushchev, then was he not wrong yesterday in not welcoming him? But we were all pro-Eisenhower yesterday—when he declared he would not meet with the Soviet leaders while under pressure of blackmail in regard to Berlin. And yet we are pro-Eisenhower today—when he proceeds to meet with Khrushchev, with the threat still hanging over us. If it is so very urgent that we should acquaint Khrushchev with the highways and byways of the United States, why is Eisenhower doing it seven long years after he first had the opportunity? Why has the same nation that implicitly endorsed the social boycott of Soviet leaders changed its mind so abruptly—to harmonize with so dissonant a change in position by our lackadaisical President? (The social history of the White House under Mr. Eisenhower will, after all, record only one exclusion and one addition during his tenure. Khrushchev was added, Senator McCarthy was ejected. And both times, the thousands cheered.) Is it a mark of loyalty to go along? What if Mr. Eisenhower had announced that, upon reflection, Red China should be invited into the United Nations? Would it be a mark of loyalty for us to assent? Or if he had decided to yield Quemoy and Matsu? A mark of loyalty to go along? And Berlin?

This afternoon Mayor Robert Wagner danced attendance upon Mr. Khrushchev. Did he do so because Premier Khrushchev is head of a foreign state and so entitled, ex officio, to the hospitality of New York's mayor? It isn't that simple. Last year Mayor Wagner ostentatiously announced his refusal to greet Ibn Saud—on the ground that Ibn Saud discriminates against the Jews in Saudi Arabia, and no man who discriminates against Jews in Saudi Arabia is by God going to be handled courteously by Bob Wagner, mayor of New York. Now, as everybody knows, Nikita Khrushchev not only discriminates against Jews, he kills them. On the other hand, he does much the same thing to Catholics and Protestants. Could *that* be why Mr. Wagner consented to honor Khrushchev? Khrushchev murders people without regard to race, color or creed—that is, on straight FEPC lines; and therefore, whatever he is guilty of, he is not guilty of discrimination, and so he is entitled to Robert Wagner's hospitality? Is that the shape of the new rationality?

It is the central revelation of Western experience that man cannot ineradicably stain himself, for the wells of regeneration are infinitely deep. No temple has ever been so profaned that it cannot be purified; no man is every truly lost; no nation irrevocably dishonored. Khrushchev cannot take permanent advantage of our temporary disadvantage, for it is the West he is fighting. And in the West there lie, however encysted, the ultimate resources, which are moral in nature. Khrushchev is *not* aware that the gates of hell shall not prevail against us. Even out of the depths of despair, we take heart in the knowledge that it cannot matter how deep we fall, for there is always hope. In the end, we will bury him.

TELL FRANCO THE WAR IS OVER

At worst, the Great Vacillation could undo the good that was accomplished by the defeat of the Republicans (let us call them what they liked to call themselves) in 1939. The agonizing indecisiveness of Francisco Franco is sapping the justification from his leadership: until one day his countrymen, even those of kindred philosophical commitment, may abominate him as an impostor whose franchise long since expired, and whose continued power derives from the fact, simply, that he has the power to exercise power; nothing more.

General Franco is an authentic national hero. It is generally conceded that he above others had the combination of talents, the perseverance, and the sense of righteousness of his cause that were required to wrest Spain from the hands of the visionaries, ideologues, Marxists, and nihilists that were imposing upon her, in the thirties, a regime so grotesque as to do violence to the Spanish soul, to deny, even, Spain's historical identity. He saved the day—but he did not, like Cincinnatus, thereupon return to his plow.

But the decision to stay on was itself a patriotic one. Spain was in danger of bleeding to death after the fray. And then a world war broke out. The pressure on all sides was great. The need was imperative for delicacy and dissimulation and contradiction and ambiguity and delay: for a national policy at the immediate disposal of a single person who might, constantly preserving just the desired balance, make this concession to Churchill this morning, that one to Hitler this afternoon, and tomorrow take a position uncongenial to both.

Hitler—the record shows—cussed Franco out continually: but the ultimate provocation, which would have brought a Panzer division to Madrid, was never forthcoming. Roosevelt and Churchill fumed at Franco's neutrality: but the cost to Spain of Allied wrath was not catastrophic. There was the petulant diplomatic ostracism of the postwar years, and miscellaneous economic discriminations. But Franco had got his neutrality, had preserved the independence of Spain, and that was what he wanted for a nation still racked by the consequences of her own tribulation.

So the war ended. What crisis warranted continued total power? Economic rehabilitation—Franco proclaimed—in a hostile world in which Communism thrives. To be sure, Spain was in sorry economic shape, and Communism was, and still is, thriving. But these were not problems that demanded immediate surgery by the intern in attendance at two o'clock in the morning: the patient was not in danger of momentary collapse. Still, the rhetoric was hammered in by engines of inculcation grown accustomed to the job of justifying one man's rule.

But this time Franco began to lose support from men—loyal followers during the civil and world wars—who felt that Franco had begun to contrive reasons why he, and only he, should govern. What, they began to ask, was the meaning of the civil war, which we fought at so great a cost, if not that there is an approach to government in Spain that is legitimate, and another that is illegitimate; and however preferable Franco is to Indalecio Prieto, or to anarchy, he is not—at least not all by himself—a legitimate governor of Spain.

There is the sense in which the exercise of de facto power tends, as the years go by, to legitimize the regime that wields it. But there are situations in which the longer power is exercised, the less legitimately is it exercised. In the one sense Franco, having been around for quite a while, has become if not legitimate, at least integrated. In the second sense, Franco's title diminishes every day. And it is for Franco the source of deep concern (for his pride is also involved) that he is not, and cannot become, the legitimate ruler of Spain on the only terms in which he knows how to rule. However sincere the respect his champions have for Franco, however reverential their tone or affectionate their esteem, they know, and he know, and history knows, that Franco did not, in virtue of his heroism in the thirties, earn the right to govern absolutely in the sixties. Moreover, until a stable, authentically Spanish, self-generative and perpetuating government is established—is the civil war quite over?

A person in a position to know informs me that the principal difficulty the king, Don Juan, and Franco have had in arriving at a basis whence fruitful discussion might proceed has had to do, precisely, with the question of the legitimacy of Franco's long tenure. Franco insists that he is engaged in the business of looking for a successor to *his* regime. Don Juan is said to insist that Franco's stewardship has merely been caretaking in character, that the king's sovereignty traces back to the character of the Spanish nation, that precisely the meaning of Franco's military victory was the reaffirmation of that sovereignty. On such formal questions the fate of nations is sometimes decided (remember the fleur-de-lis?). Don Juan does not expect, and his followers do not have in mind for him, anything like the power that once was wielded by Spanish monarchs. (On this point, Don Juan was explicit in a conversation I had with him in Portugal.) He is to be chief of state; but never chief of government. Yet restoration, it is widely felt, would mean something more than merely an esthetic or nominal reorganization of Spanish government. It would mean the re-establishment of the symbols of legitimacy in context of which Spain might once again address herself to the task of devising viable political forms. These would almost surely not be democratic; but, as surely, they would aim at the maximization of personal

liberty to a point consistent with the limitations imposed by
the character of Spanish society. "The American Constitution is an admirable document," a prominent anti-Franco,
antidemocratic Spanish intellectual told me, "but if we want
American democracy for Spain, the thing to do is not to import the Constitution, but to import Americans."

Meanwhile, Franco reigns, and reigns supreme. His is not
properly speaking a regime. It is an autocracy. There is no
reliable independent apparatus of appeal against any of his
decisions. Excepting only the Catholic Church, he dominates everything: the Falange Party, the army, the parlia-
ment, the courts, the economy, education, the press. He is
not an oppressive dictator. He is only as oppressive as it is
necessary to be to maintain total power, and that, it happens,
is not very oppressive, for the people, by and large, are
content. To put it more exactly, to the extent they are *not*
content, they do not tend to hold Franco responsible for that
discontent. The intellectuals, in hindsight, recognize the inap-
propriateness of the republic most of them once supported;
but they are restive, anxious to get on with the job of crafting
organic and responsive and durable political mechanisms.

The youth, on the other hand, are impatient to the point of
exasperation. The infinite indecisiveness of Franco, the theoretical unintelligibility of his course down myriad paths, is
making them fretful. The rhetoric of the regime, moreover,
cloys, and the exorbitance with which the accomplishments
of the regime are officially recorded is breeding a corrosive
cynicism. Could it be—the youth are begining to wonder—
that the official interpretation of the civil war is as distorted
as the official account of the economic triumphs of contemporary Spain? It would be an irony, of the very very tragic
kind, if Francisco Franco should, having saved Spain from
chaos, lead her back into it.

WILL FORMOSA LIBERATE
THE UNITED STATES? *

I HAVE lectured before to military aggregations and
I am aware of the preference of your profession for direct
action, whether military or rhetorical. The day before yesterday, at Quemoy, Captain Wang succeeded in a mere fifteen
minutes in giving his visitors a comprehensive view of the
military and strategic situation involving that perky redoubt;
but I could not hope to do so well as he, in telling you things
you need to know about the Liberal mind in America, things
which are as important to understand as is the mind of the
enemy. So let me, please, wind into this complex subject in
my own oblique way.

One learns from a study of opposites. And my experience
during the past few days in Taiwan has given me knowledge
not only of your own situation, but knowledge as well, by
contrast, of our own in America. I cannot say that I have
come to know Taiwan or its people or its officials. I can only
say that during the past five days I have engaged in Stakhan-
ovite endeavors to learn something about yourselves and
your great enterprise. I feel like Will Rogers, who came back
to New York from Russia in 1931, having made a short trip
there which included a visit to one of Russia's famous community baths. "Did you see all of Russia?" a reporter asked
the humorist when he landed. "No, but I saw all of *parts* of
Russia." I have seen all of parts of Taiwan—surely there does
not exist a Chinese or Taiwanese dish that I have not grate-
fully consumed. And surely there does not exist, in all your

* An address delivered to the National Defense Research Institute, Taiwan.

vast repository, a single resource of hospitality and kindness that I have not tasted. And I have seen something of your agricultural program, your dam building, your bureaucracy, your intellectuals, your politicians, your press, your diplomats, your soldiers, your strategists, your propagandists; but most important, I have seen something of your spirit. And it is in sharp contrast to the spirit of many men strategically situated in America. They are people who call themselves Liberals. The historians among you will immediately object that they have no title to that august designation; but the world of words is ruled by an absolute democracy: so that today in America, those people have come to be known as Liberals who in domestic affairs argue for an increase in the concentration of social, political and economic power in the hands of the state; and who in foreign policy follow the road of appeasement and withdrawal, for reasons that derive from their dependence upon a complex of philosophical heresies.

Assume that change dominates man, rather than that man can dominate change; assume that God is dead; assume that the people of the world will respond with Pavlovian predictability to material inducements; assume that it is within the power of the human will to produce instant prosperity; assume that the enemy's movement is essentially a response, however misconceived, to the legitimate social aspirations of the people; assume that nothing is more important than peace, and that the way to have peace is to compromise with the enemy; assume all those things, and those many other things that derive from them, and you have the archetype of the American Liberal. You have, in a word, Chester Bowles.

You may not be aware that in the United States there is at this moment a festering dissatisfaction with the failures of American foreign policy, and that some of those whose distress is keen have come up with the theory that the reason the free world has lost so much in recent years is because we have been, in the orthodox sense, betrayed. These persons reason schematically, as though on a blackboard—as follows:

Premise A: The United States was, in 1945, the most powerful nation in the world. Militarily it was supreme. Its allies controlled over two-thirds of the world's surface, and the overwhelming part of the world's wealth. The enemy's home base, in contrast, was racked by the ravages of war. An internal police force of three million persons was needed to maintain the Bolshevik despotism. . . .

Premise B: Fifteen years later China was gone, as was eastern Europe. Communist revolutionaries were at work through the world, the enemy had got hold of the atomic bomb and intercontinental rockets, and secured a base ninety miles from the Florida coast.

Conclusion: It can only be that American foreign policy has been subverted by Communist agents.

That analysis has a superficial appeal. But those who adopt it—and they are very few, though they have lately received much publicity—fail to understand: the American Liberal. It is he who has, by and large, most greatly influenced American foreign policy since the war. These men and women are not Communists. They are anti-Communists. The trouble is not that of motivation. The trouble is that the Liberals do not understand reality, and do not feel the devotion to our cause that alone can generate the will to victory.

Rather than illustrate what I mean by examining the Liberals' position on general categories or problems, let us bear down on the Liberals' attitude toward your own country, and your own enterprise.

They begin: The reason for the loss of the mainland was the corruption and ensuing impotence of the government of Chiang Kai-shek.

One replies: A number of things contributed to the loss of the mainland. Among them was the ambiguity of American support of Chiang during the postwar years, and the artificial exuberance and audacity of the Communist movements everywhere when the weakness of the Western will was fully realized. Would the Chinese Communists have dared do what they did had the United States, for instance, prepared to go to war if necessary in 1946 to require the Soviet Union to live up to its pledges with respect to Poland? But uncongenial facts shatter against the breastworks of Liberal dogma.

We can state as Liberal Proposition One: *Every Communist success is to be explained in terms of the internal situation.* American leadership has nothing to do with it. Thus the Liberals tell us it was the corruption of Batista that led to Castro's satellization of Cuba—it had nothing to do with any failure of the United States, during 1958 and in the early months of Castro's tenure, properly to assess, and then control, the evolution of Castro's government. In Laos, we are told, there is nothing we can do. Internal events—the aggressions of the Communists, the irresolution and confusion of the Laotian forces, the difficulty of the terrain, the poverty of the people—leave us with no alternative than merely to stand by—with perhaps an occasional trip to the scene by Lyndon Johnson to deliver grandiose elegies.

There was nothing we could do—do you remember?—to prevent the loss of Czechoslovakia, the suppression of the Budapest rioters, the Communization of Tibet, all of them allegedly the result of internal imperatives. Similarly, the Liberals are prepared to say, there is nothing we can do if a majority of the delegates to the General Assembly of the United Nations decide to recognize the government of Mao Tse-tung as the legal representative of China.

They go on. "It is unrealistic to talk about the liberation of China. What is done is done, and the best we can do is come to grips with reality."

One replies: But the facts argue that there are great possibilities, if we move decisively. The facts show that the control by the Communists over mainland China is weaker today than it was ten years ago, notwithstanding an attempted euthanasia of the middle class, a continuing program of hatred against the West, and against Chiang Kai-shek in particular. The facts show that China sits nervously by, waiting, like cordite, to be touched by a spark. Apply it, and China might burst into flames—flames which would consume the Communist leadership.

Thus we state Liberal Proposition Two: *There is no changing an adverse existing situation.*

If mainland China is in the hands of the Communists, we must proceed on the assumption that it will always be in the hands of the Communists. The United States Government made a halfhearted attempt to change the course of events in Cuba: the Liberals, including those within the Administration, disapproved of this effort to defy historical determinism. And so, the effort having failed as the result of a last-minute submission by the President to Liberal dogma, Cuba has been progressively totalitarianized. And no meaningful plans are now being made for its liberation. The scattered forces of resistance, mostly clustered in Greater Miami, face the same situation you faced ten years ago: but with this difference. They have no Taiwan to which to flee. And they have no acknowledged leader behind whose banner to consolidate. Otherwise it is much the same. They dream of liberation even as the White Russians used to do in Paris during the 1920s; but can they hope? For there is no American policy of liberation.

Change is defined, according to Liberal usage, as that which works *against* the free world. There is no such thing as "change" *away* from Communism. Did you notice that when the East Germans erected the Wall in Berlin on the 13th of August, there was no protest from the United States Government? Or rather, there was a protest, but that was all, and Khrushchev counts it a day lost when he does not receive at least one Western protest. Now our calculations are based on *the fact* of the Wall, not on the question whether we can succeed in tearing it down. In British Guiana our calculations are based on the fact that a Communist has been elected premier—not on the question whether he can be removed. In Indonesia our policy is based on the fact of Sukarno's pre-eminence—not on the question whether the anti-Communist rebels could be helped to overthrow it. And in the Far East, our policy is based on the fact of Red Chinese control of the mainland—not on the question whether we might succeed in restoring the mainland to anti-Communist control.

The Liberals go on: *An offensive by Formosa is likely to bring on a third world war, which will be the end of all of us.*

One replies: In fact, the Soviet Union will not engage in a nuclear war so long as she is convinced that the United States is ready to reply in kind, and has the capacity to do so. That is what is generally called the nuclear stalemate, or the balance of terror. It gave birth to the concept of the limited war, and it is that kind of a war of liberation which those who would re-enter China favor.

And so we come to Liberal Proposition Three: *All the roads that lead to the recovery of freedom, or to the diminution of Communist power, are closed to us, because to follow them would mean to risk nuclear war.* This is the clinching argument in all Liberal rhetoric, by which they paralyze all purposive action, everywhere in the world, that aims at the improvement of the position of the free world.

Here is the ultimate mischief that Liberalism is capable of performing, and in this respect Liberalism most clearly does the work of the Communists, the object of whose propaganda for years has been discernible: namely, to terrorize the West into inactivity by threats of nuclear war. Every year, the movement for unilateral disarmament grows. The ultimate meaning for the world of the Liberals' strategic counsels can only mean surrender.

The way to have peace and freedom for all the world is to neutralize those powers that are hell-bent on war and slavery. And the way to effect progress, on the Chinese front as on all other fronts, is militantly to encourage those rare spirits—and

I am surrounded by them here tonight—who are willing to risk their lives in order to bring freedom to themselves and their families, and to decrease the possibility of a nuclear war at some later stage when, conceivably, the enemy might outpace the United States in the development of a definitive weapon. Any sign of weakness by the free world increases the appetite of the enemy for more war and more conquest. What is more, prolonged delays could advance the ascendancy of the pacifist movement, the results of which would mean, inexorably, war, and slavery, for the entire world.

That vivid contrast, then, to which I have alluded, and from which I have learned so much from this visit, is between, on the one hand, the hopes and plans of the leadership of your movement and, on the other, the worries and fears of the leadership of the Liberal movement in America. We are more powerful than you by far; richer than you by many billions of dollars. But by your example, we may yet live. For a few stunning days, early in November in 1956, the freedom fighters of Budapest held the entire Communist world at bay. America was struck by the intensity—and efficacy—of the anti-Communist spirit, and we were breathless with wonder and admiration. But in the end, we did nothing. "For a while," Mr. Eugene Lyons, a wise and veteran American anti-Communist, remarked to me, "it looked almost as though Budapest would liberate the United States." I leave Taiwan believing that it may be your mission to liberate the United States.

HERBERT MATTHEWS
AND FIDEL CASTRO:
I got my job through
The New York Times

IT IS very much as in the early months of 1950 when, having chased the last remnants of the opposition off the mainland, Mao Tse-tung, wild with ideological lust, surveyed his kingdom, and threw himself into the job of Communizing his people. He chopped off many more heads than Fidel Castro has had so far to do in Cuba, and there are no doubt differences between Mao and Fidel, as there are between China and Cuba; but then as now, as the public slowly awoke to the meaning of what had happened, the apologists for the revolutionary forces began to retreat in increasing horror from their sometime enthusiasm. Those who had told us again and again that the Red Chinese were primarily agrarian reformers began to fade away, only to reappear, many of them, before congressional committees, which asked them the same questions they are now beginning to ask the propagandists for Castro, questions to which we desperately need the answer, now as then: *Who betrayed China? Who betrayed Cuba? Who—in the process—betrayed the United States?*

There is no longer any defensible defense of the regime of Mao Tse-tung. But here and there, there are pockets of loyalty to Castro. There is a Fair Play for Cuba Committee, which may or may not be dominated by fellow travelers, but which certainly has among its supporters some men who are *not* fellow travelers, men whose faith in Castro is livelier, alas, than freedom is in Cuba. The leader of pro-Castro opinion in the United States is Herbert L. Matthews, a member of the editorial staff of *The New York Times*. He did more than any other single man to bring Fidel Castro to power. It could be said—with a little license—that Matthews was to Castro what Owen Lattimore was to Red China, and that *The New York Times* was Matthews' Institute of Pacific Relations: stressing this important difference, that no one has publicly developed against Matthews anything like the evidence subsequently turned up against Lattimore tending to show, in the words of a Senate investigating committee, that Lattimore was "a conscious, articulate instrument of the Soviet conspiracy."

Herbert Matthews met Castro in February of 1957. To make contact with him—as he tells the story—he had to get in touch with the Fidelista underground in Havana, drive 500 miles all one night across the length of the island, using his wife as cover; and ride a jeep through tortuous dirt-road detours to avoid the patrols and roadblocks that an angry Fulgencio Batista had posted all about the Sierra Maestra mountains in the eastern tip of the island, to try to break the back of the little resistance group that two months earlier had landed, 82-strong, in Oriente Province in a diesel cutter from Mexico, pledged to "liberate" Cuba, or perish.

Matthews climbed up muddy slopes, swam across an icy river, ducked behind trees, ate soda crackers, and slept on the ground: and then, in the early morning hours, Fidel Castro came. In whispers, he talked for three hours about his plans for Cuba.

To put it mildly, Matthews was overwhelmed. From that moment on he appears to have lost all critical judgment. He became—always consistent with being a writer for *The New York Times*, which imposes certain inhibitions—the Number One unbearded enthusiast for Fidel Castro.

Castro, he told the world in a series of three articles that made journalistic and indeed international history, is a big, brave, strong, relentless, dedicated, tough idealist. His unswerving aid is to bring to Cuba "liberty, democracy, and social justice." There is seething discontent with Dictator Batista, corrupt and degenerate, after virtually 25 years of exercising power; hated by most Cubans for having installed himself as President in March of 1952 by military coup; become, now, a terrorist and a torturer. Fidel Castro is the "flaming symbol" of resistance. The fires of social justice that drive Castro on, that cause him to bear incredible hardships, playing impossible odds, with the single end in mind of bringing freedom to his people, these are fires that warm the hearthsides of freedom and decency all over the land: and they will prevail. . . .

Is Castro's movement touched by Communism? Matthews dismissed the rhetorical question with scorn. Castro's movement "is democratic, therefore anti-Communist." And, flatly, *"There is no Communism to speak of in Fidel Castro's 26th of July Movement."*

The impact of these articles all over the world was subsequently recognized even by *The New York Times* itself, normally bashful about celebrating publicly its achievements. When, almost two years later, Batista fell, the *Times* permitted itself to record jubilantly: "When a correspondent of *The New York Times* returned from Señor Castro's hideout [from that point on, by the way, Señor Castro was elevated by the *Times* to "Dr." Castro] . . . the rebel leader attained a new level of importance on the Cuban scene. Nor was the embarrassed government ever able to diminish Fidel Castro's repute again."

Foreign correspondents have been very much mistaken before. Foreign correspondents who work for *The New York Times* are no exception, as anyone knows who will attempt to reconcile Soviet history and accounts of same filed over the years by, e.g., Walter Duranty and Harrison Salisbury; who will, in a word, attempt the impossible. It is bad enough that Herbert Matthews was hypnotized by Fidel Castro, but it was a calamity that Matthews succeeded in hypnotizing so many other people in crucial positions of power on the subject of Castro. "When I was Ambassador to Cuba," Mr. Earl E. T. Smith complained to the Senate Subcommittee on Internal Security last August, "I . . . sometimes made the remark in my own Embassy that Mr. Matthews was more familiar with State Department thinking regarding Cuba than I was."

As ambassador assigned to Havana in August of 1957, Mr. Smith had been the representative of the United States Government in Cuba during the 18 crucial months that brought Castro to power, and he used just that word: Matthews' articles on Castro, he told the Senators, had literally "hypnotized" the State Department. Even as early as the summer of 1957, when Smith took over the ambassadorship from Arthur Gardner, the influence of Matthews was established—only a few months after the Castro interview in his hideout. Ambassador Gardner had met with stony resistance every time he attempted to pass on to his superiors the information he had about the nature of the Castro movement, which he was convinced—correctly, it proved—was shot through with Marxism. Gardner made himself such a nuisance that he was replaced; and his successor was instructed by Mr. William Wieland of the State Department, in charge of the Caribbean desk, to cap his month's briefing on the Cuba situation by consulting Herbert L. Matthews. Matthews told Smith that Batista was in all probability through. Castro, he said, was the man to back.

Smith went to Havana determined to do what he could, within the limits of propriety, to ease Batista out of the way. Batista pledged to hold elections in November 1958 and turn the presidency over to his successor in March 1959. The question in Smith's mind was whether he would last that long. Within two months after arriving in Cuba, Mr. Smith sincerely hoped he would; for he became convinced, he told the Senate committee, that the principal danger to the

United States lay not in the survival of Batista for a year or so, but in the rise to power of Fidel Castro who was almost certainly a revolutionary Marxist. Abundant evidence was available that he had made "Marxist statements" in Costa Rica, in Mexico, and in Bogotá; and that, dating back to his college days, he had been a revolutionist and a terrorist. Smith had even heard—and had passed the report along—that while in Bogotá, Castro had had a hand in the assassination of two nuns and a priest.

But even if Castro wasn't then pro-Communist, Smith said, his closest associates were, and this was positively documented with respect to his brother Raúl (now head of Cuba's armed forces) and Ernesto "Che" Guevara (boss of the Cuban economy).

But the ambassador's warnings were to no avail. During the succeeding 18 months, Herbert Matthews continued to write glowing accounts of the Robin Hood of the Sierra Maestra, predicting the downfall of Batista and the ascendancy of the 26th of July Movement. Others got into the act. The influential Foreign Policy Association's *Bulletin* for April 1, 1957, carried an article by Matthews on Cuba, followed by a list of "Reading Suggestions" prepared by the editors. Among them: "The best source of contemporary information of a general nature is probably the files of *The New York Times,* which published three uncensored articles on Cuba by Herbert Matthews on Feb. 24, 25, 26, 1957." The State Department went along. "Herbert Matthews ... is the leading Latin American editorial writer for *The New York Times.*" "Obviously," said Ambassador Smith, "the State Department would like to have the support of *The New York Times.*"

"Each month the situation deteriorates," Matthews exulted on June 16, 1957, a theme he elaborated in further dispatches in the succeeding months. Looking back at these reports one can only say: How right Mr. Matthews was. Batista *was* losing, and Castro *was* gaining. But Reporter Matthews neglected to give all the reasons why, just as he consistently

neglected to report on the lurid background of Fidel Castro and some of his associates. The increasing helplessness of Batista was the result primarily of the crystallization of U. S. support for Castro. During those months a fascinating dialectic went on. Matthews would write that American prestige was sinking in Cuba—on account of the aid the United States Government was giving to Batista. Our Ambassador in Havana meanwhile complained and complained to the State Department of the demoralization of the Batista government —on account of our failure to provide Batista with the aid to which, under the terms of a series of mutual aid agreements, we were bound by law and precedent to give him so long as we continued to recognize his government.

Matthews' forces proved much stronger than our ambassador's. An important segment of the press, influential members of Congress, and the Castro apparatus in Washington and New York hammered away at the State Department, urging it to desert Batista. At first the Department stalled. When Castro kidnapped 47 American servicemen in June 1958, the Government eagerly seized on the opportunity to hold up the shipment of 15 training planes that Batista was lawfully importing. "In accordance with instructions from the State Department," Smith testified, "I informed Batista that delivery would be suspended, because we feared some harm might come to the kidnapped Americans." Having yielded to blackmail, the U. S. Government then refused to deliver the airplanes—even after Castro had been prevailed upon to turn the soldiers free. Bastista's forces were becoming seriously demoralized by the growing aloofness of the U.S. Government, even while Castro was getting, the ex-ambassador went on to say, illicitly exported shipments of arms "almost every night" from friends of Castro in the United States. By November it was clear that Batista's days were numbered. On the 17th of December, Ambassador Smith received orders from the State Department to advise Batista that he could no longer exercise power, not even pending the institu-

tion of the new President a few months later—whom the
United States would not back in any case, since he had been
fraudulently elected, and didn't have the support of the
Cuban people. Two weeks later, Batista fled.

The next morning, on the first day of the New Year 1959,
Mr. Roy Rubottom, Assistant Secretary of State for Inter-
American Affairs, announced that there was "no evidence"
that "Castro is under Communist influence." Clearly he had
paid no attention to his own ambassador to Cuba. As clearly,
he read *The New York Times.*

During the 1960 campaign, both Mr. Kennedy and Mr.
Nixon expended a considerable amount of rhetoric on the
subject of Cuba. For they knew that the birth, right up
against the Florida peninsula, of what is now officially classified by the government (under the terms of the Dirksen-
Douglas Amendment to the Mutual Security Act) as "Communist" territory, is a development that has deeply disturbed
the American people. They want to know who, or what, was
the Frankenstein who created the monster.

Mr. Kennedy blasted Mr. Nixon on the grounds that Castro and Castroism had come about as a reaction against
America's tolerance of right-wing dictators—a familiar line,
advanced by those who sincerely feel it is an American obligation to purify internal Latin American politics. But Mr. Kennedy was not convincing to those who remembered that in
May, shortly before his nomination, he had said publicly
that in two respects he backed completely the foreign policy
of Mr. Eisenhower, "one of these being Cuba."

Mr. Nixon, on the other hand, pointed proudly to the dis-
appearance of a half dozen military dictators during the
Eisenhower years. He seemed to be suggesting that although
the President continued officially to beam at every leader of
every nation we formally recognize—as protocol dictated—
actually, if you looked closely, you would observe that he
was bouncing up and down on a great bellows, which blew

upon, and toppled one by one, the first rank of Latin American badmen. Beyond that Mr. Nixon did not go. He did not express a detailed curiosity about the loss of Cuba to Fidel Castro. Indeed, both candidates gave the impression that, like the State Department, *obviously* they wanted to stay on the right side of *The New York Times*. But the candidates whetted the public interest, and it is likely that the Senate Internal Security Subcommittee will pursue its investigation into the strange hold of Herbert Matthews, and the Matthews doctrine, on the men who make our foreign policy.

What will they learn about Mr. Matthews himself? That he is a scholarly, subtle man who makes and continues to make supercolossal mistakes in judgment, but whose loyalty to his misjudgments renders him a stubborn propagandist ... and an easy mark for ideologues on-the-make. So well known is he as doyen of utopian activists that when in June of 1959 a Nicaraguan rebel launched a revolt, he wired the news of it direct to Herbert Matthews at *The New York Times*—much as, a few years ago, a debutante on-the-make might have wired the news of her engagement to Walter Winchell.

Matthews was once, to use his own phrase, an "enthusiastic admirer of Facism." He turned away from facism while in Spain covering the civil war, where he took up the cause of the Popular Front with the same ferocious partisanship that earlier he had shown for Mussolini's Italy, and later was to show for Castro's Cuba. The Spanish passion is not yet expended. Mr. Matthews wrote a book in 1957 recommitting himself to the Good Guys–Bad Guys reading of a war fought by democrats and Communists against traditionalists and fascists. Always he writes with considerable sweep, and he loves to prophesy. His two most striking predictions of 1944 are that the "Franco regime is tottering" and that the disbanding of Russia's Comintern the year before was "the final indication that the Russia of 1943 and 1944 does not care to support revolutionary movements to bring about Communist states in other countries."

He has not proved over the years to be an astute judge of how to deal with Russia. "All they [the Russians] want is security," he wrote in *Collier's* in 1945. "By refusing to share the secret of the atomic bomb we are fostering Russian suspicions. . . . One can understand how they feel about our recognition of Franco, our seizure of Pacific bases, our exclusive policy in Japan, our Red-baiting press and our America-firsters. We have set up a vicious circle of mutual distrust and fear." And he is not an enthusiast for the free enterprise system, preferring the doctrinaire socialism of postwar Britain: ". . . while Britain slowly struggles toward economic order, sanity and strength," he wrote in 1946, "the British experiment will be an example [for the U. S.] to follow."

The payoff came when on July 15, 1959, Herbert Matthews wrote a front-page dispatch from Havana insisting that Castro was neither a Communist, nor "under Communist influence," nor even a dupe of Communism. Moreover, he added, there are "no Communists in positions of control." Indeed, Castro continued to be "decidedly anti-Communist." That dispatch was so brazen a contradiction of events that the *Times* reluctantly pulled him away from Cuba, as one might pull a man away from marijuana. Since then, he has not had one by-lined story on Cuba.

Subsequently, over a period of at least two years, he has continued to affirm his belief in the purity of the 26th of July Movement—but mostly in the arcane journals of the specialists (e.g., the *Hispanic American Report*), and in lectures before important audiences. The fault, he says, is ours, for antagonizing Castro, and "forcing him" to take his present hard line. One might as well argue that the Jews, by protesting the confiscation of their property and the insults heaped upon them, *forced* Hitler into genocide. And in any case, Mr. Matthews' analysis never accounted for the compulsiveness with which Cuba turned to Communism, beginning almost immediately after Castro took power.

Now and then Mr. Matthews invites attention to the fact that every one else, save himself, is out of step. "In my thirty years on *The New York Times*," he told the American Society of Newspapermen in April 1961, "I have never seen a big story so misunderstood, so badly handled, and so misrepresented as the Cuban Revolution." Those words are, as a matter of fact, exactly true: and the fault was *The New York Times'*.

The Senate subcommittee may want to know more about Matthews, and may want especially to know whether the Senate is to expect to have the honor of ratifying his appointment as Consultant Extraordinary to the State Department. Certainly it will want to examine the major premises of Matthews' position on Cuba. For it is a position that extends beyond the question of Castro, and one that is shared by many Americans, some of whom are influential with the new President. That position holds, in effect, that the United States *should* interfere, adroitly to be sure, in the internal affairs of nondemocratic Latin American nations. Matthews urged exactly that in the summer of 1958, by proposing that the United States arbitrate the differences between Batista and Castro. To have done such a thing would have been a clear reversal of United States policy—though we might rather have done that than what we did: namely, pull the rug out from under Batista, and turn the entire country over to Castro.

Another article in the Matthews position is that democracy and only democracy distinguishes the good society. Granted, he is perfectly satisfied with the kind of "democracy" that is practiced in Mexico, where everyone votes, and one party always wins; but it bears discussion whether "democracy" is the first objective of American foreign policy in Latin America, or whether it is subsidiary to other concerns, including our own national interest, and, for the Latin Americans, internal stability, economic viability and nonpolitical freedoms. (Probably the highest per capita incidence of violent deaths in any country this side of the Soviet Union has been in chaotic Colombia, a "democracy.")

A third question is whether the United States can continue, in all good conscience, to encourage Americans to invest in Latin America. Our investments there are over $7 billion— making American capital the largest single job creator in Latin America. But the Matthews position on foreign investment consists, as far as one can make out, in encouraging a) American investment in general, and b) those governments that seize, nationalize or tax to death that investment in particular. He has not, at least in any of his conspicuous writings, deplored Cuba's blithe confiscation of $800 million of American property. Symbolically, the new U. S. Administration must answer the question why, the more offensive Fidel Castro seemed to this country, the madder we got at General Trujillo.

INSTRUCTING NORMAN MAILER
ON THE TRUE MEANING OF
THE AMERICAN RIGHT WING *

I WELCOME Mr. Mailer's interest in the American right wing. On behalf of the right wing let me say that we, in turn, are interested in Mr. Mailer, and look forward to co-existence and cultural exchanges with him in the years to come. I hope we can maintain his interest, though I confess to certain misgivings. I am not sure we have enough sexual neuroses for him. But if we have any at all, no doubt he will find them, and in due course celebrate them in a forthcoming political tract, perhaps in his sequel to the essay in which he gave to a world tormented by an inexact knowledge of the causes of tension between the Negro and the white races in the South, the long-awaited answer, namely that all Southern politics reflects the white man's resentment of the superior sexual potency of the Negro male. Mr. Mailer took his thesis —easily the most endearing thing he has ever done—to Mrs. Eleanor Roosevelt, to ask her benediction upon it. She re-plied that the thesis was "horrible," thus filling Mr. Mailer with such fierce delight that he has never ceased describing her reaction, commenting that he must be responsible for the very first use of that overwrought word by that lady in her long, and oh so talkative career.

"Oh how we shall *scarify!*" the dilettante Englishman re-ported exultantly to his friends a hundred years ago, on an-nouncing that he had finally put together the money with which to start a weekly magazine. How Mr. Mailer loves to

* An opening statement, at a public debate with Norman Mailer, on "The Real Meaning of the American Right Wing."

71

scarify!—and how happy I am that he means to do so at the expense of the American Right. Not only do I not know anyone whose dismay is more fetchingly put down, I do not know anyone whose dismay I personally covet more; because it is clear from reading the works of Mr. Mailer that only demonstrations of human swinishness are truly pleasing to him, truly confirm his vision of a world gone square. Pleasant people, like those of us on the right, drive him mad, and leech his genius. Recently he has confessed that it is all he can do to stoke his anger nowadays, and he needs that anger sorely to fire his artistic furnace. The world, if it truly appreciates Norman Mailer, must be a cad; how else will he get to be President? For Mr. Mailer, to use his own phrase, has been "running for President for ten years." He means by that he wants the world to acknowledge him as the principal writer of our time. *Número uno,* the unchallenged, unchallengeable matador of all time, the biggest bull killer since Theseus. And so those of you who wish him to be President must confirm his darkest thoughts and suspicions about you, so that he may give birth to that novel of outrage—which, he gloats, will be, *"if I can do it,* an unpublishable work." Those few of us who are neither running for President, nor are needed to preserve the hideousness of this world so as to fatten Mr. Mailer's muse, are assigned by him the task of cultivating "the passion for socialism," which Mr. Mailer finds "the *only* meaning I can conceive in the lives of those who are not artists."

Mr. Mailer is a socialist of sorts, but if socialism is not his first passion, that is only because, in his capacity as an artist, he is exempt from ideological servitude. The rest of the world is divided, as I say, in two groups. First the great majority of us, who compose that terrible world he wants to write a novel about so great—so great that Marx and Freud themselves would want to read it; for they would recognize in it, says Mr. Mailer, a work that "carries what they had to tell part of the way." Those others of us, with whom he is at peace, will want to labor for socialism, he tells us; we will "want a socialist world not because we have the conceit that men would thereby be more happy—but because we feel the moral imperative in life itself to raise the human condition even if this should ultimately mean no more than that man's suffering has been lifted to a higher level, and human history has only progressed from melodrama, farce, and monstrosity, to tragedy itself."

Not very long after writing that sentence, Mr. Mailer and a dozen others, including several other presidential candidates, signed an advertisement in papers throughout the country under the sponsorship of a group which called itself the Fair Play for Cuba Committee. "The witch-hunting press," the advertisement said in almost as many words, "is suggesting that Castro's great democratic revolution is contaminated by Communism. That is hysterical and fascistic nonsense." One or two signers of that petition—Kenneth Tynan, the English critic, was one—were subsequently called before a congressional investigating committee and asked what they knew about the sponsorship of the Fair Play Committee. To Mr. Mailer's eternal mortification, he was not called, thus feeding what *Time* magazine has identified as Norman Mailer's subpoena envy. Anyway, it transpired that the organizer of that committee was a paid agent of Fidel Castro, who even then was an unpaid agent of the Soviet Union. The insiders no doubt found it enormously amusing to be able to deploy with such ease some of the most conceited artists in the world behind the Communists' grisly little hoax. There is melodrama in a Norman Mailer rushing forward to thrust his vital frame between the American public and a true understanding of the march of events in Cuba; there is even farce in the easy victimization of Mr. Skeptic himself by a silent-screen ideological con man; and it is always monstrous to argue aggressively the truth of the Big Lie. But I think the episode was less any one of these things than an act of tragedy, though without dire consequence for

the players—they are strikingly impenitent, insouciant—but
for others. The people of Cuba are also writing a book that
carries forward the ideas of Marx and Freud, a truly unpublishable book. Their suffering, for which Mr. Mailer bears a
part of the moral responsibility, they must endure without
the means to sublimate; they are not artists, who count their
travail as a stepping stone to the presidency.

Consider this. Last spring a middle-aged Cuban carpenter,
known to persons I know, received notice at his three-room
cottage on the outskirts of Havana late one afternoon that at
nine the next morning his twelve-year-old son would be
taken from him to be schooled in the Soviet Union during
the next six years. The father, who had never concerned
himself with politics, asked if his son might not, as an only
child, be spared. The answer was no. The father spent the
evening talking with his wife and sister, and on his knees
praying. The next morning he opened the door to the escort
who had come to fetch his son, put a bullet through his head,
turned and shot his wife and child, and then blew out his
own brains.

That is not merely a horror story, nor merely a personal
tragedy, any more than the story of Anne Frank was merely
an isolated horror story, a personal tragedy. It is a part of a
systemic tragedy, just as the annihilation camps in Germany and Poland were a part of a systemic tragedy, the tragedy that arises not out of the workaday recognition of man's
capacity for brutality, but out of the recognition that man's
capacity for good is equal to the task of containing at least
systemic horror, but that we are here frozen in inactivity
while the horror spreads, leaping over continents and oceans
and slithering up to our own shoreline, while those whose
job it is to contain that horror grind out their diplomatic
nothingness, and the nation's poets wallow in their own little
sorrows. The American right wing, of whom I am merely
one member, clumsily trying to say what Norman Mailer
with his superior skills would be saying so very much better

if only he would raise his eyes from the world's genital glands, are trying to understand why; are trying to understand what is that philosophy of despair, and who was it that voted to make it the law of nations, that we should yield to it; the despair that teaches us to be impotent while fury strikes at the carpenter's home ninety miles from the greatest giant history ever bred, whose hands are held down by the Lilliputian solipsists of contemporary Liberalism.

Cuba is a symbol of American Liberalism's failure to meet the challenges of the modern world. If such a thing as Castro Cuba were not possible, such a thing as the American right wing, as it exists today, would not be possible; as things are, the American right wing is necessary, and providential.

Why are we now threatened with Castro? Why should Castro ever have arisen to threaten us? There is a question, I dare suggest, the Right alone has been asking. If the President of the United States desired a clue to the answer to that question he might reflect on a scene enacted three and one half years ago at his alma mater. It was a brilliant spring evening, and Harvard had not found a hall large enough to hold the crowd. In the entire history of Harvard, it is said, there had not been such a demand for seats. The meeting was finally held out of doors. And there ten thousand members of the Harvard community—teachers, students, administrative officials—met in high spirit to give Fidel Castro a thunderous, prolonged, standing ovation.

That is why the United States has not been able to cope with Castro. (Nor before him with Khrushchev, or Mao Tse-tung, or Stalin; or, for that matter, with Alger Hiss.) We have not understood. The most educated men in our midst and the most highly trained—including those who trained the Kennedys—have not been understanding the march of history, in which Castro is a minor player, though at the moment great shafts of light converge on him to give him a spectacular brilliance. When Castro arrived at Harvard he had been five long, hectic, flamboyant months in power. He had kept the firing squads working day and night. He had reduced the courts to travesty; he had postponed democratic elections until a day infinitely distant; he had long since begun to speak stridently about world affairs in the distinctive accents of Bolshevism; he had insulted our ambassador; his radio stations and newspapers were pouring out their abuse of this country and its people. Things would become worse in the next months, and the more offensive Castro became, the madder we were all instructed to get at General Trujillo. Castro would not get such a reception at Harvard today. But today is too late. Today is when President Kennedy labors over the problem of how to contain Castro. Now, having waited so long, Mr. Kennedy must deal with the doctrine promulgated by Khrushchev on September 11, 1962, which states that "the Soviet Union will consider any attempt on the part of the Western Hemisphere powers to extend their system to any portion of the Communist world as dangerous to our peace and safety"—what we have identified at *National Review* as the Monroevski Doctrine.

The point is that no one in power seems to know exactly how to deal with Castro. No one even knows how this country is to deal, not with Castro—he is merely a particularization on the trouble—but with a much larger question. We don't know how to deal with Harvard University. If Harvard wasn't able to spot Castro for what he is earlier than it did, and show us how to cope with him, who can? And yet Harvard, so dulled are its moral and intellectual reflexes, cheered, while Castro was accumulating the power to engross the full, if futile attention of President John F. Kennedy, B.S. Harvard 1940, Ll. D. 1956, even while another of her illustrious sons, Norman Mailer, B.A. 1943, was propagandizing for a Committee to Hasten the Unmolested Communization of Cuba.

Of Cuba, the right-winger concludes, it can truly be said that she was betrayed. That melodramatic word is not being used only by the founder of the John Birch Society. It is the word—*"la gran estafa"*— being used by most of Fidel Castro's closest former associates, who had thought they were struggling all these months in the Sierra Maestra for freedom, only to find that at a mysterious political level of whose existence they were not even aware, arrangements were being made to use their hunger for freedom and reform as the engine to create a slave-state. They, the earliest associates of Castro, were not really to blame. They fought bravely, and one must not fault the working soldiery for a lack of political sophistication. But there were others whose business it was to know who did not know, and their ignorance resulted in the betrayal of those men who followed Castro blindly, only to find themselves to have tunneled out of their cell into a torture chamber.

The United States was caught by surprise? The right wing suggests there are reasons why we were caught by surprise, and that we can never be done exploring what those reasons were, and how to avoid them in the future—but all inquiries of this nature are denounced as McCarthyite. President Kennedy has told us the government was caught completely by surprise by the East Germans in August a year ago when the great wall was erected. I *believe* him—however strange it is that so massive an accumulation of standby brick and mortar could have escaped even the notice of our CIA. The result of our failure to have anticipated that wall has been to freeze the dreams of one half of Germany and chill the hopes of free men everywhere. In Laos we were surprised by the militancy of the thrust from the north and the intransigence of the Laotian insurrectionary force; whereupon we yielded, midwifing a government whose archetype we saw in Czechoslovakia just after the war; we know, but we do not learn, that coalition governments tend to become Communist governments; that who says A, must say B. . . .

So it has gone, throughout the history of our engagement with the Communist world; and only the Right, and honorable and courageous, but unrepresentative, members of the Left have had the compassion to raise their voices in sustained protest. "Never fear," our leaders sought to pacify us in 1947. "We have established a policy of containment." On the fifteenth anniversary of the policy of containment we can peer ninety miles off the Florida coast into Soviet-built muzzles.

It is said of the American right wing that we do not trust our leaders. Nothing could be closer to the truth. Our leaders are not Communists, or pro-Communists, and are not suspected of being so, notwithstanding the gleeful publicity which has been given to the aberrations of a single conspicuous member of the right wing, who made a series of statements which I would put up alongside some of the political commentary of Herbert Matthews, Gore Vidal, and Norman Mailer, as qualifying for the most foolish political prose published during 1961. The right wing, who are so often charged with wishing to escape from reality, desire in fact to introduce reality to our ideologized brothers on the left; far from fleeing world responsibilities, we wish to acknowledge that the weight of the world's problems does in fact lie squarely on the shoulders of our leaders; and draw attention to the fact that these leaders have been losing the world war; indeed, insofar as a great many human beings are personally concerned, have lost it already. If you were a Cuban who believed in freedom, would you trust the leaders of America? Or if you lived in East Berlin? Or Laos; or China, for that matter? Our leaders are not Communists but they have consistently failed to grasp the elementary logic of Communist nuclear blackmail, with the result that we have found ourselves without any strategy whatever—not even enough strategy to enforce a doctrine we felt capable of enforcing one hundred and forty years ago.

The implicit logic of those of our leaders who decline to fight for Cuba is the logic of defeat. Ultimately their arguments must, by logical necessity, come down to surrender. And indeed this exactly is the naked word that is finally being used today by a few brave cowards. "For the first time in America," Mr. Joseph Alsop wrote a year ago, "one or two voices are beginning to be heard, arguing that what ought to be done is to surrender." "*Mr. Kennedy says Berlin is not negotiable,*" wrote Mr. John Crosby in his column. "*Why isn't it? Why isn't anything negotiable rather than thermonuclear war? .... Are we going to wipe out two and a half billion years of slow biological improvement in a thermonuclear war? Over what—Berlin? I agree with Nehru that to go to war under any circumstances for anything at all in our world* [presumably excepting Goa] *in our time is utter absurdity..... I certainly think Berlin is negotiable and, as a matter of fact, Khrushchev is not even asking very much.... And after all, Communism ... is not that bad, and some day we're going to have to face up to that...*" And Mr. Kenneth Tynan, the English critic, agrees. "*Better Red than dead,*" he writes, "*seems an obvious doctrine for anyone not consumed by a death-wish: I would rather live on my knees than die on my knees.*"

Well, assuming it is death toward which we are headed as a result of our determination to stay free, let it be said that Mr. Tynan would not need to die on his knees, but rather standing up. Which is how those of his ancestors died before Runnymede, at Agincourt and Hastings, at Dunkirk, who fought for the freedom of their descendants to exhibit their moral idiocy. Mr. Crosby advances as a substitute for the slogan "Give me liberty or give me death" the slogan: "*John Crosby is too young to die.*" Let them live. There remain impenetrable corners of the Soviet Union where Messrs. Crosby and Tynan could store up their 2500 calories per day and remain absolutely free from the hounds of radioactivity, if not from the hounds of Bolshevism. But they will not go; they would have *us* all go; and they are right in suggesting that their logic, because it is in greater harmony with the inexplicit premises of American foreign policy over the years, should eventually prevail. It is at odds, after all, only with American official rhetoric, which is all wind—the tiger Schlesinger typing out a thousand-word roar once a month for the White House Department on Releasing the Bellicose Energies of the Masses. The implicit cogency of surrender will, they feel sure, overcome in due course the defiant rhetoric, and ease us into a course of conclusive appeasement. It is implied by Messrs. Crosby and Tynan that the right wing seeks a war. But in fact we seek to avoid war: and the surest way to avoid war is to assert our willingness to wage it, a paradox that surely is not so complex as to elude the understanding of professional students of the drama. The appeasers and collaborators in our midst seek to pour water in our gunpowder, and lead into the muzzle of our cannon, and leave us defenseless in the face of the enemy's musketry. There is no licit use for a nuclear bomb, they are saying in effect, save possibly to drop a small one on the headquarters of the John Birch Society. But these are in fact the warmongers, for they whet the appetite of the enemy as surely as the stripteaser, by her progressive revelations, whets the appetite of the crowd. *"However I survey the future,"* concludes Kenneth Tynan, *"there seems to be nothing noble"* in dying. *"I want my wife to have another child, and I want to see that child learn to walk."* Those in the West of civilized mind and heart are engaged in trying to make just that possible, the birth of another child to Kenneth Tynan, always assuming he has left the virility to procreate one.

Disintegration is what we conservatives see going on about us. Disintegration and acquiescence in it. The Liberal community accepts calmly and fatalistically the march of events of the past years. History will remark that in 1945, victorious and omnipotent, the United States declined to secure for Poland the rights over which a great world war had broken out; and that a mere sixteen years later—who says B, must say C—we broke into panicked flight from the responsibilities of the Monroe Doctrine, which as a fledgling republic we had hurled in the face of the omnipotent powers of the Old World one hundred and forty years ago, back when America, though not a great power, was a great nation. It is the general disintegration of a shared understanding of the meaning of the world and our place in it that made American Liberalism possible, and American conservatism inevitable.

For the American Right is based on the assumption that however many things there are that we don't know, there are some things we do know; on the assumption that some questions are closed, and that our survival as a nation depends on our acting bravely on those assumptions, without whose strength we are left sounding like Eisenhower, which is to say organically unintelligible; rhetoricizing like Kennedy, which is what comes of hiring Madison Avenue to make nonaction act; or writing like Mailer, which is to write without "beginning to know what one is, or what one wants"—the criticism of Mailer made by his friend, my enemy, Gore Vidal.

To win this one it's going to take nerve, and take courage, and take a certain kind of humility, the humility that makes man acknowledge the demands of duty. But it will take also a quiet and unshakable pride, the pride of knowing that with all its faults, with all its grossness, with all its appalling injustices, great and small, we live here in the West under a small ray of light, while over there is blackness, total, impenetrable. *"You have to care about other people to share your perception with them,"* Norman Mailer has written. But nowadays, he confesses, *"there are too many times when I no longer give a good goddamn for most of the human race."* It is tempting to observe that nothing would better serve the ends of the goddamn human race than to persuade Mr. Mailer to neglect us; but I resist the temptation, and predict instead that those liberating perceptions that Mr. Mailer has been wrestling to formulate for lo these many years, those ideas that will catapult him to the presidency, are, many of them, like the purloined letter, lying about loose in the principles and premises, the organon, of the movement the Left finds it so fashionable to ridicule.

There, in all that mess, he will, for instance, run into the concept of duty, which concept presupposes the validity of non-personalized standards. Why our great retreat from duty? Because our leaders are, when all is said and done, scared. *"We will take Berlin,"* Khrushchev said to an American cabinet officer in September, *"and you will do nothing about it."* Why won't we do anything about it? Because we might get hurt—as individuals, we might suffer; and so we rush into the great comforting bosom of unreality, who strokes our golden locks and tells us nothing will happen to us if only we will negotiate, keep sending lots of foreign aid to India, lots more sit-ins to Georgia, and lots more McCarthyites to Coventry.

The flight from reality by those who are scared . . . "I have only one life to give for my country," the Liberal says, "and my country isn't worth it." *"Could you imagine yourself living happily in a Communist society?"* the interviewer recently asked C. P. Snow, the Liberals' Renaissance Man. *"I think so,"* answered Sir Charles.

"If you had to, if somebody said you've got to live in America or live in Russia for the rest of your days, which would you choose?" *"Well, that is very difficult; I think to be honest, I could be very happy in either of them."*

Members of the right wing could not.

The true meaning of the American right wing, Mr. Mailer, is commitment, a commitment on the basis of which it becomes possible to take measurements. That is true whether in respect of domestic policy or foreign policy. For those on the radical Left with Norman Mailer, and for so many Americans on the moderate Left, the true meaning of our time is the loss of an operative set of values—what one might call an expertise in living. For them, there is no ground wire, and without a ground the voltage fluctuates wildly, wantonly, chasing after the immediate line of least resistance—which, in Cuba, is *Do Nothing*. For those, like Norman Mailer, who have cut themselves off from the Great Tradition, one observes that it is not truly important that a Laos has been dismembered, or that a great wall has gone up through Berlin, or that a Cuba has been Communized: Mailer's world is already convulsed, at a much higher level, and he has no ear for such trivia as these. For he views the world as groaning under the weight of unmanageable paradoxes, so that Euclidean formulations, Christian imperatives, Mosaic homilies become, all of them, simply irrelevant; worse, when taken seriously, these are the things that get in the way of his own absorption with himself, in the way of that apocalyptic orgasm which he sees as the end objective of individual experience.

How strange it is that all the Establishment's scholars, all the Establishment's men, have not in the last half dozen years written a half dozen paragraphs that truly probe the true meaning of the American right wing. They settle instead for frenzied, paranoid denunciations. Indeed the Left has discovered that the threat is really internal. There is no enormity too grotesque, or too humorless, to win their wide-eyed faith. I have seen some of them listen respectfully to the thesis that people in America belong to the right wing out of resentment over their failure to get their sons into Groton; and I remember the rumor that swept the highest counsels of the ADA and the Washington *Post* in 1954, that Senator McCarthy was accumulating an arsenal of machine guns and rifles in the cellar of the Senate Office Building. . . . And, of course, we all know that they continue to believe in Santa Claus.

"Therefore they took them and beat them, and besmeared them with dirt, and put them into the cage, that they might be made a spectacle to all the men of the fair." And the charge was brought against them by the principal merchants

of the city: *"That they were enemies to and disturbers of their trade; that they had made commotions and divisions in the town."* Thus John Bunyan wrote about the town of Vanity, and how it greeted those in the city who came to buy the truth.

"I am frankly all but ignorant of theology," Norman Mailer writes. If he wants to learn something about the true nature of the American right wing, I recommend to him the works of Presidents Matthew, Mark, Luke and John.

REMARKS ON A
FIFTH ANNIVERSARY *

ADMIRAL STRAUSS, my invaluable colleagues, and good friends:

I am proud beyond my powers to describe to be associated with so distinguished a list of sponsors. And they should be proud to be associated with *National Review*. Let me dispel immediately any suggestion that *National Review* is my creation, or that it depends in any serious way on my participation in it. Nothing so preposterous can be maintained save possibly by speakers at a testimonial dinner. And even if it *were* so, cannot Leonardo da Vinci worship the Mona Lisa? I could not accept the honor of sharing a testimonial dinner at which I was required to suppress my enthusiasm for a journal that collects the talents of the men you have just heard, and others, in and out of this room.

I do not suggest that all the sponsors share every opinion of every one of the editors of *National Review:* more likely not one of them shares all the opinions of all the editors of *National Review.* Certainly I do not. Indeed, anyone who did would be a schizophrenic: because some of the opinions of the editors conflict with one another, which is to be expected among serious and resourceful and inquisitive men. But we all share a few premises which are fundamental, and out of the tension of these disagreements the magazine generates, I think, a discernible vibrancy, the vibrancy, moreover, of a forward motion, not to be confused with what generates

* Remarks at a dinner commemorating the fifth anniversary of *National Review,* presided over by Admiral Lewis Strauss.

out of an attempt to conduct a dialectic between East and West, between Communism and truth. What generates from that dialectic is not truth or edification, but Pandit Nehru. And every time Mr. Nehru opens his mouth, he drives down another nail on the coffin lid of the great rationalist superstition, defended today by the reactionaries who cluster about the American Civil Liberties Union, that the free exchange of opposite ideas midwives the truth.

I make bold to say that the illustrious speakers of this dinner can take pride in their identification with *National Review* because in electing to be sponsors, some of them make yet another act of courage. *National Review* is, as Admiral Strauss suggests, organically American, rooted in the nation's deepest traditions, and beyond that even, in the deepest traditions of Western civilization: but it is precisely the deepest roots of our civilization that are out of fashion. The blooms of our society, the explosion of material well-being, the intoxicating fragrance of the notion that all points of view are equally valid, except perhaps that point of view which says they are not—these are still very modish. What is not fashionable are some of those certitudes and intuitions that most of us here in this room aim to serve—such certitudes as that there is a religious base in life, and therefore a transhistorical meaning to the human experience.

—That freedom is necessary to the development of the human personality.

—That we know enough to know that the Communist experiment, the worst abuse of freedom in history, is a violent mutation on truth, a horrible caricature on justice; that the socialized state is to justice, order, and freedom what the Marquis de Sade is to love; and that it is our solemn responsibility not to become so jaded by the continuing barbarism as to become indifferent to its depravities, as French society during the late eighteenth century became indifferent to sexual depravity: not to come to believe, after the millionth political execution, that the millionth and one becomes meaningless; not to come to believe that because there are eight hundred million slaves in the world, it will make no great difference if we add another forty or fifty thousand, who live, moreover, on a couple of desolated rocks just off the China coast.

National Review is not, of course, always engaged on such sublime pursuits. Not a week goes by that we do not need to call a point of order; or fit together the parts to show a current piece of humbuggery; or scrub down someone's shiny new proposal to expose the structure for what it is—usually Liberal totemism: these are what one might call the house-keeping chores of conservatism. It may not make points in heaven to sigh, as James Burnham has done, that Mrs. Roosevelt viewed the world as one vast slum project. Or to suggest, as Priscilla Buckley did on hearing Mrs. Roosevelt say that she would never under *any* circumstances break a picket line, that the time has come for patriots to institute a 24-hour picket around Hyde Park. Or, after due deliberation, to sum-marize, as Morrie Ryskind did, the political credo of David Susskind as reducing to the proposition: "If we would only stop regarding the monstrous things Russia does as mon-strous, she would stop regarding *us* as monstrous." Or to com-ment as Willmoore Kendall did on last year's fiscal proposal of one of our sponsors: "Senator Byrd has proposed we cut the budget by five billion dollars. *National Review* stays and raises him five." Or, in a moment of total exasperation after finishing the then current issue of the *New Republic*, to write as Willmoore Kendall again did: "Gerald Johnson, colum-nist of the *New Republic*, wonders what a football would think of the game if a football could think. Very interesting, but less relevant than to ask, What would a *New Republic* reader think of the *New Republic* if a *New Republic* reader could think?"

These are not, as I readily admit, advances upon the heavenly kingdom; but whereas man does not live by bread alone, he cannot live without it.

The sponsors of this dinner—and I speak here now not only of those whose names adorn this program, but of every one of you—know that we are probably destined to live out our lives in something less than a totally harmonious relationship with our times. Three of our most conspicuous sponsors were during their careers, rebuffed: and always for the wrong reason. Herbert Hoover was cast aside by an impetuous electorate to make way for an insouciant social adventurer who moved gaily through history, knocking about the traditions of his own country, and giving away those of other peoples, to be refashioned in the crucible of Bolshevism. Douglas MacArthur never challenged the civil authority of Harry Truman to act as commander in chief. But the appalling misuse of that power, at so great a cost in human life, led him publicly to state his misgivings, an act condemned by our Liberal spokesmen as insubordinate and inexcusable, an act in fact of transcendent patriotism which for failure to imitate, these same Liberals, just a few years earlier, had strung up a bunch of German and Japanese generals. Lewis Strauss was rejected by the Senate of the United States, and not one man in one thousand could tell you the reason why: and the thousandth would not give the right reason. Admiral Strauss' devotion to duty always singled him out as a misfit in a brawling political metropolis; but his enormous talents, his innocent integrity, caused our leaders to turn to him time and again to help with the nation's serious business. Mr. Strauss has a proud man's pride in his own standards, and before his inquisitors he calmly justified the major decisions of his career, refusing to make those easy but debasing concessions which more and more are required for admission into the entrenched political fraternity.

I think it is fair to say these are conservative virtues: Mr. Hoover's refusal to throw aside tradition in panic; General MacArthur's appeal to a higher reason than that which circumstance had imposed on the political order; Admiral Strauss' refusal to belie the standards that throughout his life had informed his public performance. These are not qualities that lead a man, nowadays, to a safe position in the public eminence; certainly they are not qualities that lead a man to the White House. We are all of us in one sense out of spirit with history, and we are not due to feel those topical gratifications which persons less securely moored will feel as they are carried, exhilarated, in and out with the ebb and flow of events. But ours is the ultimate gratification, I believe. I believe Mr. Hoover and General MacArthur and Admiral Strauss are happier men than they would be had they taken a different course when the tidal wave roared up before them. And I expect they and all of you, my good and generous and devoted friends, must be happy, as I am, to know that for so long as it is mechanically possible, you have a journal, a continuing witness to those truths which animated the birth of our country, and continue to animate our lives.

On the Edge of Politics

THE ORDEAL OF
KENNETH TYNAN

WE ARE called upon, ladies and gentlemen, to be angry along with Kenneth Tynan, Englishman, critic, Angry Young Man; and sorrowful with him too, for he has been through an ordeal, which we are to understand is really our ordeal. None of us, I warrant, will succeed in feeling quite as sorry for him as he feels for himself: the point is we are to try, and editorial writers and columnists all over the country are doing their best.

The basic story—Mr. Tynan was called before a congressional investigating committee last spring—is uncomplicated, though the account of it by Mr. Tynan in the current *Harper's* is not. This is too bad, in a man who knows how to be succinct; but we are to assume that, overcome with righteous anger, he could not write simply, or directly, or accurately. Mr. Tynan is a young man of letters well enough known among the literati in England and because of his precocious effusions against the established order (for a while he played regular piccolo for John Osborne); but he left Anger, Inc., and branched out. He went to Spain and wrote bravely about brave bulls and matadors, and turned to drama, and drama criticism.

In any event, Wolcott Gibbs of *The New Yorker* died, and the editors of *The New Yorker* invited Mr. Tynan, who was then doing criticisms for the London *Observer*, to take Gibbs' place for a year or two. He agreed, and in 1958 came over with his American wife and child and wrote excellent criticism which did not, unfortunately, exhaust his energies.

Sometime during the fall, a commercial British television company called Associated Television got in touch with Tynan and said—I am paraphrasing Mr. Tynan's account in *Harper's*—Look, old boy, let's do something to improve British-U. S. relations. Over here we have the impression that in America everybody thinks alike, that the country is in the grip of an iron philistinism; but you and I, we know it's not true, so let's put on a 90-minute television show—you produce it, we'll run it—called "We Dissent," establishing once and for all that in America there are good, brave dissenters who don't go along with American Babbitry.

To this enterprise Mr. Tynan energetically devoted himself, emerging with a list of twenty-odd "lively American mavericks" whom he invited to speak "on the state of nonconformity in general and the nature of their own nonconformity in particular."

In the arts, he selected Norman Mailer (naturally), Jules Feiffer, Alexander King, Mort Sahl, and three Beats: Allen Ginsberg, Bob Kaufman and Lawrence Ferlinghetti. Kenneth Galbraith delivered his thesis on the Affluent Society, and C. Wright Mills his about the imminence of catastrophe unless we shake off the power elite. There were speeches by Norman Cousins, Robert Hutchins, and Norman Thomas.

"America being by definition the greatest capitalist country on earth, it followed that Socialism and dissent would frequently be allied. Accordingly, I also included one admitted member of the Communist Party (Arnold Johnson); and four speakers reputedly linked with the extreme Left—Clinton Jencks, of the Mine, Mill and Smelter Workers' Union; the Reverend Stephen Fritchman of the Unitarian Church; Dalton Trumbo, the Hollywood screen writer; and Alger Hiss. ... After lengthy discussions ... we decided to exclude American dissenters of the extreme right, such as Senator Barry Goldwater, William F. Buckley, Jr., and the Imperial Wizard of the Ku Klux Klan. Their participation, it was felt, might have caused British viewers to construe the program as a slanted piece of anti-American propaganda." And that, one can see from the cast of characters selected after lengthy discussions, Mr. Tynan had no wish whatever to do.

After the program was publicized, many Americans were indignant, and Mr. Tynan couldn't, just couldn't, understand why, he said. What was wrong? Had he not merely presented a package of American dissenters to prove that there are dissenters in the United States, and that they are allowed to speak? Mr. Tynan does record that "the Messrs. Cousins, Hutchins, and Thomas wrote to me, protesting against the context in which I had placed them," and slides quickly on to other matters. He doesn't tell the fuller story, which I had from Norman Cousins last spring: namely, that when Cousins first heard about the release of the program in England he exploded—sanely, to be sure. Producer Tynan had never intimated to him or to Mr. Hutchins or Mr. Thomas that he was to be sandwiched in among persons reputedly linked with the extreme Left like Dalton Trumbo and Alger Hiss. Each one was under the impression it was to be a short program presenting only himself: not a composite program made up of propaganda by Communists, howls from Ginsberg, and a little revolutionary nihilism from C. Wright Mills. The three requested that they be given equal time to do a show over the same station called "What We Like About America."

But Mr. Tynan evidently thought there are grounds beyond which dissent becomes intolerable, and he dismissed the complaints in a one-sentence letter. The matter is not dead; indeed, a legal suit is, one would think, in order. A public figure presumably has redress if, after the curtain is drawn, he finds that he is part of a freak show.

But that was just one, the minor of two episodes that led Mr. Tynan to Götterdämmerung. Later in the spring a full-page advertisement appeared in several newspapers under the sponsorship of "The Fair Play for Cuba Committee." Among the dozen or so signatures was Kenneth Tynan's. The ad stormed against the unwarrantedly bad press Castro had received in America. Cuba is not going Communist, the statement said—such charges are smears, probably motivated by vested business interests. All Castro wants to do is "give Cuba back to the Cubans." "Having assured myself [how easily Mr. Tynan is assured the moment the drama leaves the stage!] that the factual points made in the ad were valid, I appended my autograph to the list," says Mr. Tynan. Now that was six months before Fidel Castro came up here to smooch with Mr. Khrushchev and discuss their "common aims" and "common aspirations," to be sure. And then again maybe Mr. Tynan would sign an ad tomorrow saying Khrushchev's intention is merely to give Russia back to the Russians. Still, here was an ad even Eleanor Roosevelt had refused to sign. The signers were recruited from the fever swamps of the literary Left—Jean-Paul Sartre, Simone de Beauvoir, Truman Capote, Norman Mailer, James Baldwin, that kind of thing.

It was shortly after that Mr. Tynan was hit by the thunderbolt, which is the cause of the current sensation.

He, an *Englishman,* a *freeman,* a *subject* of *Her Majesty the Queen,* was told by a subpoena to get on down to Washington and appear before an executive session of the Senate Internal Security Subcommittee.

Mr. Tynan describes at considerable length the terror he felt at the summons. He felt "a kind of nebulous chill." "Economic fears welled up." Suppose he was "publicly smeared?" "Would my American earnings be jeopardized?" Would he starve to death? And how could he even answer the committee's questions "without fatally compromising my integrity?" (He answered the questions.) He asked for a week's postponement and got it, so he had a good long night of the soul. "They were, without question, the strangest and shakiest eight days of my life."

He called around and found to his dismay that it was perfectly legal for the Senate committee to call him. He was on

American soil, over which the American government continues to have jurisdiction. There was nothing to do about it but go. He did, and wants us to know that not since Manolete went purposefully forward on his fateful encounter with Islero, was such an act of courage seen.

So Rubashov went to Washington, whence he smuggled out to *Harper's* an account of his ordeal. He is forced to paraphrase his colloquy with his interpreters. "I should like to quote verbatim, but since I have been forbidden access to the transcript, I must resort to oratio obliqua." The rules of the Internal Security Subcommittee are that a witness (or his lawyer) is entitled to access to the transcript of his testimony at any time. We must assume that the committee, if it forbade Mr. Tynan the transcript, did so in blatant violation of its own rules. The other possibility is that Mr. Tynan never requested access to the transcript, perhaps because it is a little easier to parody an event if you are not burdened by the verbatim account; a little easier to be *obliqua.*

Mr. Tynan was in Washington to answer questions about the Cuban advertisement, not the television program; but Senator Thomas Dodd, who had protested the distortions in the program in a speech in Congress, evidently took the opportunity of Mr. Tynan's presence to ask whether it had been his intention in producing the show to hold the United States up to contempt and ridicule. Tynan's answer was, obviously, No: far from it, he intended to do the United States a *favor,* as no doubt he also intended by publishing his piece in *Harper's* about his inquisition. Senator Dodd asked him how he had got in touch with the Communists who appeared on his program. He wrote them, said Tynan, having got their addresses mostly from the production staff assigned to him by Associated Television. The names of the staff, he said, appeared at the outset of the program, every one of them having received a credit line. Mr. Tynan's explanation was duly transcribed; and Mr. Tynan now reflects that he may well have ruined many careers. "Even the cutter of the show may have some very rough questions to answer should he ever apply for an American visa." (All this with an unflinching, humorless solemnity!)

Had he been paid for signing the Cuban advertisement? No. Was the advertisement paid for by the Cuban Government? He did not know. One assumes that the committee was trying to find out whether Castro has successfully launched a propaganda base in this country, and whether one of its techniques is to enlist the endorsements of gullible people. I myself should not in the least be surprised if in due course it is revealed that that is exactly what happened.* Tynan didn't put up the money for the ad, he says—and I believe him—and you can bet your bottom dollar Norman Mailer didn't, nor Simone de Beauvoir. Who did? *Cui bono?* The point is, it is the proper business of a committee charged with the internal security to explore, and if necessary to recommend, legislation designed to regulate the activities of agents of a foreign power. We do not know whether it will be established after an investigation, conducted confidentially, that the Fair Play for Cuba Committee was financed by the Cuban Government. If Tynan knows that it was not, he must have been a most useful witness, for the government needed precisely to know how *he* knew it was not. If Tynan does not know whether or not it is financed by Castro, then he can perhaps understand the committee's not knowing, and the committee's wanting to find out from anyone who might be closer to the Fair Play group what *he* knows about it. If the Fair Play for Cuba Committee *is* a Castro front, then that will probably be revealed in due course, and Mr. Tynan will presumably be grateful to Senator Dodd for relieving him of the further embarrassment of acting as an innocent mouthpiece for Cuban Communist propaganda.

---

* A few months later, the subcommittee published documentary material proving that most of the money for the advertisements was paid in cash to the executive head of the committee by Castro's representative in the United Nations.

But Mr. Tynan is not a reasoner, and his story goes on with its poetic effulgences. "Was I—and it was here that my fear melted into a deep intestinal chuckle—was I aware that President Eisenhower had made a speech in which he stated that the Castro regime was a menace to the stability of the Western hemisphere? No, I was not. And did I think myself justified in holding opinions that openly defied those of the President of the United States? I brooded . . . and then replied that I was English, and that I had been forming opinions all my life without worrying for a second whether or not they coincided with those of the President of the United States."

Now if that second question was asked exactly as Mr. Tynan quoted it, the questioner, whoever he is, is fatuous indeed; fatuous, I should go so far as to say, beyond belief, or beyond *my* belief, at any rate. I do not have access to the transcript, but I will bet Mr. Tynan the entire orchestra section at the next performance of *The Crucible* that no one said that to him. What someone might have asked him—and if no one did, I raise the point— is whether Tynan thinks it correct to come to America and pummel its citizens with his political views on essentially domestic matters. (I know of no Americans who took out ads in the English papers instructing the British Government how to cope with Cyprus.) There is no law against it, and should be none: it is a matter of taste; and though the laws of taste are uncodified, they exist, and bind lesser men than drama critics.

On this point a little more needs to be said. "As I understand it," Mr. Tynan lectured the committee after his testimony had been taken, "the function of a congressional committee is to gather information on the basis of which new legislation may be recommended. [His understanding is incomplete.]

"I cannot help finding it anomalous that a foreign visitor should be compelled to contribute to the legislative processes

of a country not his own. . . . I am modest enough to feel that
the making of American law is none of my business."

But Mr. Tynan feels the making of American foreign policy
with respect to Cuba *is* his business, does he not? He signed
an ad intended for publication in the United States, hectoring
United States citizens to change their views on Cuba. He
was not modest about *that*. He undertakes to put together a
rogues' gallery of Americans, plus a few shills, with the intention of painting a picture of America for his own countrymen so grotesque as to be unrecognizable—and which hypo-
thetically could, if taken seriously, change the policy among
nations. Let us not deny him the right to do these things; but
let him not deny our government the right to take elementary
steps designed to find out from him what he knows, if anything, that might cast light on the movements of the enemy,
and perhaps to pass judgment, to the extent a congressional
committee can, on whether he is himself an enemy, or merely
a fool.

My own impression is that he is the latter, and I do not
think it is the business of a congressional investigating committee to expose the foolishness of people just for the sake
of it. On this point the Internal Security Subcommittee presumably agrees. For it did not breathe a word of its interview
with Mr. Tynan. The quailing, cowering, angry young man
who writes of his sleepless nights, his forfeited serenity, his
sentenced virtue, his imminent poverty, blew the whole
thing all by himself, and having done his best to write his
experience into the annals of human courage, he turned a
few hundred dollars out of a complaisant American magazine, and carried on the great and lucrative English tradition
of charging the United States a handsome sum of money for
telling us how ugly we are. The Imperial Wizard and I
resent that.

THE UNEXAMINED SIDE OF
EDWARD BENNETT WILLIAMS

*For twenty years [Adam Clayton] Powell [Jr.] has been
one of the most controversial and newsworthy figures in public life in New York City. . . . His eloquent articulation of his
convictions on racial equality and his personal dynamism
have won him hordes of idolators and hordes of detractors.*

EDWARD BENNETT WILLIAMS
One Man's Freedom, p. 207

AMONG Adam Clayton Powell, Jr.'s eloquent articula-
tions of his convictions on racial equality:

On America's entry into World War II: "[As long as the
war was] yellow against yellow, white against black, and
white against white [the U. S. stayed out] . . . Pearl Harbor,
however, was yellow against white, and the war came immediately with the race baiters roaring their approval."

On racial equality and the Soviet Union: "Negro-Ameri-
cans admire and feel close to the Soviet Union. We are im-
pressed by Russia's complete abolition of racial discrimination, by the job, health and other forms of social security
which the USSR guarantees to *all* of its nearly 200 million
people, and by its consistent fight to destroy fascism and free
the colonial peoples. Negroes, therefore, generally avoid
the anti-Soviet traps set by the imperialist war-makers."

. . . And a few examples of Adam Clayton Powell, Jr.'s personal dynamism. On Martin Dies: "The sooner [Dies] is
buried, the better. He is one of the few people in history
whose body has begun to stink before it died. . . . There is
only one place fit for him to live and that's Hitler's outhouse.
We demand that the President have him arrested as an en-

emy agent. . . . The death of Dies is just as important as the death of Hitler."

On the Taft-Hartley Act: "This bill has been called a bill of rights for labor. . . . It is a bill of rights and lefts under the belt for labor, not only under the belt but in the back, in good old foreign fascist style."

On the Republican Party of Thomas E. Dewey: "Dewey is now the Crown Head and indebted servant of the worst anti-American, isolationist reactionaries ever to come on the scene. . . . Dewey and those who voted to support him in the race for the presidency hate Negroes, democracy, the President, and progress. They are the fullest expression of Southern Bourbon crackerocracy and domestic fascism."

Such eloquence and personal dynamism do indeed have a way of discouraging incipient friendships, but Edward Bennett Williams, once he becomes your advocate—that is to say, when your personal dynamism gets you into trouble with the law—*stays* your advocate, well beyond the requirements of professional duty. Witness his handling of the case of Adam Clayton Powell, Jr. in his current best seller (*One Man's Freedom*, Atheneum, $5.95), in which he has succeeded in causing most of the reviewers to believe—he treats us as though we were members of a jury, putty in his masterful hands—that here is a profound book on the sorry condition of civil liberties and civil rights. A book, moreover, which he uniquely was able to write because of the vastness of his experience and the largeness of his libertarian heart. These last are available at one thousand dollars a day, which is a highish fee, but rendered less painful by the knowledge that your case may be a chapter in a future book by Ed Williams, and from there, the proximate cause of a historical, social or juridical reform. Your case will be dealt with gently. If Edward Bennett Williams had defended Adolf Eichmann, he would no doubt have introduced him by saying: "Adolf Eichmann's steadfast devotion to his own ideas on controversial ethnic issues earned him a horde of admirers and a horde of detractors." Whereupon he would proceed, as he has done with Powell, *et al.*, to move in on the deficiencies in the legal case against Eichmann.

And who is to say there were none? What does it matter *how* Williams characterizes his clients? Are the points he raises concerning necessary reforms in congressional investigating procedures, in federal and state laws governing criminal procedures, are they not valid or invalid criticisms irrespective of whether Williams' clients are, or are not, angels or sinners? The answer to this question is not obvious. As it stands, the demands of justice are cheek-to-cheek against the rights of the individual, and when one hears it proposed that extensive radical reforms be instituted (Williams would, for instance, deny to Congress the right to exercise its informing function), one properly inquires about the balance of the reformer, about his capacity to make sound judgments; one asks whether his documentation is responsibly set forth: whether, in a word, it is credible. *One Man's Freedom,* which has overnight become a sacred book for the civil libertines, deals with a number of people and their cases, each one illustrating the need for a separate reform. About most of Mr. Williams' clients I have only an impression (though, e.g., I'd sooner trust my impression that Hoffa is a hood than I would Williams' "proof" that he isn't). I know a good deal about the circumstances behind the difficulties of two of them. One is the Reverend Adam Clayton Powell, Jr. And if Mr. Williams' treatment of the Powell case is typical of either his capacity for the truth or of his access to it, then his book should be dismissed for what it seems to me to be: a venture in cynicism, or a venture in helpless confusion. In either case, it should not, at least not by itself, be permitted to unbalance the scales of justice.

I

Mr. Williams calls his chapter on Powell "Fingers on the Scales of Justice." The fingers, it transpires, are my very own, for it is I, says Williams, who, in the pages of *National Review*, whipped up a grand jury into an unnatural frenzy by making "irresponsible charges." The result was the indictment for income tax evasion of the Rev. Adam Clayton Powell, Jr.

The case of Adam Powell is too complex to detail, even though there is a purpose in doing so now that Williams has conscripted the corpse to march in his parade testifying to the existing flaws in criminal procedural arrangements. Here it is, without unrolling the winding sheet to anything like its full length.

Says Williams in his book:

1) Adam Clayton Powell's tax affairs were being looked into by a grand jury. The jury recessed "without returning an indictment. The only proper explanation for this was that there was not sufficient evidence on which to indict." 2) *National Review*, having received a lurid account of the case from former Assistant U. S. Attorney Thomas A. Bolan, cranked up a successful campaign to incite the jury to have another and vindictive look at Powell's income tax returns. 3) *National Review* charged that the grand jury had been derailed most probably because the Eisenhower Administration was repaying Powell the favor done it when Powell announced in October 1956 that all Negroes should vote for Eisenhower. "Of course, the absurdity of the charge was quickly demonstrable from the fact that the Powell grand jury was not even empaneled until after the election." And 4) Powell was not convicted, and the case against him was ultimately dropped—conclusive testimony to the flimsiness of the original charges.

Advocate Williams declines to inform his readers that:

1) The grand jury looking into the affairs of Adam Powell had been only temporarily recessed in March of 1957, having been interrupted in mid-investigation to permit Assistant Attorney Bolan, in charge of presenting the evidence to the grand jury, to dispose of an emergency matter assigned to

him by the U. S. Attorney. After Bolan had completed his work and was ready to return to the Powell case, he was advised by his immediate superior that New York had had word from Washington that the Powell case was "too hot," and they were to let it slide. Williams does not mention that the professional tax investigators looking into the case gave the opinion to their superiors that already enough material had been accumulated to warrant indictment, nor does he record their expressed belief that continued research would yield even more incriminating evidence. He does not mention that the grand jury was never consulted about the decision to suspend its sessions even though the grand jury had the exclusive authority to decide whether or not sufficient information had been developed to warrant an indictment. He does not mention that during the 18-month interval when the grand jury was paralyzed the statute of limitations crept in to immunize Powell against any prosecution for the year 1950, around which a formidable preliminary case had been built. He does not mention that the grand jury, when it did reconvene, was so indignant over its abuse by the U. S. Attorney that it went so far as to consider voting a presentment against the U. S. Attorney's office for its conduct of the case. He does not mention that the U. S. Attorney assured the grand jury, when it reconvened, that the long interval had been spent in "evaluating" the case, and that it had all along been his intention to recall the grand jury and ask for an indictment which—what do you know?—here he was asking for. (It makes no difference that no one believed the U. S. Attorney; his was the public story, and is a part of the public history of the case, which Williams was ostensibly relating.)

2) Mr. Williams is correct in implying that the grand jury would probably not have reconvened but for *National Review*'s prodding. Although grand juries are technically autonomous, in practice they rely on the leadership of the U. S. Attorneys. The grand jury reached for its latent powers on being reminded it had them; and, in reconvening, weighed

the evidence and presumably (they too are innocent until proved guilty) agreed with the investigators for the Treasury Department and with Assistant Attorney Bolan and with the reactivated U. S. Attorney; and they voted for indictment. Williams does not mention that it was a member of the grand jury, no less, who requested that *National Review* send copies of its exposé to each member; that a separate grand jury investigated whether in doing so the editor of *National Review* had violated a law, and declined to return an indictment; that Williams' plea that the indictment against Powell be dropped on the grounds that it had been illegally obtained through the agitations of *National Review* was yawned out of court by two different judges.

3) In striking a pose of outraged innocence at the mere suggestion that the Eisenhower Administration might have promised Powell to cooperate in the matter of his pending tax investigation, Williams evidently found it necessary not to mention any of the circumstantial data that induced worldly observers to accept that hypothesis.

On July 3, 1956, the U. S. Attorney in New York announced publicly that a full-scale investigation into Powell's tax affairs would be launched immediately. The investigation had been catalyzed by evidence that grew out of successive indictments and trials of four of Mr. Powell's close professional associates. Three of his secretaries had been indicted, and one had already been convicted. The testimony heavily implicated Powell. One secretary was on trial at that moment.

As late as October 6, Powell was telling his congregation that no Negro could conscientiously "campaign for Stevenson or Eisenhower." Five days later, on October 11, having been called to testify at his secretary's trial, Powell walked in and out of the White House, called a press conference on the spot, and urged all Negroes to vote for Eisenhower.

This was a political bombshell. Powell threw himself into the cause of Eisenhower's re-election. Exhibiting what Mr. Williams has described as his eloquent and dynamic fight for racial equality, he denounced Stevenson as "a slave" to "America's fifth column of native fascists," and said that Negroes who voted for him were "traitors to their race." *The New York Times* reported that Governor Harriman had found the coincidence "strange" that Powell should strike out on so unexpected a course while the Eisenhower Administration was looking into his tax returns.

It is true that the grand jury was not empaneled until December, a month after the election; but another grand jury had been looking into his affairs for months. Nor does Williams consider the scandal that would have resulted from failing to call up a jury after the announcement had been publicly made that a thorough investigation was under way. Williams does not allude to Bolan's statements, made under oath, to the effect that he had been told to drop the case because Powell was "too hot." He does not mention that in 1960 a columnist wrote a detailed three-column exposé, based on the testimony of one of Powell's disaffected confidants, describing the exact nature of the deal made between one of Eisenhower's lieutenants and Adam Powell: a series that was not challenged, either by Eisenhower's lieutenant or by Powell. He does not mention that Senator Williams of Delaware referred to the situation as demanding congressional investigation. He does not allude at all to the general concurrence that the whole thing smelled, e.g., the Richmond *Times-Dispatch*'s summation:

> Now, we believe—and it is simply an act of faith in a man—that Dwight Eisenhower individually had nothing on earth to do with the Department of Justice's decision, in March of 1957, to suppress its case against Adam Clayton Powell. It is unthinkable, in the light of Eisenhower's whole career, that he dropped so much as a wink or a nudge or a hint that Powell's help of the autumn should thus be repaid in the spring. But the harsh, unyielding fact is that somebody, at the level of Herbert Brownell or on down the line, gave the word in March of 1957 that the heat was off; and realities

of politics are such that the prosecution of a Negro congressman from New York City is not handled in a casual fashion.
The question must be asked, and Mr. Eisenhower's administration stands under a cloud until it is answered: Who gave
the word, and why?

We do not know. We know only that it was given. When
National Review succeeded in alerting the grand jury to
what was going on, the jury met, heard the evidence (though
not by any means all of it—there was no time, with the jury's
life about to expire, to chase down enticing leads; moreover,
as we have seen, other incriminating evidence had been de-
fused by the statute of limitations); and Adam Powell was
indicted on several counts of filing fraudulent income tax
returns. I remember Murray Kempton's writing me at the
time to chide *National Review* for having upset the only
1956 Republican campaign promise that had remained intact
eighteen months after the election!

It remains to be said 4) that the case against Adam Powell
was ultimately dropped. That is an utterly irrelevant datum.
The broader question at issue is whether a grand jury was
tampered with, and the narrower question is whether Edward Williams, in making the case for a congeries of legal
and congressional reforms, is to be trusted. As far as Powell is
concerned, it is appropriate to observe that it is no more true
that all men who are found not guilty are in fact not guilty,
than it is true that all men who are found guilty are guilty.
(As *National Review* suggested some time ago, the question
needs to be raised whether the law has yet been devised
which one cannot break provided one can subsequently secure the help of Edward Bennett Williams.) Adam Powell
is legally a free man and that is as it should be; it does not
follow automatically that he was not culpable. The jury heard
evidence that, among other things, Powell had deducted
$2,536 for round-trip train fares to Washington in the course
of a single year during which he had been abroad for four
months, to justify which would have required him to travel

from New York to Washington practically every day including Sundays. He had taken a deduction, the prosecution charged, of $737 for clerical raiment which had, apparently, cost him only $2.37. Etc., etc. Williams' courtroom strategy was to dig up all kinds of deductible expenses Powell and his wife could have got away with deducting but didn't deduct, and he found here and there overstatements of income. Internal Revenue permits an overstatement of income to cancel out excessive deductions dollar for dollar, a projection of the theory that if you save one man from drowning, you are entitled to drown one man—so be it; the law is an ass, and let's keep it that way. Ten members of the jury voted to let Powell go. Two members thought he was guilty. Powell's prosecutor tried to amend a disastrously constructed Bill of Particulars which he had not drawn up, but which he was saddled with—conceivably the defective legal workmanship was the final honorable effort to redeem a political commitment—but it was too late, and the government dropped the case, which is, after all, presumably what it had wanted to do ever since October 11, 1956.

It had been, Edward Bennett Williams concludes, a "long, expensive and politically damaging trial." It was certainly long, running over six weeks. And no one is better qualified than Mr. Williams to know that it was expensive. In fact, it was not politically damaging. True, for a while it looked as though Mr. Powell was slipping politically. After he was indicted, the Democratic Party tried to shelve him: not because he had been indicted, but because he had come out for Eisenhower in 1956. The National Association for the Advancement of Colored People joined the hordes of detractors upset by Mr. Powell's eloquent articulation of his convictions on racial equality, and denounced him in the summer of 1958 as a "racialist." *The New York Times* called him "the most extreme racist in Congress." But in no time at all, absolutely no time at all, Powell had brought the Democratic Party in Harlem to its knees, taken over one of the most vital committee chairmanships in Congress, and found himself guest of honor at a testimonial dinner two months after Kennedy's election at which two cabinet members, Messrs. Goldberg and Ribicoff, sang Mr. Powell's praises. The Democrats are so much better at this kind of thing than Republicans are and the testimonial dinner went off without a hitch, which is more than can be said of the attempt to fix the grand jury.*

II

Edward Bennett Williams has gone a long way since the day when, as a total stranger, he walked into the office of Senator Joe McCarthy and volunteered to sue, on McCarthy's behalf, Drew Pearson—free of charge. Granted, any patriotic lawyer should be willing to sue Drew Pearson free of charge, but to appear as McCarthy's counselor during those days meant notoriety, which Williams clearly sought, but also the possibility—in Williams' case the certainty, considering that he had become intimate with the McCarthy household and happily frequented right-wing social events—of public identification as a McCarthyite; which presumably Williams did not want. Mrs. McCarthy recalls that she never believed, nor was led to believe, that Ed Williams subscribed to the mission of her husband, though the two were close friends. Others remember differently. Williams called me over the telephone in the summer of 1954 and asked my assistance in preparing the defense of McCarthy against the Watkins Committee, giving me clearly to understand that I should give this help at whatever personal inconvenience because the cause of McCarthy was bigger than both of us. I suggested that he secure the help of Brent Bozell, co-author

* Sequel: One week after this review was published, the Internal Revenue Department revealed that it had served Mr. Powell a bill for forty thousand dollars, representing taxes not paid, and penalties for fraudulent returns, during the late 40's. The statute of limitations prevented criminal prosecution.

of the book that had drawn me to Williams' attention (*Mc-Carthy and His Enemies*) and, moreover, a practicing attorney. Williams accepted the suggestion gleefully, called Bozell in San Francisco where he was practicing, and persuaded him to go to Washington.

Bozell and Williams differed on several tactical matters having to do with the defense of McCarthy, but Bozell never doubted that Williams truly believed in McCarthy's crusade, which those of us who encouraged it, with however many specific reservations, understood as involving, essentially, the vigorous use of the legislative arm to require enforcement of a vigorous security program weighted in favor of the government against the loyalty risk. Three years later, Bozell happened by a church hall on a Sunday evening and heard a golden voice denouncing congressional investigating committees, the Smith Act, the House Committee on Un-American Activities, upholding the *Watkins* case and the *Jenkins* case and the *Nelson* case and the whole cluster of Supreme Court decisions whose effect had been to paralyze the internal security program.

Bozell looked in, and there was his old colleague, Edward Bennett Williams, warning direfully against the perils of which their old friend McCarthy was the eponym. Fair enough. A man can change his mind. And anyway Ed Williams takes elaborate pains in the current volume to make the case for purely professional relationships, from which it is no more to be inferred that client and lawyer are ideological or felonious soulmates, than it is to be inferred that a doctor who pulls out a Democratic appendix is himself a Democrat. The question spontaneously arises, to be sure, why Edward Bennett Williams does not get up at some other church hall and declaim about the evils of Hoffaism (those evils too have been documented); or against the evils of Goldfineism (surely the attempt by a five-percenter to colonize the White House is a subject worthy of his attention?); or the evils of such as Costello (nationwide crime is also a problem); or, indeed, against the tendency of such as Adam Clayton Powell, Jr., in the name of freedom for the Negro, to develop a very special racism of their own.

This imbalance in Edward Bennett Williams, which can be understood as the occupational opportunism of a lawyer on the make (McCarthyism is a dirtier word in the circles he moves in than Hoffaism), becomes a matter of general concern when said lawyer lights on the scene as a legal statesman. Ed Williams has become the premier advocate of a wide series of reforms that aim at shoring up the positions of what one might call the defendant class. *One Man's Freedom* comes with a benediction, cautiously worded but no less surprising, from Arthur Krock, an outstanding advocate of the rights of Congress and of the individual states (Williams has little use for Congress, and one gathers he never even heard of the individual states). "The obligation of a lawyer to help assure that justice under due process of law is the right of anyone accused, however he may have transgressed," says Krock, "has never been more impressively set forth than in this book. But it is also a fascinating story of major political and social contentions, adding in several surprising particulars to the public record"—and, as we have seen, leaving out several surprising particulars from the public record. And Morris Ernst, who is widely identified with the cause of civil liberties, notes that "this book contributes more to the understanding of freedom in our republic than anything else written in recent years."

That is a most questionable contention. I do not see that the book contributes anything at all to the understanding of freedom in our republic; indeed, I would go so far as to predict that if all of Mr. Williams' recommendations were carried out, there would be precious little freedom left in our republic; in fact, it is doubtful if there would be a republic at all.

III

The statistics on the continuing rise in the crime rate have been hitting us so insistently now for so many years that we seem, as a nation, to have become completely inured to them. We deal with crime as fatalistically as the English came to deal with the nightly bombing raids during the dark days of World War II: let's hope the blighters don't hit us, but if they do, well, that's life, and there'll always be an England.

So the situation continues to grow worse, to the point where Mr. Eric Sevareid can complain, with only the normal amount of exaggeration, that in New York City the churches are empty at night, where once they were heavily attended, because the New Yorker will not grope his way back from church to home through unlighted streets for fear that, by the law of averages, his turn will have come to cross the furious path of some hoodlum or rat pack or progressively educated teen-ager.

Edward Bennett Williams is typical of our most vocal social reformers who, not understanding the circumstances, elect to spend most of their time criticizing, not the lengths to which organized crime, random crime, and quasi-legal crime have taken over the nation, but the unconstitutional, illegal, and reprehensible lengths to which our law enforcement officials and our congressional investigating committees have now and then attempted to go in order to bring the lawbreakers to justice.

Mr. Williams, who has made a great career of sticking out his tongue, in behalf of such as Jimmy Hoffa, Frank Costello, Dave Beck, and Bernard Goldfine, at those who have tried to put them behind bars, devotes himself entirely to criticizing police and congressional practices that have aimed, however clumsily, at doing something about the crime rate. His remonstrances are directed not at the Communists who seek to undermine our system, or at the monopoly leaders who rule by cracking the pates of the opposition, or at the hoodlums who rob and prey and rape, or at the manipulators who try to corrupt whole legislatures, or at the fifth columnists who carry the Fifth Amendment like an aegis and smirk at the pathetic attempts of the petty bourgeoisie to bring them to justice: Mr. Williams pleads for action to deprive the Congress of the right to exercise its traditional power to expose crime and malfeasance, to forbid the police from tapping the telephones of putative criminals, to restrain detectives from interrogating suspects. . . .

To the extent Mr. Williams is saying that this practice or that, here and there used by a policeman, is unlawful, he makes a good enough point: policemen, of all people, should not act unlawfully. But to the extent that he (or the American Civil Liberties Union) concentrates exclusively on the rights of malefactors or alleged malefactors, he is acting injudiciously. Jimmy Hoffa has rights, to be sure. But so do individual truckers, so do harassed businessmen, so do the individual members of Hoffa's union, over whom he rules like a despot. The answer to Jimmy Hoffa's overweening power would seem to be clear, though it may be true that there is not in the whole of Congress the political courage to give that answer (and this is not Williams' fault): the labor union monopolies must be broken up. Congress has been agonizing over for years the problem of the Communist conspiracy; yet every time a corrective piece of legislation is offered, the Williamses and the ACLUers weep over lost liberties. The answer to juvenile delinquents is not clear, nor is the answer clear how to deal with the Frank Costellos and the great underworld syndicates that appear to have taken over whole cities. If Edward Williams is to contribute to the understanding of freedom in our republic, he must contribute to an understanding of how to deal with contemporary threats to the freedom of the republic, and this he does not do. He feels free to defend a Hoffa or a Costello—quite properly: everyone is entitled to legal representation—why does he not, as a citizen actively concerned about pre-

serving the rights of defendants, also devote himself, in his
capacity as a citizen, to the problem of how to cope with the
criminals who are closing in on our society? As it stands now,
known members of Murder Incorporated can walk through
Central Park at night with safety, but nuns cannot. I do not
see that Mr. Williams has any ideas on how to solve the problem of which that irony is a symbol; or, for that matter, that
he shows any awareness of the problem.

Granted, it will not be easy to come up with appropriate
solutions. But should one not come up with something other
than an obsessive concern for the suspect or the defendant?
The columnist John Crosby made a semi-cogent criticism a
year or so ago in an open letter to J. Edgar Hoover saying
in effect: "Okay, so the crime rate is higher than ever. Why
don't *you*, Mr. Hoover, do something about it?" Mr. Crosby's
complaint is at least superficially appealing: if the crime
rate is up, doesn't one naturally blame the law enforcers?

What Crosby does not mention is that the political wing of
which he is a member, and whose spokesman on criminal
and related affairs Edward Williams has become, reliably
opposes, whether thoughtfully or unthoughtfully, every
measure, ranging from bills allowing New York teachers to
spank impossible students, to bills imposing the death penalty on atomic saboteurs—every measure designed to sharpen
the domestic discipline, and enforce the rights of the citi-
zenry. But Crosby has something there: his very criticisms
tend to reflect the failure of Mr. Hoover publicly to identify
himself with, and dramatize the need for, reforms aimed at
limiting crime. Why doesn't Mr. Hoover use his enormous
prestige to recommend to Congress specific revisions in the
law (granted, he has made a start in the proposed wire-tap-
ping bill advanced by Attorney General Kennedy) which
might make it possible to outwit the underworld? Any such
recommendations must reflect a continuing concern for the
rights of the individual. But so also must they reflect the
great advantages that our scientific age and our urban con-

centrations have opened up for automated crime. It is now possible for Boss Trap in New York to direct-dial Killer Joe in Los Angeles, and instruct him to deposit Recalcitrant Merchant Jones, neatly tucked into the trunk of his car, into Super-Duper GM Car-Junk Model 778, and *whee!* nothing, not a trace is left of Jones. And if Detective Smith happens to have bugged Boss Trap's telephone, all he and Killer Joe have to do is call Edward Bennett Williams, who will lucubrate over constitutional liberties; and off they will go, to continue their crusade to make the world safe from Recalcitrant Merchants.

Victims and intended victims have rights, too. Somebody should write a book about them.

IV

Edward Bennett Williams' success in winning acclamation as an architect of freedom and justice presumably derives from the use of the same skills through which he caused jurors to look at Jimmy Hoffa and Adam Clayton Powell and mistake them for the Cherubim and the Seraphim. Williams treats his readers as though they were members of a jury, and though we miss his celebrated voice and gestures, on the other hand we are not bothered by the frequent interruptions of the prosecutor. Williams' techniques are various. The first is the highly tendentious rendering of the factual situation. We have seen how he deployed the facts in the case of Adam Clayton Powell, Jr. It is so elsewhere in the book. "There were no outcries," he sighs, "from the Liberals for the unhappy victims of the [Kefauver] investigation—*and then it was the Liberals' turn, and the public was almost indifferent to the violation of their rights. Next came organized labor.*" Here is history making with verve: at a stroke we are informed, as confidently as that America was discovered by Christopher Columbus, that the congressional investigations of the 1950's were aimed not at Communists and pro-Communists and fellow travelers, but at Liberals! And then, covering his bets, he rushes forward to a yet more dazzling piece of historical impudence: the scrupulously, agonizingly fair investigation by Senator McClellan's anti-rackets committee should have brought "outcries" in behalf of the "unhappy victims" (instead it brought an attempt at remedial legislation in the Landrum-Griffin-Kennedy Bill).

"In May, 1958, a Cleveland industrialist named Cyrus Eaton made bold to criticize the FBI over a national television network . . ." "A Cleveland industrialist." That is Mr. Williams, introducing to the jury a man who happens to be a Communist Party-liner in international affairs, an adulator of Nikita Khrushchev, who on the occasion in question had attacked the FBI with the distinctive ferocity of a Communist Party hatchetman. The flotsam and jetsam of Williams' arguments wash up on the shores of reason in irreconcilable pieces, but on he goes, unperturbed. On adjoining pages he will tell us, 1): *"I very much doubt whether any juror ever saw* [Joe Louis] *in that packed courtroom, seated, and they always left before any spectator was permitted to leave his seat."* And 2): *"All of the jurors later attested that* [Joe Louis'] *appearance at the trial was meaningless insofar as the outcome was concerned."* How could the jurors attest to the impact Joe Louis had on them, if they did not even know he was there?

An extension of the technique of proceeding as though the other side did not exist is the dogmatic generality. Williams would rather asseverate about the rights and duties of Congress than get a guilty man acquitted. *"What Congress may not do is to conduct an investigation for a purpose totally unrelated to its constitutional duties. It may not, for example, conduct investigations to . . . influence opinion."* One would think that Williams was speaking as the last survivor of the Constitutional Convention. He does not bother to relate that this ill-defined stricture on the limits of congressional power contradicts the general understanding of the powers of Congress, the practice of one hundred and seventy years, and the burden of the authoritative analysis of such constitutional and parliamentarian commentators as Walter Bagehot, Woodrow Wilson, Edward Corwin, and Hugo Black (yes, Hugo Black). Williams' Amendment to the Constitution is sustained by a single *obiter dictum* of the Warren Court (in *Watkins*), from which, incidentally, the Court has since backed away (in *Barenblatt* and *Wilkinson*). "*Too many persons have forgotten that the Fifth Amendment is a citadel of Liberty, guaranteeing far more than immunity from compulsory self-incrimination.*" "Too many persons" includes the Supreme Court in 1908 (*Twining* v. *New York*)—"[the Fifth Amendment is a] useful principle [rather than] a fundamental right"; and, in 1937, Justice Cardozo, backed up by Justices Hughes, Brandeis, Stone, Roberts, and Black, who said "Justice . . . would not perish if the accused were subjected to orderly inquiry" (*Palko* v. *Connecticut*).

Yet Williams must guard against giving the jury the impression that he is unreasonable. A concession to the prosecution, every now and then, is psychologically vital. Williams has been arguing for the right of a government employee against whom secret information has been received to cross-examine the secret informant. There are those, including J. Edgar Hoover, who have repeatedly maintained that to ask the government to surface, in every relevant security case, an agent who might have spent years penetrating the Party is to levy on the nation's security an impossible price merely to effect the discreet removal of a government employee from a position to which he has, in any case, no legal right.

But hark the reasonableness of the man. "*Of course, it is possible to conjure up situations in which the disclosure of the informant's identity could do serious damage to national security. Where this is true, and where it is further true that the continuation of the accused in a sensitive job would equally damage national security*" (a fast one right there, of the kind no one is around to yell *Objection!* to. The question in security cases is not whether the government employee *would* damage the national security, but whether there are reasonable grounds for believing he *might* damage it). "[In such cases] *there is basis for exception to the over-all rule. But the truth of these facts should be certified in writing by the cabinet officer or agency chief of the affected department or agency.* [Fair enough, provided "would" is changed to "might."] *He should further certify to his belief in the credibility of the information involved. Only upon such certification should the hearing board in question be empowered to make a ruling depriving the accused of confrontation and cross-examination.* [Here we go.] *And this decision should be subject to full review by a board of appeals and, finally, full judicial review by courts which have available the concealed information that was before the board* [!]."

There is not a security official in the United States who would consider the procedures recommended by Williams as anything short of ludicrous. (And I suspect Williams knows it.) Let the FBI give the name of a secret informant to the members and staff of a federal court, to the members and staff of a court of appeals, to the members and staff of the Supreme Court, to the defendant's counsel (how is the defendant's counsel otherwise going to impeach the witness's credibility, which is the purpose of the whole procedure?)— and the "secret" informant will be ready to publish his autobiography.

But see how reasonable Williams appears?

V

And finally, there is Williams' rhetoric. It is the rhetoric of personal righteousness, with just that touch of Sunday-suit pomposity which solemnizes, and numbs. *"I was greatly moved by the plight of this man." "I entered my appearance in the case on Icardi's behalf."* (Did you ever enter *your* appearance on behalf of anyone? Shame!) *"I asked the head of the Department of Justice to afford to us, in the interest of justice, the benefits of the government's investigation."*

"My sense of fair play was so offended by all this..."
The pomposity becomes insufferable when the eagle really spreads his wings, drowning out all thought in the clatter of his clichés. *"It would be a tragic paradox if we should surrender any part of our heritage in the name of this* [anti-Communist] *effort, for we should then have done to ourselves from within what we fear most from without."* Horsefeathers. We are in some kind of a war, and that war means things like generals, bomb shelters, CIA's, kidnappings, atom bombs, tapped telephones, conscription, supergovernment, secret diplomacy, bribes, subornations, seductions, GI's getting shot in South Vietnam, Smith Acts to bear down on those in our midst who pass on the ammunition to our enemies: and all this precisely *in order* to secure the nation from the total loss of freedom. *"In 1954 the Supreme Court of the United States in a great, broad-gauged humanitarian decision held that American citizens who are required to pay the same taxes, pledge allegiance to the same flag, give obedience to the same laws, fight the same wars and die in the same battles might go to the same schools."* Does that mean they can all go to Groton? *"Fortunately we have a President who believes that nine decades is long enough for the Negro to wait to vote and that the best way to end Negro disenfranchisement in the South is the quickest way."* Fortunately, we have a President who believes nothing of the sort. The quickest way to get the vote for all the Negroes of the South is presumably to shoot every white man who tries to get in the Negroes' way. But that is *not* the best way. *"We are racing on at an ever accelerating pace to maintain a peace through mutual terror, a peace that is no peace at all."* Who says it isn't? Whatever the peace's deficiencies, Edward Williams would not be at peace to defend criminals but for the success we have had in terrorizing the Soviet Union to the point of checking her mad aggressiveness.

But the man cannot, or will not, think, except about how to win the favor of juries and law school deans. He shows evidence of absolutely genuine mealy-mindedness. Toward the end of his book he makes an idealistic quantum jump of dazzling dimensions which, typically, he introduces with a pomposity. *"I have long been convinced that the time has come to make a bold, dramatic new try at realizing man's ancient hope of world peace through law."* He wants us to can the Connally Amendment and, side by side with the Soviet Union, to submit our differences to an international court of law. *"Idealistic folly?"* he asks the jury rhetorically. *"What is the alternative?"*

Waal, the alternative is *not* to repeal the Connally Amendment. And *not* to submit national problems of life and death to anyone's authority other than our own, for so long at least as it is clear that the Soviet Union would use the court only insofar as it furthered world revolution, ignore it insofar as it didn't.

Ah, but Williams has a revelation up his sleeve for us skeptics. He has had a long talk with Mr. Platon D. Morozov, the Soviet Union's top legal representative at the United Nations, and Morozov confided to Williams that *he too* believes that the Communists should make "unqualified declarations recognizing the compulsory jurisdiction of the court"! What *are* we waiting for? Morozov's for it!

The last thing we need is to be ruled over by an international court while we live in a world with the Soviet Union in it. It would be quite unsettling enough to contemplate living under a world court—assuming the Soviet Union sank into the seas—of the kind that would have the blessing of Edward Bennett Williams. What kind of courts does he go in for? He tells us earlier in the book. *"We [in America] are blessed in the 1960's with the greatest Supreme Court in history."*

If that's the case, *this* eloquent articulator of his conviction on racial equality will vote for the *worst* Supreme Court in history, thanks very much; and, seventy times seven times, against the repeal of the Connally Amendment.

CAN WE DESEGREGATE, HESTO PRESTO?

WHAT, I am asked, is the conservatives' solution to the race problem in the South? I answer: There is no present solution to it. Such an answer appalls. It brings to mind, to move from tragedy to flippancy, the cartoon of the farmer leaning on his pitchfork and replying to the motorist: "Come to think of it, mister, I don't think you can *get* to Glens Falls from here." There are those who approach all problems as though they involved merely getting an automobile from here to there: there is always a road. There are others who know that some problems are insoluble. These last are for the most part conservatives; and I am here to defend them.

Let us begin by stressing that no matter how convinced a people may be of the wrongness of an existing situation, it does not follow that the people should be prepared to resort to whatever means may be necessary to attempt to make that situation right. That may sound obvious—the end does not justify any means; but when we examine some of the drastic proposals that are being put forward with the end of securing the rights of the Negro (e.g., a constitutional amendment depriving the individual states of their right to set up voting qualifications), the time has come to reiterate the obvious. We acknowledge, for instance, that it is wrong to drive at excessive speeds; but no state in the union seems prepared to impose a heavier penalty on the speeder than the automatic suspension of his license for thirty days. There would be less speeding, and hence less violent slaughter—the two figures, the experts inform us, are inextricably related

—if speeders were packed off to jail for a week. Even so, notwithstanding the established correlation between fast driving and aborted lives, we shrink from so drastic a penalty; and the speeding, and the deaths, go on.

Let us take the word of the predominating school of social scientists and stipulate that segregation is the cause of personality disturbances. And—mark this—not only in the Negro, but also in the white. The argument is not new; it has often been used against capital and even corporal punishment. It is not only the victim who is damaged, psychiatrists report, but also the executioner, in whom latent sadistic impulses are dangerously encouraged. No one who has contemplated a man brandishing a fiery cross and preaching hatred needs help from social science to know that the race problem has debasing effects on black and white alike.

Assume all this to be true. Assume, also, that the legal and political power is wholly at the disposal of the society to effect its point of view in the South. Assume, in other words, that *Brown* v. *Board of Education* and the supporting decisions of the Supreme Court deconstitutionalized segregated public schooling beyond the point of argument. Then assume that the raw power necessary to enforce that decision is available to the present Administration, and that the will of the nation is such as to insure that Congress will supply power where power is lacking. Should the federal government then proceed?

The list of sanctions available to the government is endless. The economic power of the federal government has in our time reached the point where it cannot be denied; cannot, in fact, be defied. If Congress can seriously entertain the question whether to spend money to aid public schooling in any state whose public schools are segregated, why can't Congress debate the question whether it is prepared to spend money for road building in a segregated state? Or for unemployment? Or for farmers' subsidies? Already the Attorney General has hinted he is considering (for purely punitive reasons) recommending to the President the removal of our large military installations from segregated areas.

In a word, the federal government is in a position to visit intolerable economic sanctions against the defiant state. Not to mention the government's arsenal of legal weapons. Why cannot the Congress (assuming always a purposive mood on the subject of segregation) pass laws increasing the penalties for those held guilty of contempt of court in a certain category of cases? And why can't the courts rule—as Professor Auerbach of the University of Wisconsin has recommended—that any state which, having fought to the end of the legal road, sets out to close down its public schools rather than integrate them, be forbidden to do so on the grounds that such action, under such circumstances, becomes not the free exercise of the state's power, but an act of defiance of a federal court? By such reasoning the federal government could take over the operation of the schools.

The crucial question arises: Will the government of the United States move in such a fashion? The answer is: Probably not; for the reason that, along the way, the ideological stamina would very likely give out, as the public contemplated the consequences of an assault of such magnitude on a whole region. Another question is: *Should* the government of the United States take that kind of action to end segregation? The answer to that is, in my judgment: No, most definitely not.

"You know, the world is hard enough and people is evil enough without all the time looking for it and stirring it up and making it worse," says Leona, in a novel by the eloquent, tormented Negro writer James Baldwin, who celebrates his bitterness against the white community mostly in journals of the far political Left. What would be accomplished by turning the legislative, judicial, and executive resources of this country over to a crash program of integration? Let us suppose the program were so successful as to make South Carolina like New York City. Recently a distinguished New York

Negro told the audience of the television program *Open End* that he did not know three white people in all of New York with whom he felt genuinely comfortable, such is the prevalence of prejudice even in this cosmopolitan center. Louis Lomax may be more sensitive, and hence more bitter, than the average New York Negro, and so unrepresentative of the state of Negro serenity in the North; but then, too, Dr. Martin Luther King is more sensitive, and so more bitter, than the average Southern Negro, and hence unqualified as a litmus of the Southern Negro's discontent. But only one of the other Negro guests on the program challenged as extreme that remarkable testament to race relations in the city under which the fires of the melting pot burn hottest.

The deep disturbances isolated by the social scientists are not, I think, of the kind that are removed by integrating the waiting rooms and the schools. It has even been revealed (*Villanova Law Review*, Fall, 1960) that the very tests cited by the Supreme Court in *Brown* as evidence that Southern Negro children were suffering personality damage, when administered in the North yielded not merely similar results, but results that seemed to indicate a greater psychic disturbance in integrated Northern Negroes than in segregated Southern Negroes! I believe that the *forms* of segregation, which so much engross us at the moment and which alone are within the reach of the law to alter, are of tertiary importance, and of transitory nature; and under the circumstances the question arises even more urgently: *Should* we resort to convulsive measures that do violence to the traditions of our system in order to remove the forms of segregation in the South? If the results were predictably and unambiguously successful, the case might be made persuasively. If a clean stroke through the tissue of American mores could reach through to the cancer, forever to extirpate it, then one might say, in due gravity: Let us operate. But when the results are thus ambiguous? Use the federal power to slash through the warp and woof of society in pursuit of a social ideal which was never realized even under the clement circumstances of a Chicago or a New York or a Philadelphia?

I say no. A conservative is seldom disposed to use the federal government as the sword of social justice, for the sword is generally two-edged ("The Government can only do something for the people in proportion as it can do something to the people," Jefferson said). If it is doubtful just what enduring benefits the Southern Negro would receive from the intervention of government on the scale needed to, say, integrate the schools in South Carolina, it is less doubtful what the consequences of interposition would be to the ideal of local government and the sense of community, ideals which I am not ready to abandon, not even to kill Jim Crow.

What, meanwhile, are the Negroes actually losing that they would not lose if the government took over in the South? One thing alone, I think, and that is the institutional face of segregation. That is important; but it is in the last analysis only a form. What matters is the substance of segregation. The kind of familiarity that might lessen racial consciousness is outside the power of the government to effect. I would even argue that it is outside the power of the government to accelerate. J. Kenneth Galbraith tells us that the ultimate enemy of myth is circumstance, and I think he is correct. If it is true that the separation of the races on account of color is nonrational, then circumstance will in due course break down segregation. When it becomes self-evident that biological, intellectual, cultural, and psychic similarities among the races render social separation capricious and atavistic, then the myths will begin to fade, as they have done in respect of the Irish, the Italians, the Jews; then integration will come—the right kind of integration. But meanwhile there *are* differences between the races which surely will not be denied by an organization explicitly devoted to the advancement of colored people. The Negro community must advance, and is advancing. The Reverend William Sloane Coffin of Yale University, returning from his whirl with the Freedom Riders, rejected the request of Mr. Robert Kennedy that the Riders withdraw to let the situation cool off with the words: "The Negroes have been waiting for ninety years." Mr. Coffin spoke nonsense, and showed scant respect for the productive labors, material and spiritual, of three generations of Negroes. A sociologist at Brooklyn College only a few weeks before had observed that never in the history of nations has a racial minority advanced so fast as the Negroes have done in America. How far will they go on to advance? To the point where social separation will vanish?

I do not know, but I hope that circumstance will usher in that day, and that when the Negroes have finally realized their long dream of attaining to the status of the white man, the white man will still be free; and that depends, in part, on the moderation of those whose inclination it is to build a superstate that will give them Instant Integration.

A REPLY TO ROBERT HUTCHINS:
THE AIMLESSNESS OF
AMERICAN EDUCATION

THERE is a sameness, both dreadful and reassuring, in the statements one is pelted with these days on the aims of American education. John Barrymore said he could induce a severe case of delirium tremens by reckoning the amount of whiskey he had drunk during his lifetime and imagining it all in a single glass (about the size of a small movie theater) poised for him to start all over again. The young college president, freshly in office, must pale at the thought of the miles and miles of clichés that stand between him and that final baccalaureate address, twenty years hence, when he will say: essentially the same thing.

What is reassuring about that sameness is that it happens to be crowding out the talk-talk-talk of the educational instrumentalists. It becomes harder and harder to find anyone of standing who will defend the theory of progressive education, let alone the enormities committed in its name. The sameness that sometimes appalls us, then, is in one respect at least a healthy sameness; it is the beginning of a negative consensus among the thinking people on an important matter, a protest against the dehumanization of the human species by that school of educational thought, or non-thought, which for years has been insisting that the supreme challenge of education is to cultivate a cheerful, mindless adjustment to one's social and material environment.

The fight, at the first phase, has been tough, and there is tough fighting, at the second phase, left to do. I date the victorious end of the first phase of the war between the forces of classical education and those of "progressive" education in 1957 with the appearance in *Life* magazine of a massive editorial barrage against what we now call the educationists. When Time, Inc. takes up a big issue in a big way, it is safe to assume that the sensitive ear of Mr. Luce has registered profound seismographic rumblings. Others had, beginning years before, pioneered. They had delivered a total critique of progressive education which disposed thinking people to listen. Mr. Robert Hutchins, Mr. Mortimer Smith, Mr. Russell Kirk, to name perhaps the three most insistent and eloquent critics of progressive education, had made it safe for *Life* magazine to speak out on the issue.

The fight that remains unwon is that of actually taking power. It is one thing to persuade the leaders of the community that a local high school has no business teaching hotel management and community hygiene in place of English and history. It is one thing to mock Columbia Teachers College for accepting as a doctoral dissertation, as it recently did, a paper on "The Cooperative Selection of School Furniture to Serve the Kindergarten Through Third Grade Program in the Garden City Public Schools." It is another actually to step in and dispossess the zealous administrators of non-education, actually shoo them out, and begin the process of re-education. That, alas, is a political fight, not an intellectual fight, and fresh and differently trained and equipped troops are needed to wage it.

Will they step forward? Here and there are hopeful signs. But final victory is not by any means guaranteed. It is comforting to tell ourselves that in a free society no fraud can survive for very long after it is publicly discredited; but alas, that is not in fact the case—as witness, for instance, socialism, which is left without serious defenders, but whose forms encroach on us year after year. The fetishes of the witch doctor may be shown to be made of nothing more than dogs' teeth and colored ink—but still the people will go to him, or tolerate him; as today, the people continue to tolerate, and to patronize, schools and colleges and universities which treat their children like half-rational biological mechanisms, whose highest ambition in life is to develop in such fashion as to render glad the rotarian heart in Anytown, U.S.A.

But why do we weary, in turn, even of the relatively enlightened statements on the aims of education that are being made by those who reject progressive education? Why does the very eloquent president of UCLA sound like the very eloquent president of Sarah Lawrence who sounds like the very eloquent president of Swarthmore who—alas—sounds, allowing for differences in syntactical resourcefulness, like an hour at the hearthside of a cliché factory?

The answer has to do with the incompleteness of their position. No matter how pleasing the fugue as it rolls along, it denies the final satisfaction until it is resolved—and all the individualistic though harmonious melodic strands come together to establish their essential unity. The critique of progressive education absolutely establishes many things—we are finally airborne: but we never land.

I think that for the most part our educators—I have specifically in mind Dr. Robert Hutchins—while they know what education is not, do not know for sure what education is.

The principal reason why they do not know and cannot know is because they are restrained from seeking educational ends, from following through, by a mystique (academic freedom) which is all promises, but no delivery. Perpetually hovering, as it does, it remains in its own highfalutin way as anti-intellectual, as nihilistic, as the assumptions of progressive education.

What are the educational aims of the good guys? All of us are familiar with the litany. I shall not quote representative educational manifestoes. I am frankly fearful of the anesthetizing effect of the prose, some of which is so exultantly sonorous as to cause the listener to drop his critical guard. (Any modern educator worth his salt will know how, without saying anything very much at all, to evoke in us a sort of dreamy and inspired confidence that we are listening to a man who is engaged in charging up the mountain of Excellence, hotly pursued by his students ...) I shall attempt instead an unembellished yet scrupulously faithful condensation of the aims of education as put forward by the typical spokesman for liberal education, as follows:

1. A student should acquire the tools of learning (e.g., he should learn to write, to reason, to memorize, to synthesize). Incontestable, I should say.

2. He should learn about the intellectual and historical experiences of others (mainly through a study of history, philosophy and literature). Again, incontestable.

3. He should learn something about the major intellectual specialties (something, e.g., about science, language, political economy). Incontestable. And we come to the purpose of education:

4. The purpose of all of which is twofold, a) to enable him to exercise, in behalf of himself, his fullest intellectual powers, and to cause him to want to do so. And b) to cause him, in behalf of others, to contribute to his community the fruit of his endowments. Incontestable.

But consider how many questions are begged by assuming that 1–2–3 will lead to 4; and that 4 sufficiently defines the aims of education.

We are, to be sure, agreed on an important postulate, namely, that for personal and social reasons it is desirable that human beings exercise their distinctively human faculties (principally the power to reason and to apprehend beauty). What is it about the aims of education, as commonly set down, that leaves us with a sense of incompleteness? The kind of incompleteness which leads, ultimately, to frustration and boredom?

Certainly we are not told how to account for the profound conflicts that sunder the educated world. If education is a civilizing experience, then why are we not entitled to correlate education and civilization? Yet it does not work out that way, does it? Educators know, or are expected to know, writes Dr. Herbert Lowry, "how vital colleges and universities are in giving leading ideas to . . . national life—all down the line. They know that education is eventually a kind of dynamite." Which exploded in our day, in various parts of the world, in socialism, fascism, and communism. Dr. I. L. Kandel has conceded the lamentable truth that "education is the most Fascist aspect of the Fascist Revolution, the most Communist feature of the Communist Revolution, and the most Nazi expression of the National Socialist Revolution."

The correlation, in other words, doesn't automatically hold. It is not safe to say: Knowledge is wisdom. In terms of sheer knowledge, sheer book learning, Lenin and Trotsky had few peers. Yet it would greatly have relieved the world had their teachers refrained from cultivating the minds, and hence the powers, of these men.

It may be argued that in worrying about Communists and Nazis and Fascists one is worrying about aberrants—intellectual mutations, who should never be allowed to distract us from the formulation of general laws. Let us suppose that is what they are—and move over to a part of the world governed by more conventional political and philosophical ideas, and put down in London.

In London there is Bertrand Russell. Lord Russell knows more about more things than, quite possibly, anyone else now living. What has it done for him? Or for us? Apart from his technical philosophical contributions of specialized significance, what has he done to ease or direct into productive channels the labors of society, or to refine the understanding? What has he done for himself? He had more than the two educations once suggested by Mr. Hutchins as requisite to marital felicity: and he has had five wives. He has explicitly rejected the Western institution of monogamy, and conventional notions of sexual virtue, in theory and practice; he has taken a very wide range of iconoclastic positions over the past thirty years, challenging at the root the basic Western convictions on: theology, ethics, the institution of the family. And now, in the plenitude of his wisdom, he advises us to yield to the Soviet Union—to yield to barbarism, rather than fight to save our institutions. "The civilized world will be destroyed!" The Great Scholar trembles, repeating the words that undermined the Roman will to resist their barbarians fifteen hundred years ago, a moral failure vividly described in one of Russell's own books. Was it the aim of the education of Bertrand Russell that he should learn in order to so instruct us? To be sure, there is a perverse consistency in his advice. He has devoted his life to challenging the validity of Western convictions—it follows they are not worth defending at the risk of war.

We put down again, this time at Cambridge, Massachusetts, and wander about the halls, listening for the wisdom that true education will make us privy to. There, until recently, was Professor John Kenneth Galbraith, insisting that the premises of our economic organization are outmoded, are merely sustained by the "conventional wisdom," which he, though not, alas, many others, has penetrated. Perhaps he is right, for he is an educated man, who did not while away his high school hours on driving lessons and life adjustment courses—but if one travels to the University of Chicago, and listens there to Professor Friedrich Hayek, at the very least as well educated a man, one is told that the way of Galbraith is the way to 1) serfdom, and 2) poverty. Mr. Hutchins, a highly educated man, even by his own exacting standards, terms nonsensical some of the views of Dr. James Conant, a highly educated man by any man's standards. Sidney Hook, a highly educated man, tells us we must emancipate ourselves from the thrall of religion, and Reinhold Niebuhr, a highly educated man, tells us that through religion we find truth, freedom, and, who knows, perhaps even salvation.

What is to be done about all those modern problems we

hear so much about, ranging from peacemaking to proliferat-
ing slums? To meet those problems we need, we keep on
being told, bold solutions; revised, renewed, upgraded, mod-
ernized thought, of the kind that will occur only to a society
that has been to schools of the kind Dr. Hutchins would
operate. But what are these solutions behind which a truly
educated public could be expected to rally? Why not ask
those men who have had the kind of education of which
Dr. Hutchins approves for a preview? What do they want
the nation to do? Well, of course, in asking that question, we
have turned on Babel. Everybody is speaking, and in different tongues. There are schools of thought, to be sure. One,
addressing itself to one area of concern, says the time is
ended when major social problems can be settled by individuals or by voluntary associations: that we must turn to
the state. There is the conflicting view, that the state is for
reasons, perhaps even metaphysical, but certainly prudential,
precisely the wrong agency through which to attempt social
reform. There are multifarious views, at daggers drawn, on
international affairs, colonialism, states rights—everything.

Ah, but if everyone were educated like Dr. Hutchins, the
"correct" or "most enlightened" voices would prevail! That,
to use a word Dr. Hutchins clearly understands, for he uses
it frequently, is nonsense. If the educated elite cannot arrive
at a consensus, why can we expect that an educated body
politic would arrive at a consensus? And even if it did, how
can we tell that the consensus of the newly educated would
be desirable? I am obliged to confess that I should sooner
live in a society governed by the first two thousand names
in the Boston telephone directory than in a society governed
by the two thousand faculty members of Harvard University.
Not, heaven knows, because I hold lightly the brainpower or
knowledge or generosity or even the affability of the Harvard faculty: but because I greatly fear intellectual arro-
gance, and that is a distinguishing characteristic of the university which refuses to accept any common premise. In the

deliberations of two thousand citizens of Boston I think one would discern a respect for the laws of God and for the wisdom of our ancestors which does not characterize the thought of Harvard professors—who, to the extent that they believe in God at all, tend to believe He made some terrible mistakes which they would undertake to rectify; and, when they are paying homage to the wisdom of our ancestors, tend to do so with a kind of condescension toward those whose accomplishments we long since surpassed.

I am saying simply that the educated elite in this country are not agreed as to what are the central problems that education aims to settle, or help settle, let alone what is their solution; that among the elite there are radical and irreconcilable differences which have nothing whatever to do with the size of the brain or the length or breadth of the education. I go further and say that when the educational elite do appear to be taking a position almost unanimously, they are often impulsive, wrong-headed, and superficial (as for instance, when for a while it was sweepingly accepted that Darwin had buried God, and that therefore agnosticism was the sign of educational sophistication; or more recently, when academic folk appeared almost in a body to accept the hysterical myth that Senator McCarthy had ushered in a reign of terror). And I conclude that there is, therefore, no currently fashionable theory of education which speaks convincingly about the social utility of a good education, and therefore no convincing demonstration having to do with the interrelatedness of good general education and social progress and harmony.

I myself am much persuaded by the position that a good education is sufficiently justified by what it renders to the individual who receives it, and that no external justification for it is needed. But even that demonstration has not been made convincingly to the people at large, and I do not think one can easily sell the community on the value of a good classical education without doing it more graphically. It

just is not that obvious to the skeptic that Latin is worth all
that work and expense, unrelated either to getting and
spending, or to making over the world in a handsomer image.
It is all very well to talk about the personal and private joys
of reading Homer in Greek, or being able to run through
Bach's partitas, or of evenings by the fire rereading a novel
by Jane Austen, but there is an intuitive suspicion abroad that
the joys are not that palpable, and that if they are—and here
the suspicion runs very deep—there are complementary disturbances which are less frequently spoken about. The suspicion is not after all ill-grounded, if we look at the evidence
about us, that "good" education tends to produce students
who may indeed read Greek plays from time to time, but
who are more discontented, more fretful, more anxious, more
resentful, less happy, than the graduated hipster whose education was in community relations and balanced diets, and
whose recreations will be confined to zooming about on a
motorboat, or sitting up watching the late, late show. That
suspicion, as I say, is very general: one has only to read representative works of the college generation of John Dos Passos
and Whittaker Chambers and Thomas Merton to understand
the impulsive cry of the despairing parent: Oh my God, must
my son receive a good education?

I do not believe we will ever be convincing in our effort
to mobilize the nation in behalf of good education until we
give the aims of that education more intelligibly. And this
we cannot do, so far as I can see, until we free ourselves of
the superstitions of academic freedom. So long as academic
freedom is understood to mean the right of the researcher to
pursue knowledge without being hindered by the law, the
doctrine is unassailable. But it does not make sense to suggest, as it everywhere is, that academic freedom should
constrain a teaching institution to keep a teacher on even if
he devotes himself to undermining the premises of the school
at which he teaches, or the society in which he lives. Such
a teacher may properly be deemed uncongruous, and any

college that so finds, ought to be as free to replace him as a community is free to dismiss a public servant for whose services there is no longer a demand.

It is especially urgent that academic freedom be abandoned in its capacity as keeper of doctrinal parity, guardian of the notion that all ideas are equal. Under academic freedom, the modern university is supposed to take a position of "neutrality" as among competing ideas. "A university does not take sides on the questions that are discussed in its halls," a committee of scholars and alumni of Yale reported in 1952. "In the ideal university all sides of any issue are presented as impartially as possible." To do otherwise, they are saying, is to violate the neutrality of a teaching institution, to give advantage to one idea over against another, thus prejudicing the race which, if all the contestants were let strictly alone, truth is bound to win.

That is voodoo. The aims of education are to forward knowledge and right conduct—at the expense of some points of view. The educated man, Russell Kirk has trenchantly said, is the man who has come to learn how to apprehend ethical norms by intellectual means. He has come to know, in a word, what is right conduct, and why one should conduct oneself rightly, and he has come to know this by understanding the rational base for such conduct. As long as universities take the position that they will not affirm one idea over against another, the faculty and officials of a center of humane learning are saying that they do not know what right conduct is. They are, moreover, saying that they never will know: for academic freedom is not conceived as a self-terminating device to be discarded on the day of the Grand Discovery. Academic freedom is conceived as a permanent instrument of doctrinal egalitarianism; it is always there to remind us that we can never know anything for sure: which I view as another way of saying we cannot really know what are the aims of education.

To say a college should not take sides because it cannot

know which side is right, or because it cannot afford the chance of taking the wrong side, is to sentence colleges to a destiny of intellectual futility, and bring education into the discredit in which so many people now hold it. If it is academically presumptuous for a college to assert, for instance, that the Western way of life is better than that of the Communists', then education has become frivolous. It is the duty of a university to pass on to its students the prodigious intellectual and moral patrimony accumulated by the generations and generations of scholars and students who agonized before us. To assume, as academic freedom implicitly does, that every child, every student, should in nonscientific matters begin again fresh, as though Plato and Aristotle and Augustine and Saint Thomas had among them reached not one dependable conclusion, is to doubt the very structure of learning; is to doubt that there are any aims at all, aside from purely utilitarian ones, to education.

If it can be said that the education of Lenin produced an aberrant, then it is tacitly conceded that standards exist by which he is judged an aberrant—standards we accept. If the giraffe leans down to the level of the donkey and says "Runt!" there is implicit an idea of a decent elevation for animals, to which the donkey does not attain. It must follow, then, that there are standards by which, taking the measure of their deviation, we judge such matters as whether Lenin or Hitler —or Leninism or Hitlerism—deserves equal attention and respect from our students: whether a university should be "impartial" to them. And if there are standards, they ought to be accounted for in any theory of education which aims to speak intelligibly. Such a theory would say something like this:

"Schools ought not to be neutral. Schools should *not* proceed as though the wisdom of our fathers were too tentative to serve as an educational base. The Ten Commandments do not sit about shaking, awaiting their inevitable deposition by some swashbuckling professor of ethics. Certain great truths have been apprehended. In the field of morality, all the basic truths have been apprehended; and we are going to teach these, and teach, and demonstrate, how it is that those who disregard them fall easily into the alien pitfalls of communism, or fascism, or liberalism.

"There is a purpose in life. It is known what that purpose is, in part because it has been divulged, in part because man is endowed with a rational mechanism by which he can apprehend it. Educators should pass on those truths, and endow students with the knowledge of the processes by which they are recognized as such. To do this is the single greatest contribution a teaching institution can make: it is the aim of education, to which all else is subordinate and derivative. If education can endow students with the powers of ethical and rational discrimination by which to discern and give their allegiance to the great certitudes of the West, we shall have a breed of men who will discharge truly the responsibilities that face them as the result of changing conditions."

I advocate indoctrination? There is a devil-word, with lots of power left in it, to tyrannize over any discussion of academic theory. In fact, it is literally impossible to act on the abstract directives of academic freedom. Just as, thank God, it is almost impossible for an individual to be entirely neutral, it is impossible for a department within a college to be neutral, or even for a college to be neutral. "Indoctrination," in the sense of urging of one doctrine rather than another, goes on all the time, and right under the noses of some of the most vociferous academic freedomites, who are often themselves the premier inculcators.

In 1959, the Harvard *Crimson* published the results of a careful questionnaire on religious and political attitudes among the students. The poll, a random-sample survey, had been prepared under the professional supervision of Professor David Riesman, a sociologist of world renown. Listen to the summation by an editor of the paper of the political half of the questionnaire:

"... whereas only a twelfth of Harvard's undergraduates describe their political temperament as 'radical,' over a seventh support full socialization of industries; more than a fifth favor socialization of the medical profession ... nearly a third believe that the Federal government should own and operate all basic industries ... a third ... favor immediate unilateral suspension of atomic tests ... a clear-cut majority ... support recognition of Communist China and a marked increase in American economic aid to other countries ... one-third prefer surrender to the Soviet Union over a nuclear world war. Two-thirds support such Welfare State projects as Social Security and Federal regional power development ... four-fifths approve of Federal aid to public secondary schools; two-thirds support national health insurance, Federal aid to private colleges and universities, government wage and price controls to check inflation; and half support Federal financial assistance to American cultural activities." Indeed, "within the College ... Federal aid is rapidly gaining the status of a magic word. Surrounded by a climate of liberalism, most Harvard undergraduates seem ready to accept increased Federal activity in almost any area of national life—from housing developments to theaters, and from farms to factories."

How did the students get that way?

"For the most part," the *Crimson* report states, "the College students did not arrive in Cambridge with these beliefs; they picked them up at Harvard. Over half admit that their political views have been strongly influenced since Freshman Registration, and, of these, seven-tenths have changed either 'from conservative to liberal' or 'from liberal to more liberal.'"

Now it may be that to indoctrinate students in political Liberalism is to lead them toward the truth—certainly Harvard appears to be acting on that assumption. But what is relevant in this discussion is not what direction Harvard is taking, but the fact that, in violation of the precepts of academic freedom, it is taking any direction at all; what is remarkable is that, contrary to the dictates of the theoretical literature that continues to pour out of Harvard, sly old Mother Harvard is not in any sense "impartial" or "neutral." The fact that you or I may happen to disagree with the political tendencies of Harvard education has no bearing on the meaning for all of us of so brazen a departure from the doctrinal imperatives of academic freedom. It means that the colleges may some day soon bring theory into line with practice, and give up all the nonsense about neutrality. When that happens, a substantial theoretical victory will have been won, and *Life* magazine may even celebrate the event with another editorial; and then we can address ourselves to the problem of which in fact are the ideas, political and philosophical, which best reflect the wisdom of the West, and will best equip us to survive the barbarian encirclement; and bring the West out alive.

I say only that the wisdom is there, and that educational theory ought to adjust to that fact. All the changing conditions we hear so much about do not affect the validity or applicability of the central directives of human conduct, and if those who are always calling for brave new solutions to our problems, like Dr. Hutchins, seem to be giving more time to calling for them than to looking for them, do not judge them harshly; they have no alternative. Burke would have treated them with tolerance, as he did his own contemporaries when he said, speaking for all the men of his age, including himself, "We know that we have made no discoveries; and we think that no discoveries are to be made, in morality; nor many in the great principles of government, nor in the idea of liberty, which were understood long before we were born, altogether as well as they will be after the grave has heaped its mould upon our presumption, and the silent tomb shall have imposed its law on our pert loquacity."

CATHOLIC LIBERALS,
CATHOLIC CONSERVATIVES,
AND THE REQUIREMENTS
OF UNITY

...the fact does remain that Catholic conservatives and liberals are often conducting a sometimes unhealthy, often unchristian—and totally unnecessary—internecine feud.

I know I speak for many when I call upon conservatives and liberals alike to begin to think seriously now of ways in which this apparent impasse can be resolved for the sake of Church and country....

Is it out of the question to hope that quiet meetings between members of both camps might be held to work out Christian ground rules for debate and to decide on a basic, minimal program for a united fight against Communism and for the promotion of justice and charity in our society?

—DONALD J. THORMAN, managing editor
of *Ave Maria,* in an editorial, October
28, 1961

MR. DONALD THORMAN has made a most pertinent suggestion, namely, that an attempt be made to formulate a "basic, minimal program for a united fight against Communism..." on which Catholic Liberals and conservatives should be able to agree. But I have truncated Mr. Thorman's sentence. Unfortunately, he did not bring it to a close where I did. He wrote, to quote the full sentence, "a basic, minimal program for a united fight *against* Communism and *for* the promotion of justice and charity in our society." (His italics.)

My considered answer to the longer question is: Any such minimal program is going to end up so minimal as to be useless. The reason why is that Catholic Liberals disagree very strongly with Catholic conservatives on how to promote justice and if it became necessary to formulate an approach on which both sides might agree, on such issues as, say, how to promote racial toleration, or how to promote industrial harmony, we'd end up with one of those ritual invocations of common purpose which are the surest disguise of sundering differences. For instance, let me suggest that the mere mention, in the previous sentence, of those hypermotive terms "racial toleration" and "industrial harmony" has already brought up the guard of the Liberal who is reading this essay.

I am not suggesting that Catholics should cease arguing about how best to serve the ends of justice and charity—in all things. I am suggesting that a serious effort be made to detach from other quarrels, to the extent possible, the argument about the Communist issue. You will remember, that used to be official policy. They called it, immediately after the war, the "bipartisan policy"; that is to say, a policy presumptively backed by both Democrats and Republicans, and held immune from normal factional analysis. The trouble with the bipartisanship of 1945–1949 is that it was pretty much bipartisan on *their* side—that is to say, on the side of what we conservatives sometimes call the appeasers; and so in due course, especially after the loss of China, many Republicans and not a few Democrats turned in their bipartisan badges, checked out their six-shooters and started to fire away at the foreign policy of Mr. Truman and Mr. Acheson. That division persists, *mutatis mutandis,* and Catholics are involved in it.

I think it was necessary that the bipartisan era should come to an end. But the virtues of bipartisanship should not be lost sight of. It is inconceivable that Catholics are not, all of them, equally interested in containing the Communists. And yet, as Mr. Thorman points out, because we are racked by differences of opinion on many matters, the unity we should be able to show on the Communist problem is lacking. Such are the developing personal antagonisms that some laymen (and priests) shun cooperation with Catholics at the other end of the political spectrum even when they seem to be saying or doing things with which they almost surely agree. May I be struck dead if I am exaggerating, but so help me I once saw in the pages of *Commonweal* a sensible anti-Communist proposal. What I should have done (I now realize) is written off a note to the editor congratulating him—though that course has its dangers too, because the editor might have felt that I was condescending to him, or—worse—he might have taken a worried look at the editorial I commended, and had second thoughts about it. In *National Review* we have printed, I say unblushingly, some articles and editorials of spectacular spiritual and strategical moment; and yet I never had a note about them, or a friendly nod, from any member of the Catholic Liberal community. And having said that, I must confess I have been guilty of the same indifference to solid anti-Communist achievement by Catholic Liberals, though, granted, on the subject of Communism they do not often pump within me the juice of admiration. But there I go—that is the kind of thing we are here to try to avoid, is it not?

Granted, temperament and pride may be the most formidable obstacles to making common cause. Still, what are the objective bases for united action? Let us attempt to be concrete. We are in search of a *minimal* program with which both sides might agree. What might I say, for instance, on the touchy subject of internal security that could win the approval of the majority of Liberal Catholics? Suppose we set down a numerical sequence, beginning with the least arguable proposal, but getting progressively provocative:

1) *The government shall maintain some kind of internal security machinery to guard against disloyalty by government personnel.* (Everybody with me?)

2) *Security officials shall have access to the files of the FBI and the CIA and other intelligence agencies of the government.* (How're we doing?)

3) *Security officials shall make an evaluation on the basis of all the data they can lay their hands on, and in the event of an adverse determination shall recommend immediate dismissal to the department head.* (Purely procedural? . . .)

4) *On receipt of a negative recommendation, the department head shall, in his absolute discretion, decide whether or not the employee shall remain in government service.* (Hmmm . . .)

5) *A government employee, having no "right" to his job, may be deprived of it without due process as commonly understood.* (Whoa! . . .)

6) *Any individual suspected of disloyalty or unreliability shall be discharged from government service whether or not he works for a so-called sensitive agency, whether or not his particular job, within the government agency, is itself sensitive. . . .* (The crowd is beginning to roar); *moreover:*

7) *If any hearing is held, which shall be at the sole discretion of the department head, the employee shall not be informed of the sources of accusations against him if there is any risk, in so doing, of exposing a counterintelligence operation. Notwithstanding, in all cases the information of secret informants will be weighed.* (Mutiny. John Cogley has fainted, and is being carried out of the room. . . .)

How far down this list, arm in arm with the conservative, will the Liberal go? My guess is somewhere down toward the vicinity of No. 4; some would go to 5, even 6. Very few would go on to No. 7.

Is this a technique by which one might put one's finger on the so-called minimal program? Should Liberal and conservative Catholics, aware that they approve proposals 1–3, join hands in opposing those who challenge these—and then separate, to fight against each other, in respect of Nos. 4–7? Assuming this is a fruitful methodological approach, it could easily be expanded, by anyone for himself, or by any man with a schematic understanding of the issues that separate Left from Right.

I myself prefer at this juncture a less schematic approach. Granted the uses of the foregoing technique, how far can we really go in understanding each other without first fully understanding Mr. Thorman's injunction, and examining its tacit assumptions? I understand that a loose syllogism has been offered, whose parts are roughly as follows:

Proposition A: Communism promotes injustice.

Proposition B: We should promote justice.

Conclusion: Those who promote justice are thereby waging anti-Communism.

Question: Is this a correct syllogism?

Answer: No, it is not, but in its coils many fine minds choke.

"We are responsible for Communism!" roars the Rev. Louis J. Twomey in the October, 1961, issue of *Act* (I assume that he roared out the words, because in his script he used both the exclamation point *and* the italics). Now if Father Twomey had meant by that that we are responsible for the imperialistic successes of the Communists, I would surely agree: it is inconceivable that the Communists could have advanced as they have done but for a morally and strategically inert West. But Father Twomey does not mean that. The Communists have advanced, he says, because of "our supreme unconcern with gross violations of justice and charity here and abroad."

Now I find that statement historically nonsensical. I believe we should make justice—because it is the right thing to do to make justice; but I do not for a moment believe that every act of justice draws strength away from the Communist movement. The temptation of the Liberal is to secularize a uniquely religious relationship. It is true that every act of justice causes the heavenly chorus to rejoice; and that every act of injustice, or uncharity, causes pain to Our Lord: in this sense, as human beings, we are each one of us in direct contact with eternity, and each day our individual ledgers reflect the success or lack of it of our daily struggle against Evil.

But it is theologically wrong, historically naïve, and strategically suicidal to assume that the forces of Communism, like those of the devil, are routed by personal or even corporate acts of justice and love. Our fight against Communism is not to be understood merely as a fight against sin: that is a fight in which each one of us is supremely engaged, and stands to lose his own soul. The other fight is one in which we are engaged as a civil collectivity, and the distinction is not between "just" and "unjust" acts in relation to fighting Communism, but between relevant and irrelevant means of fighting Communism. If you look after the medical needs of a retired and impoverished former employee, you have performed an act of love, under certain circumstances an act of justice, perhaps even, under still other circumstances, an act of mercy. Escalate your personal acts of justice, love and mercy into, if you will, Socialized Medicine —still, it cannot be established that your act, or your government's, will have anything whatever to do with staying the Communist juggernaut. For heaven's sake! Anyone who believes the battle will go to the more just, the more charitable, can hardly believe that this battle—for all the West's sinfulness—will go to the Communists!—who have made a religion out of injustice, and for whom mercy is officially catalogued as bourgeois sentimentalism. We could, of course, bring in Rube Goldberg, and ask him to work out a causal relation, and he might contrive that the old servant, if he did not get from you his medical needs, would join the local cell of the Communist Party and sound the revolutionary tocsin; but such attenuated and materialistically forged linkages are for, well, otherworldly people—people who stubbornly fail to note that a correlation has never been established between the extent of injustice and the appeal of Communism.

Father Twomey believes, for instance, that the segregation of the Negro in the South is the single greatest encouragement to international Communism. I would say the single greatest encouragement to international Communism is the existence of a class of people who can make that kind of a statement. The Communists could not care less whether there is segregation in the South, and the Negroes in the South have never been attracted to Communism on account of segregation. If every white Southerner were to miscegenate tomorrow, the Communist Party would not be set back by five minutes. The Communists view segregation merely as a point of contention within our society—which of course they will proceed to exploit, just as they will opportunize on every friction within the West (and if there were no frictions Communism would provide them).

It is one thing to say that the existence of social strife in the South generates a lesion on which the Communists can be counted to pour anticoagulants: and that being the case, the single-minded anti-Communist might argue that we should be even more opposed to the Freedom Riders than to the segregationists, inasmuch as it is the former, more than the latter, who are giving rise to the ugly explosions which the Communists exploit. To suggest that a Just Solution (instant integration, according to some) will silence the Communist carpers, is naïve: the Communists would find just as much to criticize in an integrated South as in a segregated South, just as they are finding it as easy to criticize our prodigious trade union movement as to criticize the fledgling thing of 30 years ago.

To suggest that Communism lets up its critique (or loses its appeal) as we advance toward Justice (I am letting the Liberals define the word, for the present purposes), is to be ignorant of Marxist theory and historical Communist practice. For Marxists, justice means conformity with the requirements of dialectical materialism. The so-called social reforms which Father Twomey has so much desired have, a great many of them, been adopted in Italy, where nevertheless Communism thrives. The strongest Communist Party in post-World War I Europe was in Germany—Mother of Welfare States. The *fact* of discrimination in America against the

Negro is of no more intrinsic concern to the Communists than the fact of discrimination against the Jews in Soviet Russia is of concern to them. There are, in certain kinds of segregation, problems in justice raised, and certainly problems in charity; and the Father Twomeys should, provided they are balanced in their analysis, continue to inveigh on the matter. But it is as wrong to urge the suppression of the segregationists *in the name of anti-Communism* as it is to urge the suppression of the Freedom Riders in the name of anti-Communism.

How widely is it known that the most truly integrated country in all of Africa is Angola (along with Mozambique)? There the Portuguese over a period of generations have virtually wiped out discrimination on account of color. Of what bearing has this been in the hate-Portugal drive that the Communists have mounted and are pursuing in an effort to bring disorder to the Portuguese colony?

In what three countries in Europe are the Communists the weakest? And let us see how justice, in the sense the Liberals use the word, fares in each. 1) Spain. The Communists are weak in Spain primarily because the dictator of Spain simply does not tolerate them. Go to Spain and Communize, and you will find yourself, in a very little time, either out of Spain or in jail. What has that got to do with justice? 2) Ireland. And Ireland is the poorest country in Europe, by far—but there are no Communists there to speak of, though there is much distributive injustice, one gathers. What is the reason? It is cultural, primarily. The Communists have never succeeded in making much headway in English-speaking countries. And 3) West Germany. Why? In part because the Communists there are outlawed. In part because anyone who believes Communism will augment justice, or that pro-Communism is an answer to domestic injustice, has only to turn to the man next door, who fled two weeks ago from East Germany, to find out what Communism is. Here, then, are three reasons which primarily account for the weakness of

Communism in the three countries of Europe where Communism is weakest, and not one has to do with justice; or mercy, for that matter.

No, these false correlations, and they are, alas, typical of Liberal thought on the subject of Communism, simply do not work out. I am not a pragmatist. But I believe one should be pragmatic. Lincoln wrote to Horace Greeley in the dark days of the Civil War that his aim was to keep the Union, that if he could do so by freeing every slave, he was prepared to free every slave; if he could keep the Union by freeing half the slaves, he'd let the Negro population stay half slave and half free; that if he could keep the Union by letting all the slaves stay slaves, why thus would they remain. Lincoln meant by that letter not, obviously, that the highest imaginary ideal was the survival of the Union, but that the survival of the Union was the highest ideal of which he could hope to be the instrument; the survival of the Union was his highest existential responsibility; and the Union having been secured, then, under its framework, civilized discourse would resume, and men with black faces would in due course become free. In our time, and in respect of world forces which are insurgent against civilization itself, it is I think desperately clear that the West must *survive,* or we shall have entered the longest and bitterest night in human history. To effect that survival, I am prepared to do almost anything. And as a Catholic conservative, I wish to seek out that program which is relevant to diminishing Communist power, not necessarily that program which has the highest moral sex appeal. (To this course this country is implicitly committed; hence our defense budget, for instance, is many times larger than what one might call our social, or justice, budget.)

What *is* relevant to diminishing Communist power? I touch on three points at random:

In the field of foreign aid, I would relate every penny to the anti-Communist enterprise. (If you desire to send money

for purely eleemosynary purposes, and everyone should—
and I do—do so through the missions.)

Transform the Peace Corps into a body of evangelists for
freedom, young men and women highly trained in the ways
of Communist psychological warfare who could, in behalf of
freedom, analyze, argue, explain, edify: intellectual and
spiritual legionnaires for freedom and justice.

Acknowledge that justice-as-related-to-anti-Communism
requires the liberation of the men we betrayed in Eastern
Europe. There indeed is a fusion of justice and anti-Communist activity: the redemption of the tens of millions
whom, because of a slovenly, cowardly and unimaginative
diplomacy, we turned over to their Communist oppressors,
not only defaulting on our moral obligations and diminishing
our identification with justice, but aggrandizing greatly the
enemy's power. Liberation would be an act of justice; but
primarily it must be sought as a means of weakening the
enemy. . . . This merely adumbrates the kind of thing I have
in mind, which one would hope might, upon reflection, appeal to the Liberal Catholic.

But Mr. Thorman is absolutely correct that if *any* kind of
progress is to be made in establishing a discourse between
Catholic conservatives and Catholic Liberals, it must be preceded by an improvement in one's manners, and by genuine
attempts at charity and understanding. Now here I should
like to be able to say that both sides are equally to blame
for the breakdown in communications, but to say so would
be to say something I do not believe, and that would not be
an honorable way to repay *Ave Maria*'s hospitality. It *is* true
that there *are* "conservatives," perhaps some of them are
Catholic, who believe that everyone who disagrees with
them is a Communist, or a Comsymp, or whatever; but these
are totally unrepresentative people, and to get worked up
over what a tiny and aberrant minority does, and to suggest
(as so many Catholic Liberals have done) that their behavior is typical of conservative behavior, is to sin against

reality—and justice. Conservative Catholics are quite prepared to disown irresponsible or invincibly ignorant Catholic
conservatives who make any such assertion, and will the
Liberals then disown such statements as Edward Morgan's,
quoted by Mr. Thorman in his heuristic editorial?—"The
heinous, unforgivable crime of the radical right is to leap
on such misjudgments [as the Liberals have made] as evidence of disloyalty." Will they disown such statements as
Father Twomey's, that most American conservatives are
motivated by a material self-interest? Or such ignorant statements as that of the editor of *The Sign*, to the effect that
American "ultraconservatives" are, typically, rich, com-
placent, unfeeling, ignorant, Birchite, snooping moral in-
sensates? (*The Sign*, August, 1961.)

Let us understand one another, for God's sake; and let us
not put off the day of our reconciliation. How commendable
is the effort of Mr. Thorman! We must come to know one
another. To prove my sincerity, I shall once again invite to
lunch with me, to talk over our differences, the editor of
America. I hope he will not, once again, refuse.*

* A vain hope, it proved. I have sent out into the crossroads for someone
to take the place of him who was invited.

AN EVENING WITH JACK PAAR

Saanenmoser, Switzerland. My colleagues have sent me the transcript of several Jack Paar shows, at which he and others celebrated my inhumanity to man, among other failings, notorious among which being my unintelligibility. Would I care to comment? Well, having read the transcript closely, yes, I would. For one thing, one might as well set the record straight; and besides, the time is ripe for giving a little thought to the phenomenon of boastful resistance to thought. The mistake is often made of assuming that the audience of Jack Paar is as loose minded as he is. Several of my friends, making that assumption, counseled me not to accept Mr. Paar's urgently worded invitation to appear (to answer charges made against me by Gore Vidal). If you are not show biz, they said, the only way you can make a successful appearance on the Jack Paar show is to play the part of an amiable common man, and flatter the stuffing out of Paar. Well, I didn't believe it, and still don't: but I distinguish between Paar's audience and himself. It is probably true that one cannot succeed with *Paar* without that unctuous self-ingratiation which is the trademark of so many of his most successful guests:* but the audience doesn't seem to mind a few minutes' serious talk, cast at an adult level; and so the

---

* I am indebted to Murray Kempton, see below, for calling attention to the following colloquy:

VICE-PRESIDENT NIXON. Could I ask one favor, Jack?

J. PAAR. Yes sir; you can ask any favor you'd like.

VICE-PRESIDENT NIXON. Could we have your autograph for our girls?

J. PAAR. I cannot tell you how much this means to our show. It gives us class.

real question is, can you succeed with the audience if you have not succeeded with Paar? Well, certainly he will do the very best he can to keep that from happening. I know: I tried thinking on his program, instead of emoting, and he was so traumatized it took him two and one-half shows, several gag writers, half a dozen bald lies, and a couple of character assassins to restore his composure.

I was on the show Wednesday, January 31, 1962, to answer the charge that I had "attacked" the Pope as being "too left wing." I was introduced to Paar just before the show, and we chatted together amiably for about fifteen minutes in his dressing room. What did I especially want to say? he asked. I want to set the record straight on what *National Review did* say about *Mater et Magistra*, I answered. What else? Anything you wish to ask me, I repeated. I requested only that if I were asked a question that called for a complex answer, I be given as much as one minute to answer it. Fine, he said. "I want you to leave this show feeling good—that's what I want. You know," he confided, "one of the reasons why people think we give more breaks to Liberals and left-wingers is because we have more of them on the show. But that's only because there are more of them around, more of them who are interesting people, as people. On the other side," he finished warmly, "there's just Goldwater and you." I smiled prettily, and mumbled something about my willingness to draw him up a somewhat larger list.

Well, I was on for about a half hour. During that period, in specific answer to JP's questions, I made 17 points, of major and minor importance. They were in the order given: 1) That *National Review* did not attack the Pope as a left-winger, but rather expressed disappointment, at the time *Mater et Magistra* was published, that it did not give primary attention to the Communist menace. 2) That Gore Vidal's rendition was false, and reflected his general state of hysteria in evaluating conservative activities. 3) That I consider myself a radical conservative, i.e., someone whose ideas are rooted in unchanging principles, but whose respect is great for organic growth and the body of settled opinion. 4) That Robert Welch has said irresponsible things, but that his sins cannot be visited on the membership at large of the John Birch Society; and that Liberals who criticize Welch ought to criticize extremist statements coming from their own camp, e.g., Truman's charge in 1952 that Eisenhower was anti-Semitic, and his more recent charge that members of the John Birch Society are "Ku Kluxers with their sheets off."

5) That what matters is not so much whether a political reformer is sincere, as whether what he sets out to do has objective merit. 6) That in our time, there is a role for minutemen, e.g., in Cuba. 7) That the United States is in effect at war with Cuba, so that a declaration of war would merely codify a *de facto* relationship. 8) That I wrote a book giving my views on Senator McCarthy, who was my friend; that those views are complex; that I believe anyone who studied the record closely would sympathize with much that McCarthy was trying to do. 9) That if McCarthy were to ask whether *National Review* employed ex-Communists I would, after satisfying myself of the Committee's right to ask the question, answer it: by saying there are five ex-Communists who work for *National Review*.

10) That I do not myself intend to go into politics, that I conceive the role of *National Review* to be that of providing material—thought, facts, analysis—for the opinion-makers. 11) That I like Senator Goldwater. 12) That I did not think Mr. Eisenhower was a successful President, and that I did not think history would look on Eisenhower's views as sharply distinguishable from Kennedy's. 13) That the United Nations was founded on a delusion and that we shall have frequently to circumvent it in the future, as we have in the past. 14) That there is a conservative revival among students, and that the primary reason why is because they sense the failure of Liberalism to cope with reality. 15) That the world

is not better off today than it was forty years ago, as witness
the increase in slavery, and the materialization, in the hands
of a Communist state, of the power to blow up half the world.
16) That *The New York Times'* Harrison Salisbury fell for the
Khrushchev soft line after the 20th Congress, and for much
other Communist propaganda. 17) That I consider that conservatives are the true friends of the people because their
devotion to principle and to freedom contributes the most
to the well-being and happiness of mankind.

PAAR. *Listen—all I want you to say to your people, speak to
your people, is—what—was it all right? Did you enjoy
yourself? Did we treat you all right?*
WFB. *Did you learn anything?* (Laughter, much applause).*
PAAR. . . . *I think you're sincere in what you believe; for me,
Bill, you lack all feeling for people; and in the things I
read I find no feeling for humanity.*

(One must bear in mind that Jack Paar is given to expressing *his* feelings for humanity by weeping publicly, thereby
setting standards of demonstrable humanitarianism which
those of us not trained in show biz find it difficult to compete
with.)
I answered that if that were true, it was my fault for giving poor expression to my views; not any intrinsic inhumanity in the views themselves.

PAAR. *Thank you very much, thank you very much.* (Applause. Exit WFB.)

II

In subsequent days, Paar made a great deal out of the
ensuing episode for which, as it happens, I had no responsibility whatever. How many seats would I like for my friends?
an assistant to Paar had asked me several days before. Six,

* Here, and below, I reproduce the transcript, including its description of
audience reactions and emphasized words, exactly.

please, I had said. I don't know exactly how many people fit into Mr. Paar's studio—several hundred, I should guess; but I was not made to feel that a request for six seats was unusual, or inordinate. Two of my six guests, I then told the assistant—my wife and a friend—were to drive to the country with me that same night. Would it be possible for them to tiptoe out of the studio discreetly, after I had completed my interview but before the entire show was over? Certainly, he said—just point them out to me and I'll escort them out during the commercial that follows your appearance.

That was done: and when I reached the elevator, they were there waiting for me. The other four guests stayed in their seats throughout the entire show. I subsequently learned that five members of the staff of *National Review*, on their own initiative, had joined the public queue and got tickets for the show. I was wholly unaware of their presence in the studio.

PAAR. [Immediately following the applause after I left] *I knew there was a different group in here tonight, I could tell . . . I think* [reverting to his theme] *that that's important, that you love people. I think you have to have some feeling, and perhaps—I'm sure Mr. Buckley must have— —in his writings and in the things he does I find no—no— no—humanity; I'm sorry, that's how I feel.*

Jack Paar's audiences are highly volatile. He encourages this. Accordingly, at that point, someone in the audience yelled.

VOICE. Oh baloney!
PAAR (angrily), *Well, if you don't like it, Buster, you know where the door is, don't you?* (Noise, confusion).

Whereupon some people got up from their seats, went to said door, and left the studio. Paar was undone. . . .

PAAR. *I'd like to have the lights put on in the studio, to show you 20, 30, 40 people who obviously were in—how many?*

[audience yelling numbers]—*20? How many? 10* [general chaos]—*is that all? . . . It looked like more than that leaving.*

[Next day, Thursday] PAAR. *Mr. Buckley did one thing I didn't like. He had 12 people, I believe, all told; they made a lot of noise and they applauded on cue* [how could I give cues? Paar was asking all the questions] *and laughed on cue at him and when* he *got up, they got up and left. It's quite embarrassing in the show . . . and it's also discourteous. . . . I thought that was rude of him.*

If there was rudeness, it was hardly mine. It was Buster's. He should have known Paar was joking when he showed him the door.

There were two other guests on the program Wednesday after I left: Pierre Burton, a Canadian editor, and Harry Golden, high priest of left-wing yahooism. The balance of the program Wednesday was devoted primarily to variations on the theme of

1) my inhumanity and that of conservatives in general. PAAR. *What I can't stand is that these people when they talk they have no feeling of humanity—they just don't seem to care about people.* GOLDEN. . . . *whenever you read about these rightists . . . always a skinny little guy, or a hatchet murderer—you've never seen a fat guy as a hatchet murderer —always a thin guy with hollow cheeks.* [Mr. Golden is fat];

—and 2) my unintelligibility. PAAR. *I don't think Mr. Buckley is a dangerous man at all because . . . he doesn't have the important quality of politics and that's to communicate, and Mr. Buckley, I don't think he has that.* BURTON. . . . *he doesn't say very much, you know.* PAAR. *Look, am I naïve and sophomoric when I say I don't understand everything he was saying?* GOLDEN. *You can catch a word here and there, like t-h-e* [laughter] . . . ;

—and 3) the benevolence, nay the heroism, of Jack Paar for

putting me on his show. On this theme, especially profuse was Mr. Hugh Downs, Paar's full-time sycophant. DOWNS. *I admire you for running it on the program, I really do. I think a lot of people can come on in and be what they are and be judged by the people who tune in . . . anything can be allowed on this program and it can't be harmful to the country.* And again: DOWNS. *I think he should come on television more often because I think people will see exactly what he is and he'll be judged and he'll stand or fall on that basis. . . .*

The next day Paar was so carried away by the possibilities of this great theme that he implied he had received the personal congratulations, over the telephone of the President of the United States!* *I had a—I'm not going to get into where—but I had a call today that really thrilled me because the wires, the telegrams to Mr. Buckley, were—there were a lot of wires, he got a lot of wires, and I thought Gee Whiz, you know—and we got far less than he did, and then I got a call from Washington, from a very important person, and he said, The greatest service I could do this country is to* show *these people and let them all speak and the person who called me, it really made my day. . . .* JP's day is not made by mere senators or cabinet members or ambassadors. Only by Presidents, and radical conservatives.

III

On Thursday, February 1, I had a call from Paar's assistant: What had I thought of the show? I replied (these are my exact words): "I thought it was fair enough while I was on, but I think it's a pity Mr. Paar turned it into a Hate Buckley session for the rest of the evening after I had gone." Pause. "Well," said the assistant, "Jack feels rather bad about it himself. We've received almost two hundred telegrams, and 90 per cent are in your favor. What's more, they are obviously not rigged—they come from all over the country;

* I subsequently learned: he had.

and they definitely aren't crackpot. I called to tell you Jack has decided to apologize to you tonight."

PAAR. *Let's be fair—let's talk about last night, all right? Let's admit first of all there were many wires. Hundreds of wires. And the majority of those wires, the majority of those wires, were complimenting Mr. Buckley ... whether that was, you know, his own following ... I don't know ... I talked to Mr. Buckley today. Please—I ask you to forgive me—I didn't, one of my boys did. And he said, Mr. Buckley said, that he was treated courteously and fairly while he was here, but that he thought it was unfair to talk about him when he had gone. Well, that really can't be helped, what other people say about him when he had gone. Mr. Buckley is a very controversial person, and he must realize that that's bound to come up. Many of your telegrams did say they thought it was unfair of me to mimic him after he had gone, and so did my wife. Yes, she did. He's not difficult to imitate and I did it, I thought, in jest and my wife didn't like it, and some of you didn't like it and may I publicly apologize if it offended anyone. I just did his gestures, which are quite easy to do. So I apologize for that.*

Having apologized, Paar decided to break fresh ground:

1) PAAR. *I have never mentioned Joseph McCarthy's name on this show. Ever. Nor would I. The Senator is dead. I would not bring up his name. ... Mr. Buckley brought it up. ...*

From Wednesday's transcript:

PAAR. [out of the blue]. *You were a great supporter of Mc- Carthy, right?* (I had not mentioned McCarthy's name.)

2) PAAR. *... I think that we treated him well; he asked to come on, he's an adult, he should know what he's getting into, when he comes here.*

Five minutes earlier, same night, same show:

PAAR: *I asked him on the show, and I wanted to treat him courteously.*

3) PAAR. *We have never rigged anything against anybody.*

Wednesday. PAAR. *I just got a call here. Gore Vidal's coming back tomorrow night!* Jack Paar made this statement within three minutes after I had left the stage. Paar's shows are taped three hours before they are telecast. Under the circumstances, he couldn't have received a telephone call from Gore Vidal reacting to my appearance, because the show would not go out over the airwaves for another three hours. Therefore, the "call" was not made, but was pre-planned. As the saying goes, it was rigged.

4) On the other hand, the support *I* got was, in Paar's analysis, *obviously* rigged, beginning with my "claque," see above, which performed "on cue."

PAAR: *In Hollywood, the Henry Wallace crowd was the same way. They brought their own claque.* This was another theme Paar found engrossing, and he returned to it again and again: the telegrams of protest could only have been organized. And worse, ah!—the kind of people that wrote in!

E.g., Monday, February 5: *... the mail that I have received—I'll tell you this—mail and telegrams are enormous— uh, in Mr. Buckley's favor. Oh yes. Oh yes. Yes ma'am, that is true. It is also anti-Semitic, it is also anti-Catholic, it is also threatening to have sponsors canceled; it is also threatening me. That's true. We have the letters, if you're interested....* *

And again on February 8: PAAR. *You know how many letters we got? Seven thousand letters, in two days, from this group. Nearly all in favor of them. Threatening us—threatening me—threatening to have the sponsors cancelled!*

5) Always, Mr. Paar cautioned the audience, it is wise to bear in mind that my position is, essentially, the same as the Communists', given this or that modification. *Mr. Buckley*

---

* We are interested. We asked to see the letters. NBC has not yet let us do so.

admitted there were five [former Communists working for
National Review]. . . . *I wonder why? It seems to be a pat-*
tern. All of these far-out people seem to—as you said one
night, Hugh, the circle joins here. I told you, in Germany
they have found that those who were avid Nazis are the first
now to become avid Communist police. There's a certain
kind of person who is in this kind of thing who is forever
suspicious and turning in his neighbors. And later: *Mr.*
Buckley has five Communists [sic] *working for him, by his*
own admission. That's probably the greatest group of former
Communists working anywhere that I've ever heard of. . . .
Why?

GORE VIDAL. *For the simple reason that they're attracted to*
things like Buckley because he's as extreme on the Right as
the left wing was extreme. These are absolutists and they want
a revolution . . . they've now all gone over to the right wing
. . . there's a whole theory that the Birch Society might very
well be a Communist Society.

I had said that there were five former Communists on
National Review's staff. I should have made it clearer that I
had in mind not the full-time staff, but the editorial masthead, which over the years has included, to be sure, the
names of five former Communists. If I had had the time, I'd
have added that the relatively high concentration of former
Communists who write for *National Review* might have
something to do with their attraction to a journal which, in
their judgment, truly knows how to fight an enemy whom
they intimately know. I might have quoted Raymond Aron's
statement that probably the last great fight will be fought
between Communists and former Communists. I might have
observed that a great concentration of former sinners wrote
for the Bible. But Mr. Paar would, no doubt, have found all
that unintelligible, and inhuman. Whereupon, Mr. Downs
would have too.

And finally, 6) I am against everything.

PAAR. *What is William Buckley? What is he against? From what he has written, Mr. Buckley is against:* [sic] *anti-union, anti-social security, anti-integration, anti-United Nations, anti-foreign aid, anti-income tax, anti-lower tariffs and Common Market, anti-anti trust, anti-immigration, anti-Alliance for Progress, anti-peaceful attempts to maintain the free world, anti-Supreme Court decisions, he is anti-Roosevelt, anti-Truman, anti-Eisenhower, anti-Nixon, anti-Rockefeller, and anti-Kennedy.*

Ho hum. This kind of thing can of course be done to anyone who takes a comprehensive political position. For instance, it could be said about Paar, on the basis of his categorical opposition to me, that he is by deduction anti-Free Cuba, anti-private property, anti-a strong stand against the Soviet Union, anti-a free society, anti-MacArthur, anti-Taft, anti-Jefferson, anti-Lincoln, anti-Burke, anti-Adam Smith, etc., etc., etc. And of course, I happen to be pro-non-monopoly unions, pro-voluntary integration, pro-United Nations efforts to implement the principles of the United Nations, pro-foreign aid for our allies, pro-a nonprogressive income tax, pro-the lowering of tariffs, pro-the Common Market, pro-antitrust legislation, pro-peaceful attempts to maintain the free world, pro-some Supreme Court decisions, etc.

But the best was yet to be.

IV

Gore Vidal, who phoned in asking to be put on the show to answer what I had just said three hours before he knew *what* I had said, is, in addition to being a telepathist, an intellectual, which profession cherishes the making of distinctions. Besides being an intellectual, Mr. Vidal is a friend of Paar, which friendship proved to be the dominant gene during the evening. *Notice the difference in manner and approach and reasoning,* said Paar in introducing Vidal. *You'll have different opinions, I'm sure ... Mr. Vidal [is] a friend of mine, and a very nice man. ...*

First question: What *had* I actually said about the Pope and the Encyclical?

VIDAL: *Yes, well what he actually said—and I went back and looked it up ... in the month of August, Buckley attacked the Pope in a piece in his magazine, and the piece was called "A Venture in Triviality."*

• a) I did not "attack the Pope." b) There was no "piece," merely a one-paragraph, unsigned editorial, bearing the sanction of the editors of *National Review*. c) The paragraph was not called "A Venture in Triviality." It bore no title; one phrase in it said "[the encyclical] must strike many as a venture in triviality coming at this particular time in history."

It was a vicious piece, and America, *which is the Jesuit weekly in the United States, attacked Buckley in an editorial declaring that he owes his readers an apology, unquote.*

• the demand by *America* for an apology was absolutely unrelated to the editorial in question.

And Buckley's answer to the Jesuits was: "You are impudent."

• My answer to the Jesuits was in 2,500 words, one sentence of which stated that it was impudent for *America* to ask a non-Catholic journal of opinion to apologize for a transgression (assuming it was even that) against exclusively Catholic protocol.

I mean, who is he? Here's a guy who has never worked for a living ... has never had a job.

• I had one part-time job, as a member of the faculty of Yale (1947–1951), and three full-time jobs, before going to work for *National Review*.

He's got two sisters.

• Six.

One said while she was at Smith

• It was ten years after she graduated.

. . . that the faculty was filled with Communists.

• She said four faculty members had Communist-front connections.

The other was at Vassar and started the same thing at Vassar.

• She said that at Vassar the bias was predominantly Liberal.

Meanwhile, their brother was at Yale and wrote God and Man at Yale *and said that was full of Communists.*

• My book did not suggest there was a single Communist at Yale.

He feels free to correct, through this little magazine of his, the actions of all our Presidents and the Pope, and philosophers . . . on the subject of philosophy I thought this might interest you, Jack—of Albert Schweitzer—who is one of the great men of our time, and whose philosophy is reverence for life—he wrote of Albert Schweitzer, quote: He is more destructive than the H-Bomb, unquote.

• The quotation is not from me, but from a book review in *National Review*—by a Ph.D. in philosophy. There is no presumptively binding agreement between my views and those of every one of the several hundred reviewers who have reviewed books for *National Review*.*

On the subject of integration, Mr. Buckley wrote, quote: Segregation is not intrinsically immoral, unquote. Well, that's a double negative which means I don't quite dare to come out and say I'm in favor of segregation, so I'll put it in a double negative.

• a) It isn't a double negative. b) It is a litotes, and should be recognized as such by a professional writer. The litotes has been around as a necessary rhetorical refinement for years; was frequently used, for instance, by that old evader,

---

* On reflection, I think the statement, when read in context, is wholly defensible, I would listen with respect to the argument that the views of William of Occam, a more famous philosopher than A. Schweitzer, may prove to have been more destructive than the H-Bomb.

Homer. c) I didn't write that phrase, I spoke it in the presence of a Catholic Liberal, John Cogley, who d) agreed with me.

... but that's exactly what it means, which goes against not only Catholic doctrine but I would think any humane— you put your finger on it, you know, when you said there's no humanity there.

Not bad, for one paragraph, eh? By all means, ladies and gentlemen, notice the difference in manner, and approach, and reasoning.

But Mr. Vidal was not through.

VIDAL (cont.). *I was just going to say one more thing struck me, listening to Mr. Buckley. He said (and I was quite fascinated because it's amazing the things perhaps you can just get away with, this side of libel)... He said that Harry Truman had called Eisenhower an anti-Semite and anti-Catholic.*

PAAR. *Yes, he did say that. But what—*

VIDAL. *There's no evidence that Harry Truman ever said this. Now I would like to say right now, on the air, that I will give $100 to the* National Review *which is Buckley's magazine, if he can prove that Harry Truman ever said any such thing: and if he cannot prove it, why I think he should then be regarded as what he is, which is an irresponsible liar.*

I have sent the following letter to Jack Paar:

DEAR MR. PAAR:

[I have been informed of what Mr. Gore Vidal said on your show on Feb. 1.]

1. The documentation, taken in each case from *The New York Times,* is as follows: On October 10, 1952, President Harry Truman accused the Republicans generally of supporting "the discredited and un-American theory of racial superiority." On October 17, Assistant Secretary of State Howland

Sargeant read a message from Mr. Truman to the Jewish Welfare Board in Washington. Eisenhower, Truman said, "cannot escape responsibility" for his endorsement of Senator Revercomb, "the champion of the anti-Catholic, anti-Jewish provisions of the original DP bill." Truman charged that Eisenhower "has had an attack of moral blindness, for today he is willing to accept the very practices that identify the so-called 'master race' although he took a leading part in liberating Europe from their domination."

2. The following day, Rabbi Abba Hillel Silver, ex-President of the Zionist Organization of America, expressed "shock that an irresponsible statement of that character could be made. The attempt by implication to identify a man like General Eisenhower with anti-Semitism and anti-Catholicism, is just not permissible even in the heat of a campaign."

3. Please instruct Mr. Vidal to make out a check for $100 to the National Conference of Christians and Jews.*

But Paar's sense of fair play always overwhelms his other instincts, and so, on February 5, a week after my appearance, he announced that since I was out of the country, he would not criticize me while I was gone: no sir, not Jack Paar.

PAAR. *I am, however, more than ever—leaving Mr. Buckley out of it* [understand]—*worried about what is called the "radical Right" after what happened over the weekend in California. There were the bombing of two ministers' homes out there by what they call the "radical right wing," and that's a shocking thing to me . . . almost killed a baby in a crib. . . .*

DOWNS. *I think—wouldn't it be fair also, Jack, to say that Mr. Buckley would certainly not be a party ever to the bombing of somebody's home? You know, that's—*

PAAR. *. . . . Oh, I can't believe he would. . . . But this climate of mistrust that's sprung up in this country by the now ex-*

* Sequel? G. Vidal declined a) to pay over the $100 *or* b) to give the reasons why he feels justified in clinging to the belief that I, Rabbi Silver *et al.* are irresponsible liars.

treme Right really frightens me. It does. The same as it did with the Left, only more so because the Right—they're now throwing bombs and that scares the hell out of me. I don't know how you feel about it.

Downs felt very bad about it.

V

Moral? Forget about Paar. No, on second thought, one can't really. Any more than one can forget about atmospheric pressure. But why should he know better? Who is to teach him better? The intellectuals? Vidal? "Once an argument has been classified as 'positional,' " writes Eric Voegelin,* "it is regarded as having been demolished, since the 'position' attributed to it is always selected with pejorative intent. The choice of the position selected is an expression of the personal antipathies of the individual critic; and the same argument can therefore be attributed to any one of a variety of 'positions,' according to what comes most readily to the critic's hand. The wealth of variation afforded by such tactics is well exemplified by the variety of classifications to which I have myself been subjected. On my religious 'position,' I have been classified as a Protestant, a Catholic, as anti-Semitic and as a typical Jew; politically, as a Liberal, a Fascist, a National Socialist and a Conservative; and on my theoretical position, as a Platonist, a Neo-Augustinian, a Thomist, a disciple of Hegel, an existentialist, a historical relativist and an empirical skeptic; in recent years the suspicion has frequently been voiced that I am a Christian. All these classifications have been made by university professors and people with academic degrees. They give ample food for thought regarding the state of our universities." Thus the experience of a scholar, at the hands of his fellow scholars.

* *Freedom and Serfdom, An Anthology of Western Thought*, edited by Albert Hunold (D. Reidel, Dordrecht, Holland, 1961), p. 280.

How can one blame Jack Paar, or even Vidal: who will teach them manners? Who *cares?*

They are scared folk (Vidal wrote recently that conservative thought in America is a "hymn of hatred against the common man"); and scared people know not the manners of thought; they merely extrude, in James Burnham's fleeted phrase, "a squid-like ink of directionless feeling." They are frightened at any substantive challenge even to an orthodoxy they do not wholly understand.

Anyway, here is a problem to which the Center for the Study of Democratic Institutions (*né* The Fund for the Republic) might donate some attention: namely, what *kind* of problem is it, and what are its ramifications, when the intellectual and the vulgarian unite so gladly to exhibit their ignorance to the great public? What does it bode for us? Once upon a time an intellectual stood to lose face after a display of malevolent ignorance. It doesn't seem to make any difference any more. . . .

And surely it is some sort of a threat to the national sense of humor, on which of course democratic institutions rely at moments of special stress, when a professional *comedian* can sum up his indictment in the following terms:

PAAR. *He is [even] anti-self determination for colonial peoples. . . . Here's the kind of thing Mr. Buckley has said. [An interviewer once asked him]* "You mean that the colored nations of Africa should not have the right of self-determination?"

He said: "No, not until they are ready to form governments."

And they said: "Well, when do you think they will be?"
He said: "When they stop eating each other."

That's what Mr. Buckley said. And there's that whole lack of humanity I think in his philosophy.

A FORTNIGHT WITH
MURRAY KEMPTON

Tuesday. Kempton writes today that statistics are irrelevant, that they are not nearly so useful as "free intuition." Kempton's free intuition has informed him that the steel companies could sell their products much more cheaply and still pay labor more. The companies irked K by putting on a statistical passion play whose climacteric shows that if next summer the steel unions should go after, and get, higher wages, the American companies will no longer be able to compete with foreign steel companies. K is unimpressed, and cites the electrical companies' lowering of *their* prices (by as much as 25 percent) between 1955 and 1958, after TVA refused to buy American because it could buy cheaper abroad. By refining production methods, the American companies worked their way back into the competitive picture. Moral? Go, Steel, and do likewise. Manufacturers should keep their production costs down, and operate efficiently.

But Kempton is temperamentally incapable of understanding that labor is a cost, the principal cost; and if he has any idea how the electrical companies brought down cost without doing all those things (automation, anti-makework provisions, incentive payments for overproduction) that the United Steelworkers Union is prepared to strike to keep the companies from doing, he does not tell us. Kempton's creed is: Everybody is a human being (which is true), and human beings can't be cost-accounted (which is only half true), and therefore, somehow, all economies must begin *after* paying out wages. *Ad rem* depersonalizations are necessary to social life, and are not any more inhumane intrinsically than the motions of the mother counting noses before deciding how much dinner to cook.

Ah, the capacity for systematic thought!—K never had it (he is a poet, not an exegete). Could he be got to understand, even, that if you gave your own workers everything they wanted, and then (assuming you were not bankrupted) set out to cut down costs from that point on, you're not going to make up the loss by simply cutting down executive salaries? You will shop around more ruthlessly than ever for parts and tools and piecework, to get by with the lowest possible cost; which means that you will be patronizing and encouraging the growth of firms which are *not* dominated by the behemoth unions. A most generous employer, consistent with the latitude given him by the competitive situation, can raise his workers' salaries to a point—but then he must economize elsewhere, and he will drive the hardest bargains (that is what K must mean by "making adjustments") whose effect is to make impossible at the second echelon removed the kind of munificence he himself has been able (temporarily) to extend to his own men. The struggle, then, becomes one for politico-economic leverage: Which union exercises the greatest political and economic power? That's where the money is. Other people's money. Anywhere you turn—socialism, capitalism, distributism—human beings do become, in the world of calculations, disembodied: whence economic (and political) *systems*. Every time K buys this pair of shoes rather than that one because the first is cheaper, he is doing what he would not permit the steel companies to do. He cannot grasp the implicit contradiction in (a) encouraging the steelworkers to increase their wage demands, and (b) looking, as a consumer, for the cheaper product to buy....

What would happen, one wonders, if the Devil should take the scales from Kempton's eyes, and let him see the world of economics? I say the Devil, because the Lord would not do so fiendish a thing. What a terrible end! His muse would dry up, and the pagan love song to humankind which he has been trilling for twenty years would get all hung up, under the discipline of keys, and measures, and clefs. A calamity, in a word: for Kempton, though he does not realize that theory is as liberating in social science as dogma is in theology, nevertheless, for all his confusion is as necessary to humane industrial organization as Sam Goldwyn is to idiomatic English. Linguistic solecisms remain solecisms just the same, as do also economic solecisms. But they have their uses, some of them wholly unpredictable. My guess is the Communists moved with whatever caution it can be said they did between 1953 and 1960 because they hadn't the least idea what Eisenhower was talking about, and thought a little prudence might be in order.

Wednesday. One of the most satisfying things about K is his impartial iconoclasm. There are a few, a very few, graven images he won't profane—some because he truly admires them (A. Stevenson, E. Fitzgerald); some because they are too overwhelmingly ridiculous (E. Roosevelt); and he tires of over-kill, except perhaps when dealing with institutionalized enemies (J. Eastland). I remember his writing when Roy Cohn was finally and ignominiously forced out of McCarthy's Committee, *"So help me God, I feel sorry for Roy Cohn"*—which I am sure he did, as well he might have, having for months galloped miles ahead of the posse (never did so many supererogate upon so little!). It is as distasteful to use a machine gun to deliver the coup de grace as it is to have to wait for the fourth coda to terminate a Tschaikovsky symphony. In 1960 he didn't want to go to Chicago. *"If I do,"* he told me, *"I'll knock Nixon—it's like junk. But I like Nixon!"* He does feel sorry for the mangled corpse; but it is also for artistic reasons he feels the need to back away....

Today he goes after Robert Wagner again. K, of course, immediately saw through the phoniness of the anti-DeSapio frenzy of last summer and fall (ironically, his employer was much responsible for stirring things up). K passed the day of the execution with DeSapio, following him around everywhere, closely observing his manners, and reacting prodigally to his remarkable personal gentility ("*I sometimes think that if Carmine DeSapio were running against Lucifer he would consider it ungentlemanly to mention that little trouble in heaven*"). When it was finally clear that he had been overthrown by the ideological janissaries and the playboy-reformers, there were still the conventional and highly poignant rituals to go through. And then DeSapio walked out alone, after midnight, into the streets. "*His visitor* [K's wonderfully unobtrusive way of designating himself, in all his interviews] *left him and walked into the streets and noticed that there were no slums any more, and no landlords, and the Age of Pericles had begun because we were rid of Carmine DeSapio. One had to walk carefully to avoid being stabbed by the lilies bursting in the pavements. I wish the reformers luck—with less Christian sincerity than Carmine DeSapio does. I will be a long time forgiving them this one.*"

Enter Wagner. "*The Mayor of New York,*" he writes today, opening his column, "*has hired a $40,000 a year team to improve his press relations. His image in the press already seems to any detached observer somewhat better than it should be.*" (He likes a good first sentence or two, as Pegler does. All K's sentences are good, of course—it is even suggested, by a critic on whom they happen to cloy, that they are too good. "If you try to slay your audience with every sentence," the critic once wrote me, "you run the great danger that you might succeed.") And then he goes after Wagner on highly demagogic grounds (when K is putting forth demagogy, he almost surely doesn't realize that it is what he is doing: he is still enough the old socialist to react conventionally to the old demonology...). "*If I were a union electrician at this hour, I should suggest that someone be found to preach to me besides a mayor who took a 26 percent salary increase* *two weeks ago.*" As ever, the little-manliness. It is utterly irrelevant to the question whether an electrician should get full pay for a 20-hour week (that is what the electricians in the instant case were demanding), whether the mayor of New York, commonly understood as occupying the nation's third most important electoral office, should get a salary increase from $30,000 to $40,000. And it makes no difference at all that the mayor getting the increase is, so far as being mayor goes, a notorious incompetent. He is certainly not an incompetent at getting to *be* mayor. Modern democracy holds that no man who wins landslide political victories is an incompetent, and on such matters modern democracy is sovereign. But the crack about the salary turns out to be just an aside, and K ends up back on the subject of the press agent. "[Wagner] *is the full flower of Mencken's law that no man ever went broke underestimating the intelligence of the American voter. I resent having to pay taxes for press agents to protect a man whose magnificent effrontery already makes him invulnerable.*" There aren't six men in the country who could have composed that last sentence.

Thursday. If somebody is on his way down esteem's ladder whom K as a matter of principle disapproves of (most Rich Men, most Important Men of Affairs, all conceited men), he will do everything he can to push him on down—until he is about to hit bottom, and when he is almost there, there K is, to soften the shock. Today he spends time on the eminent Carlino, the Republican Speaker of the New York State Assembly, who has been swinishly requested by a young Democrat troublemaker to elaborate on a coincidence: namely, that Carlino is a) a director of a fallout shelter manufacturing firm, and b) a legislative sponsor of a compulsory fallout shelter building program. Carlino got a big hand when he made his appearance at the opening of the legislature— a show of solidarity from men who for the most part know that there, but for the lack of sufficient opportunity, stood they. Still, there was a trace of something in the applause. . . . *"Carlino has not always been a pleasant jailer; the Democrats enjoy the obvious sag in his imperial being."* K will keep his eyes on Carlino, and if things go too badly for him, he'll give him a helping hand, you may be sure.

The big noise that day was Rockefeller, come in person with his annual message for the legislature. K is a socialist, a formal socialist—to the extent he is formally anything at all. Two years ago, after having let his membership in the Socialist Party lapse, he wrote to reinstate himself and, along with his dues, submitted a repentant and lyrical letter, which was printed in *Dissent* where, as for the prodigal son, the editors wept for joy. Why did he do it? It is a form of institutional self-flagellation. "I am an Org-bureau man," Whittaker Chambers once told me tenderly, when I questioned his statement in a letter that until the day he died he would vote the straight Republican ticket, no matter who was on it. These are the psychic requirements of intensely individualistic people. I know another genius, unfortunately without the skill to popularize his great learning and striking literary powers. He wrote recently to tell me that he had joined the John Birch Society—exactly the same thing. One would think K, as a card-carrying socialist, would welcome all steps generally conducing to socialism, e.g., Rockefeller's continual enlargement of the office of the State of New York; but K does no such thing, partly because socialism really bores him, partly because he is more struck by human ironies and formalisms and hypocrisies in any political situation than by political vectors. So: *"[Rockefeller's] address was a hash of social uplift notions ranging from a higher minimum wage to stronger civil rights legislation."* And then a gentle crack apiece at the attitudinizing of the political parties, and a smile over the congruent irony of it all. . . . *"The Republicans sat in a silence perhaps induced by the reflection that the Socialists are everywhere; the Democrats issued a statement declaring that the Governor was a petty bourgeois opportu-*

nist deceiving the toilers and then everyone trooped up to the Executive Mansion to share the Governor's buffet." That is vintage Kempton.

II

Tuesday. Incomparable. Absolutely nowhere else, save possibly in *National Review,* can you find such a thing. It is practically all quotations, and the very best evidence that selective quotations are all that is really needed to finger the nation's ironic pulse. *"Comes now Public Document 75452,"* K announces starchily, *"from the Subcommittee of the Subcommittee of the Senate Committee on Commerce, the sober record of the fall of 1960 when America was . deciding whether to move again:*

> VICE-PRESIDENT NIXON: Could I ask you one favor, Jack?
> JACK PAAR: Yes sir; you can ask any favor you'd like.
> VICE-PRESIDENT NIXON: Could we have your autograph for our girls?

"The notes on that particular meeting at the summit (PAAR: I can't tell you how much this means to our show. It gives us 'class.') *are the opening exhibit in a Senate report labeled, 'The Joint Appearances of Senator John F. Kennedy and Vice-President Richard M. Nixon and other 1960 Campaign Presentations.' That was September 11, 1960, and Nixon had packed [for the White House]. The Kennedys rallied two weeks later.*

> CHARLES COLLINGWOOD: Hello, Caroline.
> CAROLINE: Hello.
> MRS. KENNEDY: Can you say hello?
> CAROLINE: Hello.
> MRS. KENNEDY: Here, do you want to sit up in bed with me?
> MR. COLLINGWOOD: Oh, isn't she a darling?
> MRS. KENNEDY: Now, look at the three bears.
> COLLINGWOOD: What is the dolly's name?
> MRS. KENNEDY: All right, what is the dolly's name?
> CAROLINE: I didn't name her yet.

(It reminds me of Vincent Sheean, King of Gemutlichkeit, exuberantly opening the first recorded interview by a Western newspaperman with Stalin, and trying to put Stalin at ease. "Comrade Stalin, *all* the world *over* you are associated with your *pipe,* and here I sit down with you and I see *no pipe!* Where *is* your *pipe?*" "I left it at home," said Stalin.)

K continues, after having quoted much more of the same kind of thing: "*This painful, vulgar record evokes* [*the campaign*] *again, but the mystery of* [*Nixon's*] *collapse taunts us yet. Still it was a terribly close election and who can say what small mistake cost him it?*

"*There is one clue:*

> BILL HENRY, OF NBC: I am so fascinated with that little kitten. Does the kitten have a name?
> JULIE NIXON: Yes, its name is Bitsy Blue Eyes.

"*Maybe Caroline saved the package when she held off naming the doll.*"

Wednesday. Rubirosa has come to town. Fulminations, of course, are in order. But how pleasant fulminations can be, at the hands of a master. I wonder: why is he not syndicated? Is there only a single city in America cosmopolitan enough to receive him? The answer must be Yes, there is only one city in America cosmopolitan enough to receive him. And to its credit, it is the newspaper in that city whose fundamentalist leftism would not normally countenance K's ideological appoggiaturas, yet nevertheless it continues to serve—uncomplaining?—as his host.* Granted, he performs for the Liberal Establishment. Kempton is, on all important matters, Safe. (Dogmatic leftism is like junk.) But the point is, *how* does he perform? Contrast what follows with the typical fulminations of the editorial page of the same paper. "[*Rubirosa*] *was Inspector of Embassies for the Dominican Foreign Ministry, a position from which he was removed by his country's*

---

* Mr. Kempton has gone to the *New Republic,* as editor-at-large.

new government last week after 24 years of carrying his dip-
lomatic passport into some of the most distinguished boudoirs
in the architecture of international relations." Rubirosa's
presence, it transpires, had been politely requested by a
grand jury seeking to know the circumstances of one of
Trujillo's uncannily efficacious death wishes for his political
enemies, this one dating back to the thirties. But Rubirosa
declined to go. The evidence against him was *"admittedly*
wispy and arose from the unfortunate coincidence that any
member of the Dominican Republic's tiny middle class is apt
to be related either to a victim or to an assassin or to both."
Sociologists please note how, in one sentence, to describe
an era.

Thursday. The undeniable labor union is, of course, the principal extra-government threat, in America today, to individual or, for that matter, collective freedom. He knows this,
and writes often as though he were, if only casually, somehow aware of it: but the effect is like that of a cardinal writing about Pope Alexander VII—somehow, when you are with
the rascal, you have got to come out sounding pro-Pope. The
situation is this: A tough, strategic, and solidly entrenched
New York labor union is in a position to simply turn off the
construction business in New York, bringing unemployment
to hundreds of thousands and panic to the financial houses.
The energumen is Local 3 of the Electricians' Union. This is
a satrapy inherited by one Van Arsdale, a labor aristocrat of
a breed which an American Djilas ought to write about. This
much K does not shrink from. *"[Arsdale's union is] that ulti-*
mate peril to the established order: the second generation of
established wealth afflicted with a social conscience." You
will see that K's use of the word "afflicted" is sarcastic.
Remember that: you are otherwise liable to forget it. . . . *"Van*
Arsdale inherited Local 3—although no one who knows him
would deny that he improved the property." K loves an
oxymoron: *"and here he was talking about the general wel-*

*fare. Society, he said, needed the shorter work week; there
was no other way to establish full employment and opportunity for the young."*

Now K knows, and has made clear, that he has introduced
us to Mr. Mountebank. But before going on he asks himself,
as always he does provided he is dealing with someone who,
loosely speaking, is associated with the American Left, or
Left's institutions: Is he a nice guy? What is Van Arsdale
like? (I myself don't know Van Arsdale. But I wish Kempton
would go a little less on his own personal soundings. He
might reflect on Albert Jay Nock's lament, surveying his
career as first editor of *The Freeman,* "Where talent is the
question, I have always had the surest sense, and would be
worth a ducal salary to any one in search of it. But as a judge
of character, I have never been able to distinguish a survivor
of the saints from the devil's rag-baby.") *"I like Van Arsdale
better than any other functioning labor leader I know"*—prepare for a dividend: almost always conjoined, by K, to any
character reference which might appear sentimental—*"in
fact, I even like him."*

"But"—well, now, but what? What about a union which
proposes to extort by the use of blackmail a fee for its services
which will seriously affect the budget of millions of New
Yorkers? Will K proclaim a Hundred Years' War, as he would
have against the electrical companies under like circumstances? Or against doctors, some of whom earn, because
they have no Van Arsdale, less than a New York City electrician of Local 3? Here K is all-ideologue, though like Rubashov, he knows, isolates, and even revels in the weaknesses
of the heroes whom fortune has visited upon him. *"But hereditary wealth is, of course, seldom logical; it is insulated
against ruthless scrutiny of the source of its wealth. For
example, the nation should plan as a nation, but I should
hate to be a New Jersey contractor attempting to sell figures
in Local 3's territory. There should be an opportunity for all,
but Local 3 is for all practical purposes a closed union, limited*

by genetics; I should hate to be a Puerto Rican bringing only a shining face and an open heart to my application for an apprentice permit." Sounds bad for Van Arsdale? Wait. "*[But] if society* [how did society get into this?] *denies his urge to serve the common laborer* [when did that happen?], *he will at least serve the elite. And in the process, he does us all the service of reminding us for the first time in years of how a union ought to act, which is outrageously."* The last refuge of ideologues is the sociologization of plain matters of right and wrong. "*Show me,*" K concludes, "*a good union that isn't occasionally outrageous."* Article 3, Section 4, Paragraph 5, anybody's ethical code book: Beware the "humanizing" sin. . . .

III

Tuesday. K is fascinated by the Right—especially by the hard Right, so-called, though today he writes about routine Republican developments. ("*I have discovered the definition of a radical,*" he told me once over the telephone. "*It is anyone whose name is preceded by 'so-called.'*" He had had difficulty, a few days before, getting a Montgomery taxi driver who would consent to take him to the home of Martin Luther King. He solved the problem by asking a driver to take him to the home of "the so-called Martin Luther King.") K is the principal chronicler of hard-Right activities, and knows his way about the Right labyrinth with ease. He has no trouble at all mixing easily with those whom the next morning he will berate with a passionate wit. As a matter of fact, K has no enemies, and that is an unusual estate for a man with so forked and active a tongue. "Everybody likes me," he told me once from a hospital bed. "That is one of my major failings. For instance, take my book—it got only favorable reviews!" He was grievously disappointed. His book was not seriously criticized because it is hard seriously to criticize Kempton, as it is difficult to criticize seriously—whom else? I have given the matter five minutes' thought and I can't come up with anyone so intensely partisan to whom all is forgiven, and whose most outrageous statements are allowed to rest in peace. Perhaps there is no one else with that blend of art, compassion, and personal appeal. One night sitting at the dais at a testimonial dinner for Roy Cohn, before the festivities began, I was talking to him across the table. Someone nudged me from behind. "Do you know who you are talking to?" Senator Joe McCarthy whispered. "Yes," I said. Actually, if the Reign of Terror had known K (or read him), he'd have got on fine with him (McCarthy had no difficulty with infinitely less personable left-wingers). He sought merely to do me a favor—he was the most considerate of men. Often he had been ambushed, and he thought perhaps I might at that moment have my foot on a land mine (as it turned out, I had).

This morning K speaks of the emergence of Romney as a presidential contender. Like a gravometer, he is attracted to the irony in the situation. "*. . . a former lobbyist for the Aluminum Company of America and present $150,000 auto executive comes forth now as spokesman for the neglected common man, and the Republicans who dislike him may have to take him and Walter Reuther who likes him will have to find reasons to fight him.*" K is always surprised when undiscriminating institutional obligations rope in other men. But he also sympathzes with them, for more than the usual reasons; he is himself so often heaved about by ideology's wayward storms.

Wednesday. Black Wednesday. He sulks over the West Virginia Medical Association's successful resistance to the attempted bureaucratization of medicine by the Kerr-Mills Bill (Senior Citizencare), and in spite of a grandiose literary whoop into the subject (a 150-word quotation from Heller's *Catch 22,* of dubious relevance), he leaves at least this reader feeling, Hooray for the doctors.

Thursday. Back to the Right. A hilarious look Inside Sokolsky, et al. *"Sharonology is the study of the internal struggles
of the American Right, as Kremlinology is the study of the
internal struggles of the Politburo, the materials in both cases
being incomprehensible documents and speakers' lists at din-
ners. It takes its name from Sharon, Conn., birthplace of ..."*
your visitor. K has spotted George Sokolsky going after anti-
Communist evangelist Dr. Fred Schwarz. For unknown reasons, K does not treat the more exotic subject of Sokolsky's
new-found enthusiasm for J. F. Kennedy and all his works,
which is the buzz-buzz of the Right at this moment. *"Sokolsky has even taken after Dr. Fred Schwarz, director of the
Christian Anti-Communist Crusade. Schwarz is an Australian,
and Sokolsky feels that anti-Communism is an American
enterprise; he is high tariff in all things."* Fulton Lewis, Jr.,
K observes, has become a security risk in some quarters of
the hard Right because *"[as] an honored speaker at the
Human Events Forum in Washington the other day ... he
abused the privileges of the rostrum to attack certain un-
identified flying objects who confuse the issue by thinking
that everybody is a Communist."* (K is master of what Martin
Greenberg, reviewing Randall Jarrell's imperishable *Pictures
at an Institution,* called the "tall epigram.") What is *Human
Events?* *"[It is a newsletter with]* certain leftist deviations
(*it is not quite convinced that the Public Health Service is
consciously plotting to poison us all by fluoridating our
water*), *but is respected by Robert Welch as a source of
information on minor aspects of the conspiracy."*

Ah, the conspiracy. Dwight Macdonald once made a semi-
sensible point, namely, that McCarthy's chronic exaggera-
tions (I deny they were as exaggerated as Macdonald's exaggeration of them) had the especially mischievous effect of
persuading the public, time after time deprived of its scalps,
that in fact there *were* no serious Communist conspirators in
our midst—which of course (Macdonald's point) there are.
Here Kempton is at his absolute, unbeatable worst. It has

been said there is no theological question Billy Graham cannot vulgarize; so there is no issue touching the Communist
problem that Murray Kempton cannot sentimentalize. The
Communist enterprise, or at least that part of it that goes on
in this country, is in his opinion *opera bouffe* (*Cosi Fan Tutti
Atomica*). I have never seen a pointed sentence by Murray
Kempton on the subject of the Communist problem at home:
once again, the systematic refusal to face the systematically
demanding question: to which, in this case, among others,
Sidney Hook has tried to face up to, systematically, in his
book, *Heresy Yes, Conspiracy No.* "The trouble with Kempton," Hook once said, "is he thinks with his stomach." (The
trouble with Hook, says your visitor, is he doesn't think often
enough with his stomach.) Hook is right here. I give you the
locus classicus, K's report on the election of the new president
of the CPUSA. *"It is impossible to look at Miss [Elizabeth
Gurley] Flynn without collapsing into the molasses of the
American dream. She is the aunt Dorothy longed to get back
to from Oz. . . . If the old-fashioned virtues really had any
impact on our culture, the disenchanted of our society would
rush to this dear sister's bosom. . . . [She has] a face that
would be irresistible on the label of an apple pie mix."* Had
enough? Well, this apple-pie hater is going to give you more.
. . . *"The evil is not them [the members of the Communist
Party], but a society which . . . demands a vast establishment
of policemen, Congressional committees, and disgusting laws
to protect us from them.* [! Who on earth would undertake
to protect Kempton from Them? That is more than an affluent
society could afford!] *You could sum up the domestic history
of a dozen years just by printing a picture of Elizabeth Gur-
ley Flynn and putting under it the caption 'From 1948 to
196– a great nation was afraid of this woman!' But what
generation unborn could possibly be expected to believe
that?"*

There are other problems more likely to urge themselves
on generations unborn. The incumbent young generation in

Cuba will wonder less why some Cubans were afraid of Fidel Castro, than why other Cubans were not. Kempton's glands are, alas, no substitute for the humorless appraisal of the role of the Communist parties in the free world. He is foremost among those the burden of whose thought is that it is the grave responsibility of the free world to ensure the serenity of those in their midst who would subvert their freedom. E. Flynn's face is, after all, no more pleasing than poor Kerensky's. One has the feeling that the poet Kempton, whose grasp of reality so often surpasses that of the humdrummers whom destiny has charged with the evolution of our destiny, is resigned to turning over the future to the prosaic men who are poetically benighted; just so long as he can be around to write the requiem for our time. A fine requiem it would be. And your visitor, to the extent he is ever tempted, where such solemn issues are involved, would care greatly to see that requiem, for it would be monumentally grand. But it would be easier reading if one knew that unborn generations would never wake.

THE LAST YEARS OF
WHITTAKER CHAMBERS

"Where is Renoir's 'Girl with the Watering Can'?"
I asked the attendant at the entrance to the National Gallery.
I walked up the flight of stairs, turned left through two galleries, and spotted her near the corner. It was only 12:25 and
I had the feeling he would be there at exactly 12:30, the
hour we had set. I sat down on the ottoman in the center of
the room. I could see through the vaulted opening into the
adjacent galleries. I saw him approaching. It could only have
been he, or Alfred Hitchcock. Five months had gone by
since he had been at my home in Connecticut, but we were
never out of touch; almost every Sunday afternoon I would
call him, and we would talk, at length, discursively, and
laugh together, between the strophes of his melancholy.
(And every now and then—rarely, now that he was back at
school—I would receive one of those letters.) The Sunday
before, he had told me he was to be in Washington on the
8th of June.

I was surprised—he loathed Washington, and probably had
not been there three times in ten years, although he lived
only two hours away. Perhaps, I wondered, one of those
infrequent meetings with Nixon—though Nixon was in California now. Perhaps yet one more meeting with the FBI.
I had told him I would schedule my own business for the
same day. He had asked me to keep the evening open, and
we agreed to meet for a private lunch. "You've guessed what's
up, haven't you?" he said, his face wreathed in smiles. "I
haven't the least idea." "John!" he said proudly. We went off

185

talking excitedly. His son would be married that afternoon, and I was to go to the wedding and the reception. "Where shall we eat?" "I don't know," I said—I couldn't, on the spur of the moment, think of the name of a single small restaurant in Washington which might be reasonably proof against Chambers' being recognized—we had had that difficulty so often in New York, when he used to come to *National Review* on Tuesdays and Wednesdays. "I can't think of any place," he said helplessly. "I know!" I interjected. "We must eat at L'Espionage" He smiled.

It wasn't open. We lunched somewhere, and talked and talked for the hour and a half we had. We walked then to the Statler and sat in the corner of the huge lobby. At that moment a reporter I had recently come to know approached me. I rose quickly and stood directly between him and Chambers, whose anxiety for the privacy of his son was intense (the press all but took over at his daughter's wedding seven years before, and the entire family had taken elaborate precautions to keep this wedding out of public view). The reporter talked on and on, but my taciturn answers finally discouraged him; we shook hands and he left. I turned around. But Chambers was gone.

We met again at seven, in the blistering heat, at the church at Georgetown where a few months earlier John Fitzgerald Kennedy, Jr. had been baptized. Whittaker and his wife Esther, slight and beautiful, with her incomparable warmth; a genial couple, old friends of the Chambers from Baltimore; with his wife and sons, his steadfast friend Ralph de Toledano, who met Chambers during the Hiss trial, and wrote *Seeds of Treason;* the bride's parents, a sister of the bride and a friend of the groom. We went from there to a private room at the Statler, where we drank champagne (for the first time in my life, I saw him take a drink) and ate dinner. Whittaker was quiet, but I think he was very happy. I thought back on a letter several years old. *"John's parents live for John, and for little else. In 1952, I sat and reckoned—so many years*

I must live to get John to his majority. It seemed an impos-
sibly long course. Now each day is subtracted from the year
that is left. . . . The day I finished the last section of Witness,
I took the copy into town and put it in the mail myself. Then
I returned to the little house at Medfield, where, for about
two years, I had written alone. I sat down at my now need-
less table and thought that now, perhaps, God would permit
me to die. I did not really wish this—much less, I now know
than I then supposed. And I could not pray for it because
of the children. I thought that I must live until they reached
their majority, at least, so that they would be beyond the
reach of men in the legal sense. They would be their own
man and woman. In John's case, this meant some five or six
years. It seemed to me an almost unendurable span of time.
In the past year I have found myself inwardly smiling be-
cause only a few months of that span are left. I have been
saying to myself: I am free at last. . . ."

The bride and groom left. We got up to go. After saying
good night all the way around, I drew Whit aside and made
him listen to an irreverent story, which shook him with silent
laughter. I never knew a man who so enjoyed laughing. I
waved my hand at him and went out with the de Toledanos.
As we stepped into the elevator I saw him framed by the
door, his hand and Esther's clutched together, posing while
his son-in-law popped a camera in his face; a grim reminder
of all those flashbulbs ten years before. I never saw him
again. He died a month later, on July 9, 1961. Free at last.

I first met Chambers in 1954. An almost total silence had
closed in on him. Two years earlier he had published *Witness.*
In the months before the book appeared there was a considerable nervous excitement. The book had been postponed
several times. Chambers would not let the publishers have it
until he was quite through with it. (He told me with vast
amusement that a prominent journalist had volunteered to
ghost the book for him.) When the preface of *Witness* ap-

peared as a feature in *The Saturday Evening Post,* that issue of the magazine sold a startling half million extra copies on the newsstand. The book came out with a great flurry. The bitterness of the Hiss trial had not by any means subsided. For some of the reviewers, Hiss's innocence had once been a fixed rational conviction, then blind faith; now it was rank superstition, and they bent under the force of an overwhelming book. But the man was not grasped by the reviewers, who treated *Witness* as a passion play acted out by archetypes. "I am a heavy man" (*Ernst Mensch*), Chambers once wrote me, to apologize for staying two days at my home. There is a sense in which that was true. But he never appreciated, as others did, the gaiety of his nature, the appeal of his mysterious humor, the instant communicability of his overwhelming personal tenderness; his friends—I think especially of James Agee—took endless and articulate pleasure from his company.

Witness was off to a great start. But, surprisingly, it did not continue to sell in keeping with its spectacular send-off. The length of the book was forbidding; and the trial, in any case, was three years old, and the cold sweat had dried. Alger Hiss was in prison, and now the political furore centered about McCarthy. Those who did not know the book, and who were not emotionally committed either to Chambers' guilt or innocence, seemed to shrink even from a vicarious involvement in the controversy, to a considerable extent because of the dark emanations that came out of Chambers' emotive pen, depressing when reproduced, as was widely done, in bits and snatches torn from the narrative. "It had been my impression," Hugh Kenner, the author and critic, wrote me recently, "before reading *Witness,* that his mind moved, or wallowed, in a setting of continuous apocalypse from which he derived gloomy satisfactions, of an immobilizing sort. The large scale of *Witness* makes things much clearer. It is surprisingly free from rhetoric, and it makes clear the genuine magnitude of the action which was his life:

a Sophoclean tragedy in slow motion, years not hours. I think Communism had an appeal for him which he doesn't go into: the appeal of large-scale historic process, to which to surrender the self. The self awoke and fought its way clear by a superbly individual action (look how his attention comes awake when he is itemizing his essentials for escape; a weapon, a car, etc.). As a Communist he sleepwalked to heavy Dostoyevskian music ... the constant note was surrender to a process larger than himself; and the heroic quality comes out in the interplay between this essentially musical mode of existence (the terminology is Wyndham Lewis') and his constant awareness of the possibility, the necessity, of equilibrium, choice, the will poised freely amid possibilities. It's in the texture of the *Witness* prose, the narrative line making its way freely through the rhythms, sonorities, declarations; through the organ-tones of plight."

In 1954 I asked if I might visit him. He had written a long-standing friend, Henry Regnery, the publisher of my book on Senator McCarthy, to praise the book, while making clear his critical differences with McCarthy. ("... *for the Right to tie itself in any way to Senator McCarthy is suicide. Even if he were not what, poor man, he has become, he can't lead anybody because he can't think.*") A few months after the book was published, he was struck down by a heart attack, and it was vaguely known that he spent his days in and out of a sickbed, from which the likelihood was that he would never again emerge physically whole. He managed one piece for *Life* during that period; otherwise he was silent. I had every reason to believe that I would be visiting Jeremiah lying alongside a beckoning tomb. The letter telling me I might come began with gratifying vivacity. But the gloom closed in before he had come to the end of the page. "*The score,*" he wrote, "*as the points are checked up, daily and boldly, more and more convinces me that the total situation is hopeless, past repair, organically irremediable. Almost the only position of spiritual dignity left to men, therefore, is a kind of stoic silence, made bearable by the amusement of seeing, hearing and knowing the full historical irony that its victims are blind and deaf to, and disciplined by the act of withholding comment on what we know."* And then—inevitably, because Chambers did not want to curse a stranger with his own profound gloom: *"This may well be more of a posture than a position, and, happily, none of us will be permitted to assume it, or could, without violating our own articulate imperative."*

I found him in bed. The doctor had forbidden him even to raise his head. And yet he was the liveliest man I think I ever met. I could not imagine such good humor from a very sick man, let alone a man possessed by the conviction that night was closing in all over the world, and privately tortured by his continuing fear that the forces aligned against him would contrive to reorder history, impose upon the world the ghastly lie that he had testified falsely against Alger Hiss, and so erase his witness, his expiation for ten years' complicity with Communism. (*"If the West cannot use the Hiss Case to its own advantage, the Hiss forces will use the case, against the West; a kind of historical law of opposite and equal reactions seems to be in play."*) We did not, of course, speak of Hiss, nor did we for several months; though later he spoke of him, and of the case, with relaxation and candor. But we must have talked about everything else, and I left later than I should have, hustled anxiously to the door by a wife who knew she was all but powerless to enforce the doctor's rules.

As he began to recover he was, for a while, greatly renewed by physical and spiritual energy which were dialectically at odds with his organic ill health and his intellectual commitment to the futility of all meliorative action. I talked with him about the magazine I proposed to publish and asked whether he would join the staff. To my overwhelming surprise the answer was, Yes—he might do just that. But not, he warned, if the journal was to be a sectarian enterprise, intended for a semiprivate circulation. We corresponded through the summer. He was to make up his mind definitely during the fall, after we visited again. I made the mistake in one of my letters of expressing exorbitant hopes for the role the magazine might hope to play in human affairs. He dashed them down in a paragraph unmatched in the literature of supine gloom, even though finally resisting despair. *"It is idle,"* he rebuked me, *"to talk about preventing the wreck of Western civilization. It is already a wreck from within. That is why we can hope to do little more now than snatch a finger-nail of a saint from the rack or a handful of ashes from the faggots, and bury them secretly in a flowerpot against the day, ages hence, when a few men begin again to dare to believe that there was once something else, that something else is thinkable, and need some evidence of what it was, and the fortifying knowledge that there were those who, at the great nightfall, took loving thought to preserve the tokens of hope and truth."*

The tokens of hope and truth were not, he seemed to be saying, to be preserved by a journal of opinion, not by writers or thinkers, but only by activists, and I was to know that he considered a publication—the right kind of publication—not a word, but a deed. Though Chambers was a passionately literary man, always the intellectual, insatiably and relentlessly curious, in the last analysis it was action, not belletrism, that moved him most deeply. He could write, as he did of Arthur Koestler: *"If you re-read* Darkness at Noon *at this late hour you will see how truly it is a book of poetry. I re-read it recently. I came to the part where, after his break-down, Rubashov is permitted a few minutes of air in the prison yard. Beside him trots the Central Asian peasant who has been jailed because, 'at the pricking of the children,' the peasant and his wife had barricaded themselves in their house and 'unmasked themselves as reactionaries.' Looking sideways at Rubashov in his sly peasant way, he says: 'I do not think they have left much of Your Honor and me.' Then,*

*in the snow of the prison yard and under the machine-gun
towers, he remembers how it was when the snow melted in
the mountains of Asia, and flowed in torrents. Then they
drove the sheep into the hills, rivers of them, 'so many that
Your Honor could not count them all.' I cannot go on reading
because I can no longer see the words. To think that any
man of my time could have written anything so heart-tear-
ingly beautiful, 'wonderful, causing tears.' "*

But in time I began to understand why in 1932 he resigned
as editor of the Communist *New Masses*, where he had
already earned an international reputation as a writer, to go
scurrying about the streets of Washington, Baltimore and
New York, carrying pocketfuls of negatives and secret phone
numbers and invisible ink. . . . *"One of the great failures of
Witness is that there was no time or place to describe the
influences, other than immediate historical influences, that
brought me to communism,"* he wrote me. *"I came to communism . . . above all under the influence of the Narodniki.
It has been deliberately forgotten, but, in those days, Lenin
urged us to revere the Narodniki—'those who went with
bomb or revolver against this or that individual monster.'
Unlike most Western Communists, who became Communists
under the influence of the Social Democrats, I remained under the spiritual influence of the Narodniki long after I became a Marxist. In fact, I never threw it off. I never have. It
has simply blended with that strain in the Christian tradition
to which it is akin. It shaped the particular quality of my
revolutionary character that made me specially beloved (of
course, it is wrong to say such things, but it is true) even
among many of the crude, trifling American Communists; so
that* [one among them] *could say to a* Time *correspondent
with whom she found herself junketing in East Germany
after World War II: 'I simply cannot believe that Whittaker
Chambers has broken. I could believe it of anybody else, but
not of him. . . .' And, of course, it was the revolutionary quality that bemused Alger*—mea culpa, mea maxima culpa.

"*I remember how Ulrich, my first commander in the Fourth Section, once mentioned Vera Zasulich and added: 'I suppose you never heard that name.' I said: 'Zasulich shot General Trepov for flogging the student, Bogomolsky, in the Paviak prison.' And I remember the excited smile with which he answered (Ulrich was a Left Socialist Revolutionist, not a Communist): 'That is true. But how do you know that?'*

"*Like Ulrich, I may presume in supposing that the name of Ragozinikova is unknown to you. But the facts are these. In 1907, the Russian government instituted a policy of systematically beating its political prisoners. One night, a fashionably dressed young woman called at the Central Prison in Petersburg and asked to speak with the commandant, Maximovsky. This was Ragozinikova, who had come to protest the government's policy. Inside the bodice of her dress were sewed thirteen pounds of dynamite and a detonator. When Maximovsky appeared, she shot him with her revolver and killed him. The dynamite was for another purpose. After the murder of Maximovsky, Ragozinikova asked the police to interrogate her at the headquarters of the Okhrana. She meant to blow it up together with herself; she had not known any other way to penetrate it. But she was searched and the dynamite discovered. She was sentenced to be hanged. Awaiting execution, she wrote her family: 'Death itself is nothing.... Frightful only is the thought of dying without having achieved what I could have done.... How good it is to love people. How much strength one gains from such love.' When she was hanged, Ragozinikova was twenty years old.*

"*In Witness, I have told how Sazonov drenched himself with kerosene and burned himself to death as a protest against the mistreatment of others. And I have told what that meant to me at one moment; how, had my comrade, Sazonov, not done that, there would not have been a Hiss case as we know it. This spirit persisted in the Fourth Section as late as 1938 [Jones] knows nothing of such people except as a legend. That is why, though [Jones] is transfixed with as many arrows as Sebastian, he simply does not understand the source of the glance that the Saint bends upon the bowmen. I need scarcely underscore the point at which that strain of the revolutionary spirit blends with a Christian élan, or why it was imperative for Communism to kill it out."*

Activism. From the Narodniki to the Republican Party, in one defection. During that period, Chambers believed that there was only a single man, among all those who had the slightest chance to succeed Eisenhower at the White House (Eisenhower was down with his heart attack and it was generally assumed he would not run for re-election), who had any idea of what Communism was all about. I drove down to Westminster with a friend we had in common to get from him—it was on the eve of the publication of our first issue—his final word. The word was No. There were several reasons why he declined to leave his farm in Westminster and trudge back to New York to resume his professional life (he had all along insisted that if he joined us, he would come regularly to the office, even though we were content to let him peck away at his typewriter in the dark basement of his farmhouse). But the predominant reason was that he would not associate himself with a journal which might oppose Eisenhower's re-election, in the unlikely event he were to run again, or even be indifferent to his prospects for winning; let alone any magazine that might oppose Nixon's nomination in the event Eisenhower withdrew. Chambers the activist reasoned that under the existing circumstances, a vote for Eisenhower was actually a vote for Eisenhower's Vice-President. He puffed away at his pipe.

It was an awesome moment. A climaxing disappointment. It was rendered tolerable by one of those master strokes of irony over which Chambers and I were to laugh convulsively later. My companion was Willi Schlamm, former assistant to Henry Luce, an old friend of Chambers in the hard anti-Communist cell at Time, Inc., and a colleague, from the very beginning, in the *National Review* enterprise. Schlamm is a Viennese, volatile, amusing, the soul of obduracy, and a conversational stem-winder. He had been in on the negotiations with Chambers from the very first, and was modestly certain he could bring his old pal Whit along by the terrible cogency of his arguments. But as we drove down to Maryland from New York, Schlamm got progressively hoarser. Two minutes after we arrived, laryngitis completely closed in. Whittaker was wonderfully attentive—aspirin, tea, lemon, whiskey, bicarbonate, all that sort of thing. But at one point he turned to me, when Willi was out of sight, and gave me a huge, delighted wink.

So he stayed on his farm, and worried. He had a great deal to worry about. There was a pending libel suit against him by a minor actor in *Witness,* and Chambers felt that he had been fighting completely alone. "*Your letter* [stating that his friends were standing by] *did me a lot of good at the right moment. . . . When I go into court with the litigious Mr. X three days hence, I shall not feel, as until now I have had to feel, that I am just as alone in 1954 as in 1948. It is a somewhat freezing feeling.*"

And Alger Hiss had come out of prison arrantly proclaiming his innocence. "*Alger came out more fiercely than even I had expected. . . . His strength is not what it was. But that it exists at all is stunning. Every time that, in the name of truth, he asserts his innocence, he strikes at truth, utters a slander against me, and compounds his guilt of several orders. . . . It is this which squirts into my morale a little jet of paralyzing poison. . . .*"

His son John was having the normal son's difficulties at college. "*John, like most sensitive youths, is a great nuisance to himself and to many others. He often stirs me to rage. . . . There come moments, even with a beloved son, when we are moved to nod assent to what Karl Brandt once said to me: 'Don't you know that boys at that age are poisonous, simply poisonous?'*"

His broken health, together with a grim financial situation, contributed to a great restlessness. *"I do not even have the capital to farm halfheartedly, and I cannot, as in the past, make good the capital by my own labor power. This inability to work the place is perhaps the greatest burr in my mind at that angle. It torments me since, among other disabilities, I have no talent for being a country gentleman.... But we have long been as poor as rats."*

And then, during that period, he reached the psychological low point of his later years, as he sweated in philosophical bedrock, gathering his thoughts: *"I have been splashing about in my private pool of ice water."* Again, *"I have ceased to understand why I must go on living."* Again, *"The year was, for me, a long walk through the valley. No one but me will ever know how close I came to staying in it."* What was the trouble? *"It had to do with my inability to fix the meaning of the current period of existence in some communicable way. I knew the fault lay in me. So that, all the while I was trying to write, I was simply trying to grow."*

But he came out of it. *"Between Christmas ... and New Year, I woke, one dawn, from a dream in which I had been singing (in German, but not aloud, of course) a marching song. In my half-waking state, I continued to sing the song to the end, which goes:* Hell aus der dunklen Vergangenheit/ Leuchtet die Zukunft hervor—*Bright, from the darkness of the past/ Beacons the future. From what depths had this song risen, which I had not sung (or heard sung) for decades? But the song was only a signature. What was wonderful, incredible, was the sense of having passed from one dimension into another; a sense of ordered peace, together with an exhilaration ('at last I am free'). I had touched bottom and was rising again to the surface; and, to rise, I had cut loose a drowning weight of extraneous this and that.... The dream was, in fact, the turning point of my late years. I take it that such a dream is a recapitulation; it prepares itself, as Camus*

says of suicide, 'like a work of art, secretly, in the heart' with-
out the artist's being aware of the process."

He could write, finally: "Ehrenburg has just made one of
the most memorable utterances of the time: 'If the whole
world were to be covered with asphalt, one day a crack
would appear in the asphalt; and in that crack, grass would
grow.' I offer the lines as the irreducible terms on which the
mind can have hope in our age."

Eisenhower ran and was re-elected. Nixon was safely Vice-
President. Six months later Chambers wrote me to say he
wanted to sign up with *National Review*. Having made the
decision, he was elated. After years of isolation and intro-
spection, he was like a painter who had recovered his eyesight. He felt the overwhelming need to practice his art.
How many things he wanted to write about, and immediately! Mushrooms, for one thing. Some gentleman, in an act
of supreme conceit, had recently published a ten-dollar book
of mycology, heaping scorn on one of Chambers' most beloved species of toadstools. Camus. What a lot of things
needed to be said instantly about the *Myth of Sisyphus!*
Djilas' *The New Class* was just out and most of the critics
had missed the whole point. . . .

I rented a one-engine plane and swooped down on him at
Westminster to make our arrangements. For my own reasons
I had to make the round trip in one day, and I wanted to act
immediately on Chambers' enthusiasm. He met me and we
drove in his car to his farm. He told me the last time he had
driven to the little grassy strip at Westminster, on which
reckless pilots venture occasionally to land, was to greet
Henry Luce, who had soared in from Washington to pay him
an unexpected visit some months after Hiss's conviction. I
remarked that such, obviously, is the traveling style of very
important publishers. If he would not acknowledge that
common denominator between me and Mr. Luce, I added,
then he might recognize this one: such is the style of pub-

lishers who employ Whittaker Chambers. He laughed, but told me my manner was grossly imperfected. When Luce arrived, he said as we bounced about on the dusty dirt road in his open jeep, he had waiting for him at the airport a limousine to drive him to Chambers' farm. I made a note for my next landing. . . .

He would not go to New York after all. To do so would be not merely to defy his doctor's orders, which he did regularly almost as a matter of principle, but to defy Esther's wishes, which was something else again. He would work at home. I begged him to desist from what I had denounced as his sin of scrupulosity. During the preceding eighteen months, since the Laryngitis Conference, he had twice volunteered to do a piece for *National Review*. One, I remember, was to be an answer to Dwight Macdonald's unbalanced attack on *National Review* in *Commentary*. He had suggested a deadline of two weeks after we spoke. Ten weeks later he abandoned the project. Meanwhile he had done thirteen drafts. He would not show me any of them.

I was disappointed, but not altogether surprised. I had had a dozen letters from him describing the fate of other letters he had written me. (*"To your gladdening letters, I wrote a close-set, three-and-a-half-page reply, which I have just had the pleasure of setting a match to. . . ."*) At least once he burned a book-length manuscript. (*". . . I have burned a book half the size of* Witness, *and consider it one of my best deeds. . . ."*) As soon as he regained consciousness after one coronary attack, whose relative ferocity he was sure would end up killing him, he groped his way down to the basement to destroy another great pile of manuscripts.

He wrote on yellow second sheets, by hand, in pencil. Then he would rewrite and rewrite. Then—sometimes—he would type out a third or fourth draft. Then, after a few days, he would often destroy that. "Let *us* judge whether what you write is publishable," I pleaded. "You have no judgment on such matters. There should be a constitutional amendment forbidding you to destroy anything you write, without the permission of a jury of your superiors, to which I hereby nominate myself." He chuckled. Underproduction would not be his trouble any more, he said: the way he was feeling he would bury us with copy, and before long I'd be sending him literary tranquilizers. . . .

But, five weeks later, he wrote me to say he must resign: he could not bring himself to submit to us what he had written. I cajoled him, and one day a five-thousand-word manuscript arrived, on "Soviet Strategy in the Middle East." (*"Talk, here in the farmlands"* [it began], *"is chiefly of the heaviest frost of this date in a decade, and what it may have done to stands of late corn. Yet it cannot be said that we are wholly out of touch with the capitals of the mysterious East—Cairo, Damascus, Baghdad, New York. . . ."*)

Two months later, after struggling with the book for eight weeks, he submitted a long review of Ayn Rand's *Atlas Shrugged*. (*"Somebody has called it 'excruciatingly awful.' I find it a remarkably silly book. . . . In any case, the brew is probably without lasting ill effects. But it is not a cure for anything. Nor would we, ordinarily, place much confidence in the diagnosis of a doctor who supposes that the Hippocratic Oath is a kind of curse."* Miss Rand never forgave me for publishing it. (To this day, she will walk theatrically out of any room I enter!)

A few months after that he wrote about the farm problem, clearly as an insider. (*"Perhaps* [in the future the socialized farmer] *will not be able, in that regimented time to find or frame an answer* [to why he lost his freedom]. *Perhaps he will not need to. For perhaps the memory of those men and women* [who fought socialism] *will surprise him simply as with an unfamiliar, but arresting sound—the sound of spring-heads, long dried up and silent in a fierce drought, suddenly burst out and rushing freely to the sea. It may remind him of a continuity that outlives all lives, fears, perplexities, contrivings, hopes, defeats; so that he is moved to reach down and touch again for strength, as if he were its first discoverer, the changeless thing—the undeluding, undenying earth.")*

And then a piece defending the right of Alger Hiss to travel abroad, while denying that Hiss can be said to have paid his debt to society. (*"The Hiss Case remains a central lesion of our time. That is why, ultimately, I cannot say . . . that Alger Hiss has paid any effective penalty. For precisely he can end the lesion at any moment that he chooses, with half-a-dozen words."* Chambers knew that his absolute endorsement of the right of anyone to travel would bring criticism from certain quarters on the Right. No matter. *"Woe to those who grope for reality and any approximate truth that may be generalized from it, in the no man's land between incensed camps. History and certain personal experiences leave me in little doubt about the fate of such seekers. They are fair game to the snipers of both sides, and it is always open season. But while Mr. Hiss hurries to his plane or ship, and the snipers wait for the man to reach, in his groping, the point where the hairlines cross on their sights, I may still have time to sort the dead cats into tidy piles—those from one camp, here; those from the other, there. As one of my great contemporaries put it: 'Anybody looking for a quiet life has picked the wrong century to be born in.' The remark must be allowed a certain authority, I think, since the century clinched the point by mauling with an ax the brain that framed it."*)

That piece was picked up by *The New York Times*, which also had run a paragraph calling attention to Chambers' joining the staff of *National Review*, a story picked up by AP. He bore the publicity he got with resignation, though it clearly upset him. If Chambers could have taken a bath in invisible ink, I have no doubt he'd have done so. He loathed publicity, even as he loathed gossip. (He passed on a piece of news to me once which, he admitted, he had got second-hand—Esther had it over the telephone: *"I think it is true. Or so Esther tells me. For, at the first tinkle of the bell, I rushed outside to feed the fish in the pond. Because they do not bark, and do not know the secrets of Washington."*) In preparing this article I looked in *Who's Who* for Chambers' birth date but his name was not listed. I looked in the 1952 edition; no entry there either. I wrote a furious letter to *Who's Who*—which (I had previously noted) studiedly ignores the existence of all interesting people—to ask why they discriminate against anyone who isn't a Congressman or a rich dentist. But this time they had me: Chambers had for ten years refused to complete the biographical questionnaires they had repeatedly sent him. When the news got out that he had joined *National Review*'s staff, he received a telephone call from *Time* magazine's Baltimore stringer requesting an interview. Sorry, Chambers said, as he always did to any member of the press who wanted to see him on official business. Like *Who's Who, Time* refused to take notice of the affairs of anyone so ungrateful as to refuse to cooperate with its opinion-gatherers (*Who's Who,* after all, could have got all the information it needed from *Witness*). The *Time* reporter wired the New York office, snootily declining to pursue a story about so uncooperative a subject, and, for good measure, sent Chambers a copy of it.

At about that time, I remember, *Newsweek* ran a story under its regular feature heading, "Where Are They Now?" (i.e., the Heroes [or Villains] of Yesteryear). Chambers, *Newsweek* Periscoped, was still living in the farmhouse where he had buried the famous papers in a pumpkin; he never budged from the farm; and was hard at work on a new book. I wrote to *Newsweek* to say their account was interesting, except that: a) Chambers had moved from the farmhouse in question (during the preceding winter it had almost burned to the ground), and was now living in a little house at the other end of his farm; b) that he was working, and had been for a year, for *National Review,* and came regularly to New York; and c) that he had temporarily abandoned work on the new book. *Newsweek* ran no correction. If *Newsweek* had run an incorrect report on Chambers, clearly it was Chambers' fault. He should have kept *Newsweek* better informed on his movements.

But notwithstanding his desire for privacy and his temperamental dislike for New York (*"New York you need to exploit, and I never learned how"*), Chambers decided in the summer of 1958 to come here every fortnight to spend two days in the office, writing editorials and short features for *National Review.* He would arrive on the train from Baltimore at noon and come directly to the editorial lunch, always out of breath, perspiring in his city clothes. He was always glad to see his gentle friend, John Chamberlain, his longtime colleague from Time, Inc. He liked his little cubicle at *National Review* which, five minutes after he entered it, smelled like a pipe-tobacco factory. He puffed away ferociously, grinding out his memorable paragraphs. Everything he wrote had intellectual and stylistic distinction and, above all, the intense emotional quality of the man who, fifteen years before, had said of the Negro spiritual: *"It was the religious voice of a whole religious people—probably the most God-obsessed (and man-despised) since the ancient Hebrews. . . . One simple fact is clear—they were created in direct answer to the Psalmist's question, 'How shall we sing the Lord's song in a strange land?' . . . Grief, like a tuning fork, gave the tone, and the Sorrow Songs were uttered."*

Yet anyone meeting Chambers casually, without preconception, would say of him first that he was a highly amusing and easily amused man. The bottomless gravity seldom suggested itself. He was not merely a man of wit, but also a man of humor, and even a man of fun. Often, in his letters, even through his orotund gloom, the pixie would surface. (*"Would that we could live in the world of the fauves, where the planes are disjointed only on canvas, instead of a world where the wild beasts are real and the disjointures threaten to bury us. Or do I really wish that? It would take some nice thinking for, perhaps, toasted Susie is not my ice cream. Per-*

haps you should make a transparency of [Gertrude Stein's 'most perfect sentence'] *and hang it as a slogan outside the windows of the* National Review: *'Toasted Susie is Not My Ice Cream.' It might catch you more subscribers than Senator McCarthy at that.")*

On Tuesday nights we worked late, and four or five of us would go out to dinner. By then he was physically exhausted. But he wanted to come with us, and we would eat at some restaurant or other, and he would talk hungrily (and eat hungrily) about everything that interested him, which was literally everything in this world, and not in this world. He talked often around a subject, swooping in to make a quick point, withdrawing, relaxing, laughing, listening—he listened superbly, though even as a listener he was always a potent force. He was fascinated by the method and scope of James Burnham's interests, and the sureness of his analytical mind, though Chambers' own thoughts were so resolutely non-schematic that he tended to shrink from some of Burnham's grandiose constructions, even while admiring the architecture. They made for a wonderful dialectic, Burnham's *sostenutos* and Chambers' enigmatic descants. The next morning, press day, he was at his desk at eight, and we would have a sandwich lunch. At five he was on the train back to Baltimore, where his wife would meet him. And on reaching his farm he would drop on his bed from fatigue. Three months after he began coming to New York, he collapsed from another heart attack.

Six months later, in the summer of 1959, he felt well enough to indulge a dream, more particularly his gentle wife's dream, to visit Europe. She had never been there, and he had been there only once, in 1927, the trip he described so evocatively in *Witness*. We drove them to the airport after a happy day. I noticed worriedly how heavily he perspired and how nervously his heavy thumbs shuffled through the bureaucratic paraphernalia of modern travel, as he dug up, in turn, passports, baggage tags, vaccination certificates, and airplane tickets. His plans were vague, but at the heart of them was a visit to his old friend, Arthur Koestler.

They were at Koestler's eyrie in Austria for a week, an unforgettable week.

"*Alpach, where AK lives, is some four hundred meters higher into the hills than Innsbruck. While we were flying from Paris, the worst landslide since 1908 (I am only quoting) had destroyed several miles of the only road up. Nevertheless, we got through, by jeep, on a road just wide enough for a jeep, and not always quite that. On my side, without leaning out at all, I could see straight down several hundred feet. Happily, the Austrian army was at the wheel of the jeep. K, waiting at the point where our trail emerged, was thinking of the most amusing headlines: 'Whittaker Chambers crashes over Alpine Trail on secret visit to Arthur Koestler. British Intelligence questions surviving writer.' There in Alpach we spent some days about which I cannot possibly write fully. Perhaps, some moment being right, it will seem proper to try to recover certain moments. Perhaps. Then K had the idea to wire Greta Buber-Neumann:* 'Komme schleunigst. Gute weine. Ausserdem. Whittaker C.' '*Come quickest. Good wine. In addition, WC.' In case you do not know, Greta Buber-Neumann is the daughter-in-law of Martin Buber, widow of Heinz Neumann, most dazzling of the German CP leaders (shot without trial), sister-in-law of Willi Muenzenberg (organizer of the Muenzenberg Trust, killed by the NKVD while trying to escape the Gestapo). Greta herself spent two years as a slave in Karaganda. By then, the Moscow-Berlin Pact had been signed, and the NKVD handed her (and many others) over to the Gestapo on the bridge at Brest-Litovsk. Then she spent five years in German concentration camps, mostly at Ravensbrück. . . . Impossible to tell here this story of her lifetime, which makes the* Odyssey, *for all its grandeur, somehow childish. . . . So there we sat, and talked, not merely about the daily experiences of our lives. Each of the two men had tried to kill himself and failed; Greta was certainly the most hardy and astonishing of the three. Then we realized that, of our particular breed, the old activists, we are almost the only survivors....*"

They went on to Rome ("*In Rome, I had to ask Esther for the nitroglycerine. Since then, I've been living on the stuff ...*"), Venice ("*I came back to Venice chiefly to rest. If it were not for my children, I should try to spend the rest of my life here. Other cities are greater or less great than something or some other city. Venice is incomparable. It is the only city I have ever loved*"), Berlin ("*I feel as though I had some kind of a moral compulsion to go at this time ...*"), Paris ("You will look up Malraux?" I wrote him—I remembered the gratitude Chambers felt on receiving a handwritten note from Malraux, who had just read *Witness*: "You have not come back from hell with empty hands." "*Malraux is busy*," Chambers replied: "*If he wants to see me, he will know where to find me*").

"*Europe,*" he concluded one letter, "*has almost nothing to say to me, and almost nothing to tell me that I cannot learn just about as well from the European press and occasional European tourists in America; or correspondence.... Give* [the Europeans] *the means, and these dear friends, that noble Third Force, will cut our bloody throats. As people, they are stronger than we are, and they know it ... their disdain for us is withering. Give these superior breeds the economic power to see us at eye level, and they will see right over us....*"

Within a few weeks he got sick again, and abruptly they flew back; and again he was in bed.

He wanted to resign from *National Review*. It was partly that his poor health and his unconquerable perfectionism kept him from producing a flow of copy large enough to satisfy his conscience. Partly it was his *Weltanschauung*, which was constantly in motion. Chiefly he resisted *National Review*'s schematic conservatism, even its schematic anti-Communism. "*You ... stand within, or at any rate are elab-*

orating, a political orthodoxy. I stand within no political orthodoxy. . . . I am at heart a counter-revolutionist. You mean to be conservative, and I know no one who seems to me to have a better right to the term. I am not a conservative. Sometimes I have used the term loosely, especially when I was first called on publicly to classify myself. I have since been as circumspect as possible in using the term about myself. I say: I am a man of the Right." But a formal withdrawal would mean the final institutional wrench. Emotionally he was drawn to us. "*Could I join you,*" he had written as long ago as 1955, on deciding not to join us, "*that might end my loneliness; it might spell hope. It is, in fact, the great temptation. My decision is, therefore, made across the tug of that temptation.*" Chambers, the individualist, believed strongly in organization. He believed, for instance, in the Republican Party. Not the totemic party of *John Brown's Body* as sung by Everett McKinley Dirksen, but the Republican Party as a Going Organization. "*I shall vote the straight Republican ticket for as long as I live,*" he told me. "*You see, I'm an Orgbureau man.*" ("I expect," I replied after the 1958 elections, "that you will outlive the Party.") He easily outmatched my pessimism. Already he had written, on the New Year before the elections, "*I saw my first robin this* A.M., *sitting huddled, fluffed up and chilly on a bare branch, just like, I thought, a Republican candidate in 1958.*" And when the returns came in: "*If the Republican Party cannot get some grip of the actual world we live in and from it generalize and actively promote a program that means something to masses of people—why somebody else will. There will be nothing to argue. The voters will simply vote Republicans into singularity. The Republican Party will become like one of those dark little shops which apparently never sell anything. If, for any reason, you go in, you find at the back, an old man, fingering for his own pleasure some oddments of cloth. Nobody wants to buy them, which is fine because the old man is not really interested in selling. He just likes to hold and to feel...").*

But the day had to come, as I knew it would. *"This is my resignation from NR,"* he wrote sadly toward the end of 1959. *"This is a retype of the beginning of a much longer letter...."*

He had made up his mind to do something else. He enrolled at Western Maryland College as an undergraduate. *"Most people incline to laugh. I think they feel that it is such a waste on all sides since I shall not be around long enough to put it to any use of the kind people call 'good.' I've considered that. I do not wish to die an ignoramus. If I can bring it off in terms of health, energy, time, application, then I think the world should let me try. The world is desperately ignorant at the moment when it has most reason to know with some exactitude...."*

Several reasons why he should take this course were instantly clear to me. He had quit *National Review.* He had failed to complete the book that Random House had been expecting for six years. (That book is now being assembled for publication.) He did not want to sit at home, half crippled and denied the life he would, I think, have liked most to lead, the life of a dawn-to-dusk farmer. Chambers was all Puritan about work. Idleness was utterly incomprehensible to him. Even when he was home and without formal obligations, he was unremittingly active, working, reading, writing, beginning at four or five in the morning. At night he often watched television, and then early to bed.

But there was another reason. In Europe, Koestler, whose book *The Sleepwalkers* Chambers had read just before leaving, had said to him sharply: "You cannot understand what is going on in the world unless you understand science deeply." Very well, then, he would learn science. And so the author of *Witness,* former book reviewer and foreign editor for *Time,* author of profound essays on history and theology and politics, of exhaustive articles on the Renaissance and the culture of the Middle Ages, writer of what a critic has called the most emotive political prose of our time, whose voice John Strachey had called, along with those of Orwell, Camus, Koestler and Pasternak, the "strangled cry" of the West in crisis, a sixty-year-old man fluent in French, German, at home in Italian, Spanish and Russian, went back to school.

I remembered suddenly that the hero of *The Sleepwalkers* was Johann Kepler. And I remembered the first question in an examination in physics I struggled with at Yale: "State," it said, in those hortatory accents common to government forms and college examinations, "Kepler's Laws." I hadn't been able to state them, let alone understand them. So Chambers would learn about Kepler. God help us.

He threw himself into his work. Science courses galore. And, for relaxation, Greek, Latin and advanced French composition. Every morning he drove to school and sat between the farmers' sons of Western Maryland, taking notes, dissecting frogs, reciting Greek Paradigms, working tangled problems in physics. Home, and immediately to the basement to do his homework. Everything else was put aside. He signed up for the summer session, of course, but in the interstice between terms (*"First day of summer break, and I am wild with liberty. I was still standing by hanging on to the ropes, when the final bell sounded"*) he drove north to see his daughter, and spent the day with us on a hot afternoon during the summer. How do you get on, my wife asked him, with your fellow undergraduates? "Just fine," he said. "In fact, I have an admirer. A young lady, aged about nineteen, who shares with me the carcasses of small animals, which the two of us proceed, in tandem, to disembowel—the college can't afford one starfish per pupil, let alone one piglet. For months while we worked together she addressed me not a word, and I was afraid my great age had frightened her. But last week, all of a sudden, she broke silence. She said breathlessly: 'Mr. Chambers?' 'Yes,' I answered her anxiously.

'Tell me, what do *you* think of *Itsy Bitsy Teenie Weenie Yellow Polka-dot Bikini?*' " He broke down with laughter. He hadn't, at the critical moment, the least idea that the young lady was talking about a popular song, but he had improvised beautifully until he was able to deduce what on earth it was all about, whereupon he confided to his co-vivisectionist that it happened that this was absolutely, positively, indisputably his very favorite song, over all others he had ever heard. Her gratitude was indescribable. From that moment on they chirped together happily and pooled their knowledge about spleens and livers, kidneys and upper intestines.

I imagine he was a very quiet student, giving his teachers no cause whatever for the uneasiness they might have expected to feel in the presence of so august a mind. Only once, that I know of, was he aroused to take issue with one of his teachers.

"*An incident from my Greek class, which has left me in ill favor. We came on a Greek line of Diogenes: 'Love of money is the mother-city of all the ills.' Opinions were invited; and when my turn came, I answered with one word: Nonsense.' That was too vehement, but there was a reason. Behind me was sitting a Junior, who manages on a scholarship or grant or something of the kind, and whose college life has been made a misery by poverty.... All things considered, he is a pretty good student; but his sleepiness makes him an easy professorial butt. In addition, he is not a particularly personable youth. To say in the presence of such a case, 'Love of money is the mother-city of all ills ...'—is why I answered 'Nonsense.'... I offered in Greek: 'A lack of money is the root of many ills.'... I thought I could speak with some freedom since there can scarcely ever have existed a man in whom love of money is as absolutely absent as in me. I don't even get properly interested in it. Oh, I also offered (while authority was being bandied) St. Thomas Aquinas' 'Money is neither good nor bad in itself: it depends on what is done with it.' But St. Thomas seems not to be in good standing. So, down the generations go the blinded minds, blinkered minds, at any rate. But I wonder what Master Jones, the impoverished Junior, thought about it. I did not ask. He, like the other Greeks who were doing most of the talking, is a pre-divinity student—pre-Flight, as they call it happily here."*

During examination weeks he was in a constant state of high boil. He slaved for his grades. And he achieved them, even in the alien field of science; all A's, or A–'s; once, as I remember, a humiliating B+. After the winter, his fatigue was total, overwhelming. *"Weariness, Bill,"* he wrote in the last letter I had from him, shortly before John's wedding, *"—you cannot yet know literally what it means. I wish no time would come when you do know, but the balance of experience is against it. One day, long hence, you will know true weariness and will say: 'That was it.' My own life of late has been full of such realizations."*

He learned science, and killed himself. Those were the two things, toward the end, he most wanted to do.

"Why on earth doesn't your father answer the phone?" I asked Ellen in Connecticut on Saturday afternoon, the 8th of July. "Because," she said with a laugh, shyly, "Poppa and the phone company are having a little tiff, and the phone is disconnected. They wanted him to trim one of his favorite trees to take the strain off the telephone line, and he put it off. So . . . they turned off the phone." I wired him: WHEN YOU COME TO TERMS WITH THE PHONE COMPANY GIVE ME A RING. But he didn't call. The following Tuesday, I came back to my office from the weekly editorial lunch—I had thought, as often I did, how sorely we missed him there in the dining room. As I walked into my office I had a call. I took it standing, in front of my desk. It was John Chambers. He gave me the news. A heart attack. The final heart attack. Cremation in total privacy. The news would go to the press later that afternoon. His mother was in the hospital. I mumbled the usual inappropriate things, hung up the telephone, sat down, and wept. *"American men, who weep in droves in movie houses, over the woes of lovestruck shop girls, hold that weeping in men is unmanly* [he wrote me once]. *I have found most men in whom there was depth of experience, or capacity for compassion, singularly apt to tears. How can it be otherwise? One looks and sees: and it would be a kind of impotence to be incapable of, or to grudge, the comment of tears, even while you struggle against it. I am immune to soap opera. But I cannot listen for any length of time to the speaking voice of Kirsten Flagstad, for example, without being done in by that magnificence of tone that seems to speak from the center of sorrow, even from the center of the earth."*

For me, and others who knew him, his voice had been and still is like Kirsten Flagstad's, magnificent in tone, speaking to our time from the center of sorrow, from the center of the earth.

Outside Politics

THE THREAT TO THE
AMATEUR SAILOR

I

VERY early in my very brief career as an oceangoing sailor I read with considerable interest the chapter in one of H. A. Calahan's "Learning How" series on selecting the ideal crew. The subject has continued to absorb me, both as an abstract problem, and as a practical matter. At about the time I was getting together a crew for the Newport–Annapolis Race I read a magazine article which posed the question, What are the proper qualifications for crew members on a transatlantic race?

The author's answer—he should be able to make a long splice from the masthead—struck me, at the time, as a perfectly serviceable symbolic requirement for the useful crew member; so drugged was I by the propaganda of cultism. I coasted along for several days at peace with that generalization until some devil prompted me, apropos nothing at all, to ask the crew of my boat, *The Panic*, at a moment when we were sprawled about the cockpit and deck having supper, "How many of you know how to do a long splice?"

Of the six persons I addressed, five did not know how. Two or three of them had once known how, but had forgotten. The sixth said that under perfect circumstances he probably could negotiate a long splice. What, I asked him, did he consider perfect circumstances to be? Well, he said, lots of time, nobody looking over his shoulder, nothing said about the esthetic appearance of the splice once consummated, and maybe a sketch to refresh his memory in the event it should lapse.

Not, in a word, from the masthead.

I felt no embarrassment, I hasten to add, in putting the question to my crew, because I do not myself know how to make a long splice, or even a short one. I intend, one of these days, to learn, as I intend, one of these days, to read Proust. Just when, I cannot say; before or after Proust, I cannot say either.

I mean to make two points. The first is that the crew on the race in question was a perfectly competent crew *according to my standards,* the standards of an amateur; and the second, that the cultists are these days, as far as sailing is concerned, winning a creeping victory over us amateurs. And then, of course, I have an exhortation: Amateurs of the world unite! What you stand to lose is your pleasure!

What are the standards I am here to defend? At this point I must be permitted an autobiographical word or two detailing my own experiences with, and knowledge of, sailing.

Sailing has always had an irresistible allure for me. At twelve, I persuaded my indulgent father to give me a boat. Cautiously, he gave me a boat *and* a full-time instructor. The boat was a 16-foot Barracuda (a class since extinct), and I joined the variegated seven-boat fleet in Lakeville, Connecticut, as the only member under twenty-one.

The Wononscopomuc Yacht Club, whose only assets were a charter, an aluminum trophy donated by a local hardware store, and $2 per year from each of the boats, was fortunate enough at the time I joined it to be adminstered, or rather reigned over, by a retired commodore whose passion for ritual and discipline imposed upon the carefree fleet a certain order. From him we got a knowledge of, and respect for, the rudiments of yachting, and even some of the niceties. We learned, too, something about the rules of racing (although I infer from the animadversions of an adjacent skipper at the

starting line at a recent race that some of the rules have
since changed). After virtually every round (we raced three
times a week) the commodore would buzz around the fleet
in a squat canoe propelled by four melancholy ten-year-old
camp boys, informing us of the delinquency of our racing
strategy, and of the great swath we had that day cut into
the rule book.

Dutifully, we would file our protests. Having done so, we
would meet some evening during the following week—never
less than three days after the offense, for the commodore required at least that much time to reflect on the enormity of
the offense, and to weigh carefully the conflicting demands
of justice and mercy. After an elaborate exposition of the
problem, he would pronounce, ponderously, sentence.

This ranged from disqualification to, on the lenient days, a
terrible warning to which, of course, was attached public
obloquy.

So it went for three years; 50 races per season, rain or
shine. The war interrupted all that, and I did not sail again
until a few years ago, when I bought a 14-foot Sailfish.

The Sailfish pricked the curiosity of my six-foot-five, 250-
pound brother-in-law, Austin Taylor, who had never sailed
before.

Austin regulates his life on the philosophy that tomorrow
we may die and hence he was soon urging that we buy a
cruising boat and move around a little bit. In the summer of
1955, a persuasive yacht broker parlayed our desire for a nice
little cruising boat into *The Panic*. Austin's size provided the
rationalization.

The Panic is* a lovely 42½-foot, steel-hulled cutter, stiff,

* *The Panic* was destroyed during a recent hurricane. Professor Hugh
Kenner wrote of her: "She had done much for her friends, in the summers
before her side was stove in. She had taken them all around the Sound,
and along the New England coast, and even to Bermuda (thrice), and
shown them Wood's Hole, and the Great Fish, that eats taffrail logs, and the
Kraken, and the strange men of Onset with their long faces, and perfect
Edgartown; and lapped them at night gently to rest; and given them the
wind and sun and often more rain than they knew how to be comfortable

fast, built in Holland in brazen disregard of American handicap rules. Her CCA rating is a merciless and zenophobic 34.4, putting her up in the company of the racing machines, which she is not. Our first race was the Vineyard Race of that September. Our large genoa and spinnaker arrived two hours before the start. A crew was hastily put together by a friend who knew the race, and the rigors of ocean racing. We did not come in last, but that was not, the skipper commented ruefully, because we didn't try. We learned a great deal and resolved to enter, the following year, the exotic race to Bermuda.

What kind of a sailor, then, do I consider myself? I am perfectly at home in a small boat, and would, in a small boat race, more often than not come in if not this side of glory, perhaps this side of ignominy. I know enough of the elements of piloting to keep out of normal difficulties. I have a spectacularly defective memory, so that I am hopeless in recognizing even landmarks I may have set eyes on a thousand times, and therefore not a naturally talented pilot.

When my radio direction finder works, I can work it. I am studying celestial navigation (how it works, not why). My instructor would classify me as a medium-apt student, though my attendance record has been erratic. I know my boat reasonably well and even know now why it suddenly sank at a slip a year or so ago, mystifying me (I was a thousand miles away when it happened) as well as the experts. I am reasonably calm, reasonably resourceful, and have reasonable resistance to adversity. Those are my credentials. And the question before the house: Are my credentials high enough? And the corollary question, high enough for what?

Herewith my first collision with a cultist.

Second only to the fear of God, the beginning of wisdom is the knowledge of one's limitations. That much wisdom

---

in; and made for them a place of adventure and refreshment and peace; and taught them this, that beyond illusion it is possible to be for hours and days on end perfectly and inexpressibly happy."

Austin Taylor and I exhibited in resolving to ask someone with considerably more experience than we to take command of *The Panic* on the race to Bermuda. The name of a highly experienced sailor known slightly to Austin Taylor suggested itself. Parkinson (let us call him) had met Taylor in the course of business in downtown New York, and identified himself as an enthusiastic and seasoned sailor. He had his own boat (I think it was an 8-meter) but it was ill-equipped and unsuited to the Bermuda ordeal. Parkinson had approached a mutual friend with the idea of getting a berth aboard *The Panic*. Instead we offered him, and he promptly accepted, Command.

There followed eight or so of the most hectic weeks of my life. Parkinson had not only got control of *The Panic*, he had got control of me, my wife, my child and my dogs in the bargain. (Austin Taylor fled to the Philippines and stayed away a year.) My life, I think it is accurate to say, was at his disposal. To begin with, the crew was seated at lunch; and before we knew it there had been duly constituted some one dozen committees, each of which had three members and a chairman, meaning about four committees for each member of the seven-man crew.

Each committee had an area of responsibility. There was, for example, the Safety Committee (flares, life jackets, dye markers, etc.), the Navigation Committee (HO 211, six pencils, etc.), the Bermuda Reservations Committee, the Food Committee, the Supplies Committee—ten or twelve in all. Parkinson suggested I go to work on my backwardness by doing a little remedial reading. Without even glancing at the list he furnished me, I turned it over to my secretary and asked her to secure the books. A week later anyone gazing at my desk would have taken the occupant for the curator of a maritime library. Moreover, I had the distinct feeling that, at Newport, Parkinson would examine me and, if I did not measure up to his final standard, I would probably see the start of the race from the committee boat.

Beginning that weekend in February, Parkinson and one or two of his associates (he had promptly filled out half of the crew with his expert friends) started coming to the Muzzio Brothers boatyard in Stamford to brood over *The Panic*. Parkinson is a highly efficient and useful human being, and I do not mean to underrate the services he performed for *The Panic* in the succeeding six weekends: but I could not avoid getting the impression that he liked to fuss over the boat partly for the sake of it; and arriving at the conclusion, upon meditation, that in liking to do so, he is one of a breed.

I believe, to give an example, that my concern that the standing rigging in my own boat be sound is as lively as his own. But whereas I am satisfied to inspect the rigging cursorily, and otherwise repose my faith in professional riggers whom I retain to go over the rigging every year, Parkinson spent hours feeling every strand of wire, and fingering every screw and bolt for signs of wear, or fatigue, or restiveness of the subtlest kind. *The Panic* had no secrets left when Parkinson was through with her. She might as well have gone to bed with a psychoanalyst. I soon learned that the Bermuda race began the day we took on Parkinson: which meant, really, that it was too long a race.

We foundered, curiously, on a triviality, but one on which I decided, providentially, to take a stand.

Nothing, as I say, was being left to take care of itself. And so in one connection or other (probably the chairman of the Supplies Committee brought the matter up) the question arose what to take along in the way of liquor. "There will be no liquor consumed during the race," Parkinson said, with rather arresting firmness. I rose to the bait, and said I thought it reasonable to permit members of the watch going off duty to have a drink, if they chose.

In races, Parkinson said patiently, one does not drink liquor until one crosses the finish line. I said: "One undoubtedly knows more about the traditions of ocean racing than I do. But," I added, warming a little bit to the subject, "some traditions are rational and some are not, and I think it reasonable, in such a case as this, to ask One to bring intelligence to bear on the subject rather than submit unquestioningly to doctrinaire propositions minted by our nautical forebears. Is it your assumption," I asked jocularly (it was a mistake to be jocular with Parkinson), "that the Battle of Trafalgar would have been won sooner had One reminded Admiral Nelson of Tradition in time to recall the ration of rum he had recklessly dispensed to the fleet immediately before the engagement?"

Parkinson explained that crossing the Atlantic Ocean in a small boat requires an alert crew. I explained that I was aware of the fact, and was not suggesting a drunk, nor even, for those on watch, a drink; that I thought reasonable men could distinguish between a drink and a drunk. I suggested, as the subject began to carry me away, that his position was fetishistic, that unless he could defend it more reasonably, it must be written off either as superstition or as masochism or as neo-spartanism, and that I was anti-all three. Parkinson said that no boat of which he had charge would dispense demon rum to the crew, and that was that. I told him liquor would be on board, and those who wanted it could have it. . . .

Late that night he called me dramatically to say that he and his associates were pulling out of the crew, on the grounds that my attitude toward sailing was too frivolous. Parkinson's replacement, an engaging, highly skilled and wonderfully permissive Middle Westerner, arrived for the trip two (2) days before we set out from Newport. He was relaxed and competent and congenial. (There was liquor aboard, by the way; and, further by the way, in the four-day trip we probably averaged two drinks apiece.)

We did rather creditably, as a matter of fact; halfway in our high-powered class. Parkinson, who had joined another boat, came in two days after we got to Bermuda, second to last in the fleet. I am not implying divine justification here, or even empirical corroboration of my theories. If Parkin-

son was in charge of his boat I am certain things were tidier
and better ordered than on *The Panic,* and that it was his
boat's fault—or the cruelest ill luck, against which no committee however diligent could have shielded him—that we
trounced him so decisively. I am merely saying that if I
should be guaranteed the Bermuda Trophy provided I raced
with Parkinson aboard, I should say thanks very much, but
no thanks: I like to sail, and I like to sail well; and I'd love
to win the Bermuda race. But when I step on a boat I do
not wish to pursue ordeal, for ordeal's sake; we amateurs
want to sail. Sail—remember?

I almost always end up with a crew one or two members of
which have had very little sailing experience. This is some
sort of handicap in a race, no doubt about it. When at the
helm in a boat the novice will too often luff up, or bear away
and lose position. Leading the jib sheet, he will at least once
in the course of the race gird the winch counterclockwise.
Ask him to rig a preventer and he rushes forward with a
boom vang. Almost surely he will pronounce leeward leeward, and who knows the measure of Triton's vengeance on
the boat where that enormity is perpetrated?

I have seen consternation on the faces of the more experienced members of the crew at such evidences of inexperience
or even ignorance, and I do not myself pretend to imperturb-
ability when they occur.

But shouldn't one bear in mind other factors? The annoyances, *sub specie aeternitatis,* are trivial. The mistakes seldom
make a marginal difference, particularly in a long race, if one
doesn't, to begin with, own a gold-plater. And there are other
things to be weighed. You are introducing a friend to an
awesome experience. You see him learn his way about much
faster than ever he would on a cruise. There is aboard a person or two upon whom the wonder of it all works sensations
of a distinctive freshness; and there is vicarious pleasure to
be had in bringing such pleasure to others. The novice is a
friend, and to other common experiences you have shared,

you now add that of sailing. One must make certain, of course, that there is enough aggregate experience aboard to cope with emergencies: so that the levy is not on the well-being of other crew members, but on their patience, and, to some extent, on their chances—so very remote, anyway, in the company *The Panic* keeps—for hardware.

Let us face it, the oceangoing race is largely an artificial contest. Will the best boat win? It is impossible to weigh the relative merits of different boats except by one standard at a time. In ocean races the boats are not alike; each boat represents an individually balanced set of concessions to speed, safety, comfort, and economy. A noble effort is made by ingenious statisticians and measurers to devise a Procrustean formula that will leave all boats identical; but it is a failure, and all of us, in our hearts, know it. The handicap rule is a Rube Goldberg contrivance designed to succeed in the kind of tank-test situation which Nature, in her sullen way, never vouchsafes us.

If *Cotton Blossom* and *Niña* were both manned by automatons and sailed around a given course a thousand times, on a thousand consecutive days, the chances are very good that the corrected times of the two would not once coincide. The contest, then, given differing characteristics and differing relative speeds of boats in different tacks and under different conditions, is not really between boats.

Is it between crews? Again, only if the boats are identical, or nearly so. A good crew will get more out of a boat than a poor crew, but the only generalization that this permits is that a given boat will do better with Crew A than it would have done with Crew B: meaning, if you want to make a contest out of it, that Crew A beat Crew B. But that is a hypothetical contest; in reality, a boat can only sail, at any given time, with a single crew. What, then, can be proved between competing crews on different boats? Not very much.

There is, finally, a feature of ocean racing that can make a shambles of the whole thing. The poorest judgment can, under capricious circumstances, pay the handsomest rewards. Crew A, out of an egregious ignorance and showing execrable judgment, elects to go around Block Island north to south while the seasoned and shrewd Crew B makes the proper choice under the circumstances, and goes south to north. The wind abruptly and inexplicably changes, and has the effect of whisking A in and stopping B dead in its tracks. Ridiculous, isn't it? What satisfaction am I entitled to feel if I beat the fabulous Rod Stephens? I should feel an ass; for given the presumptions, there could be no clearer demonstration of my inexpertness. That a playful providence should have elected to reward folly and punish wisdom does not mitigate my offense against sound judgment.

It will be objected that, after all, the facts are that 10 percent of the boats win 75 percent of the hardware. True. But what does the statistic prove? Merely that fast boats with digestible handicaps, or slow boats with exorbitant handicaps do best. Not more. One cannot set up, in the way that one can in class-boat races, or in tennis or golf matches, a ladder which will reflect with reasonable accuracy the relative proficiency of ocean racers.

Wherein, then, does the contest lie, in the sport of ocean racing? It is, I think, a contest with oneself. It lies in the demands made upon the crew by the boat, the weather, and the crew itself. There is of course the formal race, within the general framework of which that contest takes place. And there is the delusive tendency to feel that one's position in the fleet exactly reflects the quality of one's response to the challenge. But that is false.

The challenge for all of us, in every boat, takes place in context of our total experience with, and our total preoccupation with, sailing. It is absurd to expect that the casual sailor whose mind, week in, week out, is very much on other things shall have acquired the expertise of an Alan Villiers; and it is barbarous to suggest that that sailor, given the failure to meet the standards of a Villiers, is either presumptuous or impudent in participating in ocean racing. The challenge, I say then, lies in setting the sails as quickly as you know how, in trimming them as well as you know how; in handling the helm as well as you can; in getting as good a fix as you can; in devising the soundest and subtlest strategy given your own horizons; in keeping your temper, and your disposition; and above all things, in keeping your perspective, and bearing in mind, always, the essential meaning of the experience.

All these things are, by definition, since the standards are subjective and not objective, as "well" done by amateurs as by professionals. In one sense, better done. The amateur, though his failures will be more abysmal than the professional's, can also soar to greater heights. He is more often afraid, and therefore more often triumphant; more often in awe, hence more often respectful; more often surprised, hence more often grateful. When did the crew of *Finisterre* last experience the exultation that comes to the amateur crew on expertly jibing their spinnaker?

I should be glad to describe the sensation to Mr. Carlton Mitchell.

II

WHEN we ducked inside the harbor at Newport, two hours after sundown, the sudden stillness was preternatural. The spinnaker was down for the first time in three full days. The wind stopped blowing on our necks and the water, finally, was calm, for now we were shielded from the southwesterly that had lifted us out of Chesapeake Bay and carried us on the long second leg of the race, right to Newport. That sudden stillness, the sudden relief, caused us, out of some sense of harmony, to quiet our own voices so that it was almost in whispers that we exchanged the necessary signals as we drew into an empty slip at Christie's wharf. We tied up, doing our work in silence, dimly aware that the boat that had crossed the line a half mile behind us was groping its way to the slip opposite.

A searchlight pierced the darkness and focused for an instant on our distinctive red bowsprit. "Oh my God," we heard a voice, in muted anguish, "*The Panic!*" The man with the flighlight, aboard the famous *Golliwog*, deduced how poorly his boat must have done—behind *The Panic!* We felt very sorry for *Golliwog*. In reversed circumstances, we too would have felt ashamed.

I and *The Panic* are arrant beginners in the sport of ocean racing. We are bumptiously amateur, and appear to have a way of provoking the unreasoned and impulsive resentment of sailors whose view of ocean racing tends to be a little different from my own. That resentment is wholly spontaneous and, I like to feel, evanescent. I distinguish it sharply from the highly mobilized and systematic displeasure that I have here and there engendered in proud professionals.

I have even been scolded in public by one sailor who announced that he would take his stand by precisely these professionals, some of whose tendencies I have here and there criticized. We experts, my critic said, have made it possible for you sub-amateurs to sail in ocean races without breaking your necks. Your corresponding obligations are 1) to stop being amateurs just as soon as you possibly can; and 2) to show a little reverence for the experts, to whom you are so solidly indebted.

I gather that my failure to proceed with satisfactory speed toward goal Number One above, and my inconsistent adherence to rule-of-the-road Number Two are, perversely, my qualifications (I have no others) to write at all on the subject of ocean racing.

Let me begin by saying that I am a conservative, and that the worship of excellence is a part of the conservative creed. Indeed, I abhor the indifference to excellence which I suggest is, nowadays, the hottest pursuit of our society. Nor do I underestimate the importance of what the social scientists call "expertise"—the body of expert operative knowledge in any field. It is hard for me to believe, therefore, that in declaiming so impassionately about the great contributions the experts have made toward ocean racing, anyone could understand himself to be arguing with *me*. How can *anyone* question the usefulness of such lives or, particularly in the very act of putting that knowledge to practical use, speak lightly or condescendingly of their attainments?

I would not count it a life wasted that was consumed in the development of the definitive snatch block, heaven knows. I have merely, here and there, suggested that the principal difficulties of the beginning ocean sailor are 1) the mystifying lack of expertise in much of what goes into ocean sailing; and 2) the tendency, in some experts, to desiccate the entire experience by stripping it of spontaneity, of wonder; the tendency to demand the kind of reverence for the experts that belongs to the sea.

I have not made a study of the tribulations of novitiate sailors, and I pass off my own without any suggestion that I am writing about universal experience. If what I have to say turns out to be not at all useful to others, then I apologize for wasting their time. If it turns out that I have something useful to say, then I am pleased beyond words finally to have contrived a way to requite, in some small measure, my large debt to the sport of sailing.

One reads a great deal in primers on boat buying about the practices of unscrupulous men. I have no doubt that such men exist. It is natural that they should, for confidence men notoriously gather around the commodities that dreams are made of—money, power, women, boats. But I am singularly fortunate in never having been handled by one. From the outset, I have dealt with honest men, genuinely concerned to satisfy the desires of the owners of *The Panic* while, to be sure, making an honest living out of it. It is against such a framework that I discuss my first point above and, by lurid autobiographic detail, make my point about the perplexing inexpertness of experts.

The Panic is a looker. I would not know what to say to anyone who was not instantly captivated by her appearance. We fell in love with her at first sight, and decided, on second sight, to buy her. How much did the broker (remember: a wholly honest one) think we would have to spend to put her in racing shape? He thought and thought about it, and made careful notes. Five hundred dollars, he decided.

I am not sure how much we have spent on *The Panic* (and the experts would not even now designate her as being a racer). The original mistake, most of them would say (now!) was made on that Dutch drawing board, but it is no exaggeration to say that we have bought her, so to speak, two or three times. (I intend to will my boat bills to the museum at Mystic, so that future beginners can have a detailed idea of just where the mines are buried.)

Let us take one item. *The Panic* proved to have a terrible weather helm. When it began to blow, and particularly when we had to shorten headsails, we used to measure the force needed to keep the boat on course in terms of horsepower. Racing to Bermuda in 1956 we would wear out a helmsman every half hour, even with the aid of a becket made out of several strands of thick shock cord. We determined the next winter to do something about it.

Now even beginners can figure out that a weather helm results when the center of effort is too far aft. Let me try to put that more intelligibly. A weather helm will result when a greater area of sail is exposed to the wind aft of the fulcrum point of the boat than forward of it. The obvious way to correct the situation is to move the whole rig forward. But in large boats that is not feasible. So I took the problem to the experts. What should I do? What would *you* recommend? (One minute of silence, while you think. . . .)

Well, the experts reasoned, let us increase the sail area forward, to compensate the pressure aft. How? No room on top, because it's a masthead rig already. What, then? A bowsprit.

A bowsprit! A bowsprit! the cry rang out from consultant to consultant, from boatyard to rigger, gaining volume as it traveled through the echo chambers of expertise. We were so intoxicated by the proposal that we ordered it executed without delay: on with the bowsprit.

Well, all it involved was constructing a 39-inch steel section with a couple of sheaves for the anchor chain and a bobstay, welding it on, yanking out the woodwork and pulpit, machining and installing two new stanchions and chocks: and there we were. But, of course, the headstay had to move forward. So in came the riggers and moved it forward. The headstay having moved forward, the forestay could not linger behind—so off it went—another stainless steel cable and installation. Then, what do you know, the spinnaker pole—too short now. A new pole.

But you couldn't have a bigger pole without a bigger spinnaker—so you just increase the size of your spinnaker, a matter of a couple of weeks' work by a couple of expert sailmakers. Then you find your headsails are hanging down, as what dope couldn't have figured out, now that, the headstay being strung out, the angle is changed. So you recut them. Having done so, you find that the deck plates are just plain no use where they are—they have to be changed, to reflect the new angle of descent of the headsails.

And then the horrible moment when, realizing we had increased the area of the fore-triangle, we called in the Measurer. He surveyed the revised boat with the sadistic satisfaction of the headmaster of Dotheboys Hall confronting a refractory student: severe punishment was in order. Up soared our rating.

That's all there was to it.

And it didn't work worth a damn. Before, the helm had only been bad in fresh air. Now when the wind freshened you had to reduce headsail or luff the main, or both. There went the advantage of the bowsprit. In light airs, the increase in comfort was barely noticeable; the increase in speed not noticeable at all. The experts never thought of that.

The problem continued to be serious, so last winter we started at the other end. At the suggestion of the estimable Mr. Bill Muzzio, of Muzzio Brothers Boatyard, we bade good-by to the sails and journeyed below, to the keel. If we could not change the center of effort, we could change the center of lateral resistance. We proceeded to extend the keel *aft,* adding about twenty square feet. The operation involved virtually rebuilding the after half of the boat—new rudder pipe, new tiller, new lazarette. The result was miraculous. We now have no helm at all. The boat is beautifully balanced. Question: Could we not have been spared our first experience?

Take our radio direction finder. Our first one was Dutch. It sort of worked, but the signal was not really satisfactory. We asked a top firm of marine electricians to recommend and install the very best thing available. In came a Bendix loop and a war surplus airplane Bendix radio direction finder. That was three years ago. Every three months, that is to say, every time I have desperately needed it and it refused either to work at all, or else to work well enough to yield an intelligible signal, I write a letter of complaint to the electricians. In response to my complaint, they bear down on *The Panic* and "fix" it. They will then demonstrate the quality of its performance as we sit in our slip in Stamford; and sure enough, WOR turns out to be located in New York City.

Three days later, surrounded by fog off Block Island, Point Judith turns out to be in Pennsylvania, and Montauk has begun to sail off toward Iceland at about forty miles per hour. I report my complaint. We repeat our performance. The same thing happens again. I repeat my complaint. This has gone on for three years. An exception?

There's our radio telephone. Never fear, I reassured my apprehensive wife on purchasing the boat, the Radio Corporation of America will never permit us to be truly separated. Ten percent of the time, I get through to the marine operator. The other times, she doesn't hear me—not a word. I'd much prefer it if the set didn't work at all, because then one could buy new tubes, or something. In come the electricians. We have tested the telephone, they will report to me.

"Got a check from the New York marine operator on four different stations. The perfect power effect is ten. Your set got three tens and a nine."

"Yes, I know," I say. "Only it doesn't work for *me*, when *I*, not *you*, want to use it. What should I do? I now have radio aerials that are the pride of the electronic industry. If I am on a port tack, I can switch to a port aerial, freeing the antenna of any leeward encumbrance. The aerial is exquisite. The telephone has been checked fifteen times. Only it doesn't work. Why? *I* don't know. *I* never said *I* was an expert."

In a piece I wrote for *Motor Boating,* I made the claim that unlike the fusspot sailers, I was prepared to repose my faith in professional riggers, to whom I would say, simply, "Please give me first-rate rigging"—and I would not insult them by following them around, making a strand-by-strand examination of their handiwork.

I am beginning to modify my views. Not because, as Norris Hoyt would have it, my respect for the expert increases; but rather because of my faith in him having diminished, I begin to realize that though I am not inclined that way, I shall probably have to become, before I am done, not only an electronics engineer but a rigger.

Here is what I mean: On the first race to Bermuda, coming back, the backstay parted where the stainless steel cable fitted into an insulator which had to do with the aerial (in those days, before the alterations, the aerial didn't work on the backstay, whereas now it doesn't work on the shrouds). "What do you know!" the rigger exploded when I held the sundered pieces in my hand, "that aerial insulator is tested for five million pounds' (or something) pressure."

"Yes," I said, "only it didn't work."

In the most recent Bermuda race we were sailing along and . . . *bang* . . . the headstay, no less, was gone, parted at the turnbuckle. We had been sailing alongside *Finisterre* (a brief encounter). On the way back, in the airplane, where I had the honor to meet him, Carleton Mitchell asked what had gone wrong, that the entire crew should have rushed forward so excitedly to the bow. I told him.

"Oh, yes," he said. "I had the same trouble once. Now I don't use a turnbuckle at the headstay at all. I do all the adjusting on the backstay turnbuckle. You do, of course, have a double toggle on your headstay, don't you?"

Never in all my life was I so anxious to please, but I just couldn't pretend to know and get away with it.

"What is a toggle?" I asked sheepishly. He explained (I assume the reader knows). Well, it turns out, we *didn't* have a double toggle, we had only a *single* toggle. Why? The people who rigged *The Panic* rigged one of the contestants for U. S. representation in the America's Cup Race (come to think of it, the boat didn't qualify). If a double toggle is obviously the thing to do, why wasn't it done? Are there two points of *view* about double toggles? Why aren't they ventilated? Why don't some people come forward as single toggle men, prepared to fight to the finish double toggle men? But no. There appears to be no expertise in the making on the subject.

Oh yes: on the way back from Bermuda, the topping lift parted. *And the main halyard parted.* It seems there was a strain where the Tru-lok fitting ran up against the sheave at the top of the mast. Why hadn't the experts caught that? Because *they* are inexpert? Or because there is inexpertise?

The point I labor so clumsily to make is that I suspect it is the latter, and that the beginner, buffeted as he especially is by the marauding experts, has the sharpest insight into the fact. The rigger who splices a wire around a thimble with loving care has a regard for, and takes a pride in, excellence. And if he does it "correctly" he is an expert. But if the splice does not hold the wire around the thimble as it is designed to do, then there is insufficient expertise in the matter.

It happens all about us. Masts break—for no very clear reason. Boats sink at the slip, and all the king's horses and all the king's men cannot figure out why. This telephone will work every time, and that one won't. This paint works beautifully on this hull, and that hull, with the identical paint, will look, in a week or two, as though it had impetigo.

But we are dealing, are we not, with laws of nature which, at the level we speak of, can be assumed to be constant? Hume, dismissing miracles, said he would sooner believe that human testimony had erred than that the laws of nature had been suspended. Is it miraculous then that John's radio works and William's does not? I should consider it the most rational explanation yet offered if my electrician would inform me that my radio telephone does not work because of the absence of miraculous conditions.

But he does no such thing, nor do the riggers, or painters, or engine makers (engines! What a temptation to write about my engine!), or sailmakers, or meteorologists, or ropemakers. The fact of the matter is they are half craftsmen (and excellent craftsmen, at that) and half medicine men who, due to the absence of experience in the design, manufacture and maintenance of boats, do not know what they are up against and hence traffick in sheer charlatanry.

My advice to the beginner? Read all those books and listen to all that advice with high skepticism. There is much there to learn, but there are many, many uncharted seas, and the man who tells you with that robust certitude that is characteristic of the expert's rhetoric (viz. Mr. Calahan's advertisements) that the way from A to C lies via B is very likely to be quite, utterly wrong. There are compensations in the situation. Think how much the amateur can accomplish for himself! If anyone is of a mind to conquer, there is a great deal around to subdue. And if anyone has the stomach for high adventure, I wish he would bear my radio telephone in mind.

The second point I have made, and I do not want to be tiresome about it. Hilaire Belloc was driven to a rage at the very thought of racing a cruising boat. It was never very hard to drive Belloc into a rage, but in this case he surely had a point, and if he had participated in some of today's races, he would have felt fully justified. Cruising boats, offshore boats of varying design, are made for cruising; and to race them, Belloc seems to feel, is like seeing how fast you can play a symphony: the very point is lost.

I disagree, obviously, for I race; and will race again and again, in all likelihood. But I do believe that the dangers that most horrified Belloc are pre-eminently there, that one has only to go down to a yacht club, survey the ministrations tendered to a 12-foot racing dinghy, extrapolate, and you have an idea of the way you may find yourself spending your life if you race a 40-footer to win.

I can understand an amateur's mothering a dinghy, or a Comet, or a Star—or even an International Twelve-Meter— with the kind of loving care necessary to eliminate those marginal seconds and half seconds, but I do not understand why such a thing is done when disparate boats race each other under the colossal, though conscientious, hoax that is The (handicap) Rule. I do not understand, because the con-tent—multiplications, square roots, and long divisions not-withstanding—is essentially a phony.

I have seen the obsession with high fidelity displace the enjoyment of music. I have known bright people who devel-oped into crashing bores as they transmuted ocean racing into a neo-Spartan and never-ending ordeal which, even when it gives pleasure, gives a pleasure that is totally unrelated to the generic source of pleasure in sailing: which is the sea and the wind.

I have a notion that the inertia of our age, the perfect expression of which is the Western paralysis in international affairs during the past half century, has had the effect of extravasating the natural physical and moral energies of some people into athletic channels. I can understand the lure of the total workout, expressed in sailing by the devotion of twenty hours a week, thirty weeks a year, toward the perfection of one's yacht and the forwarding of one's competitive position. Only I say such as they threaten the sport as surely as some of the new critics threaten the art of poetry. And I say to the beginner, don't let them tyrannize over you, or you may never recapture your romance.

I am solidly for amateurism in ocean sailing. I have lost, as I indicated above, faith in the very existence of the expertise before which, even did I know it to exist, I should not be disposed to humble myself in quite the manner that some deem appropriate. I am quite serious in saying that I idolize Carleton Mitchell because he is a professional who, one can tell by reading what he writes, derives an amateur's pleasure out of his trade. (Has anyone noticed that there is no rasp in Mitchell's writing? That is the sign.) He would never, I think, stultify the sport by discouraging its discovery by beginners, as so many people are likely to do.

Of the eight or ten people who regularly race *The Panic*, nowadays, it is fair to say that by contrast with the gold-platers, our boat is crewed by rank beginners. And before the comment gets made that this is all too visible to any boat a half mile away from *The Panic*, let me say, brother: Think what you like. Let us go, amiably, our amiable ways. Just rescue me if I fall overboard, as I would you, and get out of my way when I'm on a starboard tack. I make no other demands.

Do I have advice for a beginner? Yes. If you intend to race, buy a racing boat. They are just as comfortable nowadays. But remember, they are much, much more expensive. If you buy a boat that is afflicted with an unviable rating, and then

race it, you will—unless you exercise a solipsist's self-discipline
—fret, and be unhappy.

Do you know about the Law of Rusher's Gap? Well, it
especially applies to ocean racers. Rusher's Gap is the gap
beyond the gap that one anticipates. Apply it generously in
your calculation of costs. Assume your upkeep will be five
times what you first anticipated. Especially the first year or
two. Assume no one has yet invented a radio telephone. Take
four extra turnbuckles everywhere you go and a hundred
cable clamps, to say nothing, of course, of a complete hardware store.

Have your drink (singular) before dinner. The first couple
of days out, take a sedative when your turn comes to go off
watch, and take a stimulant when you get up. That will catapult you, rather than drag you slowly by the hair, into the
new and very different rhythm of life aboard an ocean racer.
Wear an eyeshade when trying to sleep during the day. Do
not assume it is possible to stay dry when you go forward
in a heavy sea. (The only way to accomplish that, a friend of
mine has observed, having tried every other way, is to strip
naked and get completely vulcanized at the home port.)
Race your boat hard. And pay no attention to the results.

WHAT DID YOU SAY?

I RECENTLY spent the better part of a day with a college student who had much on his mind to tell me. I in turn was much interested in what he had to say. But after an hour or so I gave up. It wasn't that his thinking was diffuse, or his sentences badly organized. It was simply that you couldn't understand the words. When they reached your ear they sounded as faint as though they had been forced through the wall of a soundproofed room, and as garbled as though they had been fed through one of those scrambling devices of the Signal Corps. "Somi iggi prufes tometugo seem thaffernun."

"What was that?"

(*Trying hard*) "So mi IGgi prufes tometugo seem THAaffernun."

"Sorry, I didn't quite get it."

(*Impatiently*): "So MY ENGLISH PROFESSOR TOLD ME TO GO SEE HIM THAT AFTERNOON." And on with the story. By which time, let us face it, the narrative has become a little constipated: and soon I gave up. My responses became feigned, and I was reduced to harmonizing the expression on my face with the inflection of his rhetoric. It had become not a dialogue but a soliloquy, and the conversation dribbled off.

I remarked on the event later to a friend who works regularly with boys and girls of college age. "Don't you understand?" he said. "*Nobody* at college today opens his mouth to speak. They all mumble. For one thing, they think it's chic. For another, they haven't got very much to say. That's the *real* reason why they are called the Silent Generation. Because nobody has the slightest idea what they are saying when they *do* speak, so they assume they are saying nothing."

It isn't a purely contemporary problem. Two generations ago Professor William Strunk, Jr. of Cornell was advising his student E. B. White to speak clearly—and to speak even more clearly if you did *not* know what you were saying. "He felt it was worse to be irresolute," White reminisces in his introduction to *The Elements of Style*, "than to be wrong. . . . Why compound ignorance with inaudibility?"

I remember when I was growing up, sitting around the dining room table with my brothers and sisters making those animal sounds which are only understood by children of the same age, who communicate primarily through onomatopoeia. One day my father announced after what must have been a singularly trying dinner that exactly four years had gone by since he had been able to understand a *single* word uttered by any one of his ten children, and that the indicated solution was to send us *all* to England—where they *respect* the English language and teach you to OPEN YOUR MOUTHS. We put this down as one of Father's periodic aberrations until six weeks later the entire younger half of the family found itself on an ocean liner headed for English boarding schools.

Mumbling was a lifelong complaint of my father, and he demanded of his children, but never got, unconditional surrender. He once wrote to the headmistress of the Ethel Walker School: "I have intended for some time to write or speak to you about Maureen's speech. She does not speak distinctly and has a tendency, in beginning a sentence, to utter any number of words almost simultaneously. Anything the school can do to improve this condition [the school did not do very much—Ed.] would be greatly appreciated by us. I have always had a feeling [here Father was really laying it on, for the benefit of his children, all of whom got copies] that there was some physical obstruction that caused this, but doctors say there is not."

Frustrated by the advent of World War II and the necessity of recalling his children from England before they had learned to OPEN THEIR MOUTHS, my father hired an elocution teacher and scheduled two hours of classes every afternoon. She greeted her surly students at the beginning of the initial class with the announcement that her elocution was so precise, and her breathing technique so highly developed, that anyone sitting in the top row of the balcony at Carnegie Hall could easily hear her softest whisper uttered onstage. Like a trained chorus we replied—sitting a few feet away—"What did you say? Speak up!"WE DID NOT GET ON. But after a while, I guess we started to OPEN OUR MOUTHS. (There are those who say we have never since shut them.)

No doubt about it, it is a widespread malady—like a bad hand, only worse, because we cannot carry around with us a little machine that will do for our voices what a typewriter does for our penmanship. The malady is one part laziness, one part a perverted shyness. Perverted because its inarticulated premise is that it is less obtrusive socially to speak your thoughts so as to require the person whom you are addressing to ask you twice or three times what it was you said. A palpable irrationality. If you have to ask someone three times what he said and when you finally decipher it you learn he has just announced that the quality of mercy is not strained, or that he is suffering the slings and arrows of outrageous fortune, you have a glow of pleasure from the reward of a hardy investigation. So let the Shakespeares among us mumble, if they must. But if at the end of the mine shaft you are merely made privy to the intelligence that the English professor set up a meeting for that afternoon, you are entitled to resent that so humdrum a detail got buried in an elocutionary gobbledygook which required a pick and shovel to unearth.

I do not know what can be done about it, and don't intend to look for deep philosophical reasons why the problem is especially acute now. . . . I nevertheless suggest the problem be elevated to the status of a National Concern. Meanwhile, the kindergartens should revive the little round we used to sing—or, rather, mumble:

> *Whether you softly speak*
> *[crescendo] Or whether you loudly call.*
> *Distinctly! Distinctly speak*
> *Or do not speak at all.*

LETTER FROM JAPAN

WE ARE about to leave Japan, as ignorant about what is going on here as we were when we arrived three days ago. But that is no excuse for not writing about Japan, as any opinionated publicist will tell you, carbon copy to Internal Revenue. It happened that all five of our contacts here were, for one reason or another, *hors de combat,* so that we were left attempting to communicate with two guides, the most amiable of men, but whose combined knowledge of English was insufficient to cope with a question concerning the whereabouts of the "convenient place" (genteel Japanese for "lavatory") (genteel English for "toilet")—let alone cope with questions concerning the shogunate of Premier Ikeda. My single conversation while in Japan with a non-Japanese was conducted over the telephone, with the Spanish Ambassador, to whom I relayed the greetings of his son in New York. I managed to extravasate into a wholly nonpolitical exchange of pleasantries the question: "How does it go with the government in Japan?" "It goes well," he said; "it is a very stable government." If the Spanish Ambassador says a government is stable, I say the viewing is worth passing along....

Otherwise, it was mostly shrines. Goodness, but the Buddha is a beshrined man. In Kyoto alone, which was the capital of Japan for a thousand years, up until 80 or 90 years ago (by the way, everything in Japan happened "80 or 90 years ago." Especially fires and industry. Upon introducing almost any building, the guide will say: "The original burned down 80 or 90 years ago, but has been rebuilt. . . .")—in Kyoto, there are 200 to 300 shrines, great and small, mostly a little decrepit, but every one of them with the characteristically upturned ends, the gentle, almost imperceptible upward lilt in the railings and the eaves which transmute an essentially stodgy structure into a fitting monument to a people whose lives are fastidiously symmetrical, but who are softened by just a touch of blitheness.

If my guide is correct (or if I understood him correctly), religion in Japan is a depressed area. Especially since the war's end, he said, there has been a loss of interest in religion (and one notes, a corresponding national passion for getting and spending). How many of his classmates at Kyoto University are practicing Buddhists? "About ten." "Only 10 percent?" I expressed surprise. "No—ten peoples, in totality," he said. What about Christianity? Roughly two percent of Japan is Christian, at least formally Christian. Is Christianity growing? I asked. Not really. Lots of people go to Christian schools. But, he said, they go there primarily "to train their conversations." (Our guide had not gone to a Christian school.) What percentage of his classmates are Communists? About 20 percent. Were they upset by Russia's detonation of the big bomb? Yes, very upset, and they do not upset easily, he said: for instance, they were not much upset when the "right-wing student" (in Japan, "right wing" is the ultramontanist monarchist, the high nationalist, the ferocious religionist) "put a knife in the chief of the socialists" a year ago. Would he say the influence of the Communists among the young was increasing or diminishing? Diminishing, he said—because the standard of living is rising. I let the implied correlation go by. That morning, a commentator had summarized the foreign policy section of a report filed the day before by Mr. Saburo Eda, the Secretary-General of the Central Committee of the powerful Socialist Party: "The language used in Eda's report prompts one to ask whether a Japanese socialist would feel any qualms in joining the 22nd

Congress of the Communist Party, USSR, and applauding Nikita Khrushchev enthusiastically."

Do you mind if I ask *you* a question? the law student smiled cagily. Is it true that in America no one is allowed "to talk about Communism"? "No," I said, "that is not true. That is largely Communist propaganda. But it is true that in America no one is allowed to say anything is Communist propaganda." He did not understand me, but then neither would many Americans have understood.

The strain of intercommunication was taking its toll. It requires a dozen exchanges to effect the transmission of a single piece of intelligence with an "English-speaking" guide. Sample, as we looked at the imposing gate outside the Imperial Palace in Kyoto, through which no mortal man may pass, only the Emperor himself—the palace where the emperors, who lived there a thousand years until 80 or 90 years ago, still go to be crowned:

"Does the Emperor travel a great deal?" "Yes, he lived here for one thousand years." "No, does he now travel very much?" "He lives now in Tokyo." "Yes, I know—but [slipping inevitably into pidgin English] does he go all over Japan very much now?" "He is here when he is coronated many years ago." "But [reducing the scope of the inquiry] does—he—come—now—here—still—now—often?" "Yes, when he is coronated. And [pointing to one of the great buildings in the imperial compound] that is where he goes when he wishes to mediterate."

So it goes, It is hard on the visitor. It is not merely this guide. Yesterday it was the Tokyo guide, and my question, issuing from the shock of having been billed 75 cents (U. S.) for a glass of orange juice that morning, was "From where do you import your oranges?" "From Tokyo Bay," he said. *Don't pursue it,* my wife nudged me ferociously. As ever, I yielded—more, I relapsed into a sullen silence, forever abandoning the conversational initiative. "In Osaka," he said, as we drove through what is surely the most endless of all the cities in the world, "the people here are famous for sticking to money." "What on earth can he mean?" I whispered to my wife. "He means, ass, that in Osaka they are notoriously stingy." I settled down, using my wife as the interpreter's interpreter, and we drove on to Nara, where the emperors lived one thousand and 80 or 90 years ago, and we left the car to walk through the famous, tranquil park, with the pastel pine trees, and the thousand stone columns, waist high, where gifts are offered, or were offered—most of them are empty now—for the propitiation of the gods who let them down during the great recent war. Throughout the park tame deer wandered, nuzzling up to the tourists for food. Why do the deer have no horns? I asked Mr. Maezakawa. "They are taken away," he explained, "because sometimes the deer stick the children." I need not have asked the question at all because just then we came upon a large official sign, thoughtfully explaining everything in Japanese and English. The sign read: *Deer are now in puberty season. Be aware. Bucks sometimes hurt people with their horn.*

The day we left, the government of Japan announced its decision not to accept the kind offer of Mr. Sargent Shriver to endow Japan with 100 Peace Corpsmen as English teachers. To accept them, the foreign office disclosed, would be for Japan to appear as an underdeveloped nation, which she most definitely is not, and has not been for 80 or 90 years.

WHY DON'T WE COMPLAIN?

It was the very last coach and the only empty seat on the entire train, so there was no turning back. The problem was to breathe. Outside, the temperature was below freezing. Inside the railroad car the temperature must have been about 85 degrees. I took off my overcoat, and a few minutes later my jacket, and noticed that the car was flecked with the white shirts of the passengers. I soon found my hand moving to loosen my tie. From one end of the car to the other, as we rattled through Westchester County, we sweated; but we did not moan.

I watched the train conductor appear at the head of the car. "Tickets, all tickets, please!" In a more virile age, I thought, the passengers would seize the conductor and strap him down on a seat over the radiator to share the fate of his patrons. He shuffled down the aisle, picking up tickets, punching commutation cards. *No one addressed a word to him.* He approached my seat, and I drew a deep breath of resolution. "Conductor," I began with a considerable edge to my voice. . . . Instantly the doleful eyes of my seatmate turned tiredly from his newspaper to fix me with a resentful stare: what question could be so important as to justify my sibilant intrusion into his stupor? I was shaken by those eyes. I am incapable of making a discreet fuss, so I mumbled a question about what time were we due in Stamford (I didn't even ask whether it would be before or after dehydration could be expected to set in), got my reply, and went back to my newspaper and to wiping my brow.

The conductor had nonchalantly walked down the gauntlet of eighty sweating American freemen, and not one of them had asked him to explain why the passengers in that car had been consigned to suffer. There is nothing to be done when the temperature *outdoors* is 85 degrees, and indoors the air conditioner has broken down; obviously when that happens there is nothing to do, except perhaps curse the day that one was born. But when the temperature outdoors is below freezing, it takes a positive act of will on somebody's part to set the temperature *indoors* at 85. Somewhere a valve was turned too far, a furnace overstocked, a thermostat maladjusted: something that could easily be remedied by turning off the heat and allowing the great outdoors to come indoors. All this is so obvious. What is not obvious is what has happened to the American people.

It isn't just the commuters, whom we have come to visualize as a supine breed who have got on to the trick of suspending their sensory faculties twice a day while they submit to the creeping dissolution of the railroad industry. It isn't just they who have given up trying to rectify irrational vexations. It is the American people everywhere.

A few weeks ago at a large movie theatre I turned to my wife and said, "The picture is out of focus." "Be quiet," she answered. I obeyed. But a few minutes later I raised the point again, with mounting impatience. "It will be all right in a minute," she said apprehensively. (She would rather lose her eyesight than be around when I make one of my infrequent scenes.) I waited. It was *just* out of focus—not glaringly out, but out. My vision is 20-20, and I assume that is the vision, adjusted, of most people in the movie house. So, after hectoring my wife throughout the first reel, I finally prevailed upon her to admit that it *was* off, and very annoying. We then settled down, coming to rest on the presumption that: a) someone connected with the management of the theatre must soon notice the blur and make the correction; or b) that someone seated near the rear of the house would make the complaint in behalf of those of us up front; or c) that—any minute now—the entire house would explode into catcalls and foot stamping, calling dramatic attention to the irksome distortion.

What happened was nothing. The movie ended, as it had begun, *just* out of focus, and as we trooped out, we stretched our faces in a variety of contortions to accustom the eye to the shock of normal focus.

I think it is safe to say that everybody suffered on that occasion. And I think it is safe to assume that everyone was expecting someone else to take the initiative in going back to speak to the manager. And it is probably true even that if we had supposed the movie would run right through the blurred image, someone surely would have summoned up the purposive indignation to get up out of his seat and file his complaint.

But notice that no one did. And the reason no one did is because we are all increasingly anxious in America to be unobtrusive, we are reluctant to make our voices heard, hesitant about claiming our rights; we are afraid that our cause is unjust, or that if it is not unjust, that it is ambiguous; or if not even that, that it is too trivial to justify the horrors of a confrontation with Authority; we will sit in an oven or endure a racking headache before undertaking a head-on, I'm-here-to-tell-you complaint. That tendency to passive compliance, to a heedless endurance, is something to keep one's eyes on—in sharp focus.

I myself can occasionally summon the courage to complain, but I cannot, as I have intimated, complain softly. My own instinct is so strong to let the thing ride, to forget about it—to expect that someone will take the matter up, when the grievance is collective, in my behalf—that it is only when the provocation is at a very special key, whose vibrations touch simultaneously a complexus of nerves, allergies, and passions, that I catch fire and find the reserves of courage and assertiveness to speak up. When that happens, I get quite carried away. My blood gets hot, my brow wet, I become unbearably and unconscionably sarcastic and bellicose; I am girded for a total showdown.

Why should that be? Why could not I (or anyone else) on that railroad coach have said simply to the conductor, "Sir"— I take that back: that sounds sarcastic—"Conductor, would you be good enough to turn down the heat? I am extremely hot. In fact, I tend to get hot every time the temperature reaches 85 degr—" Strike that last sentence. Just end it with the simple statement that you are extremely hot, and let the conductor infer the cause.

Every New Year's Eve I resolve to do something about the Milquetoast in me and vow to speak up, calmly, for my rights, and for the betterment of our society, on every appropriate occasion. Entering last New Year's Eve I was fortified in my resolve because that morning at breakfast I had had to ask the waitress three times for a glass of milk. She finally brought it—after I had finished my eggs, which is when I don't want it any more. I did not have the manliness to order her to take the milk back, but settled instead for a cowardly sulk, and ostentatiously refused to drink the milk —though I later paid for it—rather than state plainly to the hostess, as I should have, why I had not drunk it, and would not pay for it.

So by the time the New Year ushered out the Old, riding in on my morning's indignation and stimulated by the gastric juices of resolution that flow so faithfully on New Year's Eve, I rendered my vow. Henceforward I would conquer my shyness, my despicable disposition to supineness. I would speak out like a man against the unnecessary annoyances of our time.

Forty-eight hours later, I was standing in line at the ski repair store in Pico Peak, Vermont. All I needed, to get on with my skiing, was the loan, for one minute, of a small screwdriver, to tighten a loose binding. Behind the counter in the workshop were two men. One was industriously engaged in servicing the complicated requirements of a young lady at the head of the line, and obviously he would be tied up for quite a while. The other—"Jiggs," his workmate called him—was a middle-aged man, who sat in a chair puffing a pipe, exchanging small talk with his working partner. My pulse began its telltale acceleration. The minutes ticked on. I stared at the idle shopkeeper, hoping to shame him into action, but he was impervious to my telepathic reproof and continued his small talk with his friend, brazenly insensitive to the nervous demands of six good men who were raring to ski.

Suddenly my New Year's Eve resolution struck me. It was now or never. I broke from my place in line and marched to the counter. I was going to control myself. I dug my nails into my palms. My effort was only partially successful:

"If you are not too busy," I said icily, "would you mind handing me a screwdriver?"

Work stopped and everyone turned his eyes on me, and I experienced that mortification I always feel when I am the center of centripetal shafts of curiosity, resentment, perplexity.

But the worst was yet to come. "I am sorry, sir," said Jiggs deferentially, moving the pipe from his mouth. "I am not supposed to move. I have just had a heart attack." That was the signal for a great whirring noise that descended from heaven. We looked, stricken, out the window, and it appeared as though a cyclone had suddenly focused on the snowy courtyard between the shop and the ski lift. Suddenly a gigantic army helicopter materialized, and hovered down to a landing. Two men jumped out of the plane carrying a stretcher, tore into the ski shop, and lifted the shopkeeper onto the stretcher. Jiggs bade his companion good-by, was whisked out the door, into the plane, up to the heavens, down —we learned—to a near-by army hospital. I looked up manfully—into a score of man-eating eyes. I put the experience down as a reversal.

As I write this, on an airplane, I have run out of paper and need to reach into my briefcase under my legs for more. I cannot do this until my empty lunch tray is removed from my lap. I arrested the stewardess as she passed empty-handed down the aisle on the way to the kitchen to fetch the lunch trays for the passengers up forward who haven't been served yet. "Would you please take my tray?" "Just a *moment*, sir!" she said, and marched on sternly. Shall I tell her that since she is headed for the kitchen *anyway*, it could not delay the feeding of the other passengers by more than two seconds necessary to stash away my empty tray? Or remind her that not fifteen minutes ago she spoke unctuously into the loud-speaker the words undoubtedly devised by the airline's highly paid public relations counselor: "If there is anything I or Miss French can do for you to make your trip more enjoyable, *please* let us—" I have run out of paper.

I think the observable reluctance of the majority of Americans to assert themselves in minor matters is related to our increased sense of helplessness in an age of technology and centralized political and economic power. For generations, Americans who were too hot, or too cold, got up and did something about it. Now we call the plumber, or the electrician, or the furnace man. The habit of looking after our own needs obviously had something to do with the assertiveness that characterized the American family familiar to readers of American literature. With the technification of life goes our direct responsibility for our material environment, and we are conditioned to adopt a position of helplessness not only as regards the broken air conditioner, but as regards the overheated train. It takes an expert to fix the former, but not the latter; yet these distinctions, as we withdraw into helplessness, tend to fade away.

Our notorious political apathy is a related phenomenon. Every year, whether the Republican or the Democratic Party is in office, more and more power drains away from the individual to feed vast reservoirs in far-off places; and we have less and less say about the shape of events which shape our future. From this alienation of personal power comes the sense of resignation with which we accept the political dispensations of a powerful government whose hold upon us continues to increase.

An editor of a national weekly news magazine told me a few years ago that as few as a dozen letters of protest against an editorial stance of his magazine was enough to convene a plenipotentiary meeting of the board of editors to review policy. "So few people complain, or make their voices heard," he explained to me, "that we assume a dozen letters represent the inarticulated views of thousands of readers." In the past ten years, he said, the volume of mail has noticeably decreased, even though the circulation of his magazine has risen.

When our voices are finally mute, when we have finally suppressed the natural instinct to complain, whether the vexation is trivial or grave, we shall have become automatons, incapable of feeling. When Premier Khrushchev first came to this country late in 1959 he was primed, we are informed, to experience the bitter resentment of the American people against his tyranny, against his persecutions, against the movement which is responsible for the great number of American deaths in Korea, for billions in taxes every year, and for life everlasting on the brink of disaster; but Khrushchev was pleasantly surprised, and reported back to the Russian people that he had been met with overwhelming cordiality (read: apathy), except, to be sure, for "a few fascists who followed me around with their wretched posters, and should be horsewhipped."

I may be crazy, but I say there would have been lots more posters in a society where train temperatures in the dead of winter are not allowed to climb to 85 degrees without complaint.